"La Vía Campesina is the most important transnational social movement in the contemporary world. They are the leading edge of resistance against neoliberal economic globalization. This book is must-read history and analysis for scholars and activists alike."
PETER ROSSET, CO-COORDINATOR, LAND RESEARCH ACTION NETWORK (LRAN)

"Finally a book from the inside of global resistance by farmers to corporate takeover of the food, seeds and land on which all life depends. This magnificent analysis exposes the pitfalls that await popular movements, beset on all sides by neo-comprador NGOs, corporate newspeak, World Trade Organization manipulations, internal division and funders' cooptation. How La Vía Campesina survived and thrived to champion food sovereignty, gender equity and global grassroots solidarity is an inspiring tale, beautifully told."
TERISA TURNER, ASSOCIATE PROFESSOR, SOCIOLOGY AND ANTHROPOLOGY, UNIVERSITY OF GUELPH, ONTARIO, CANADA.

"La Vía Campesina has become one of the most dynamic and creative elements in the global justice movement. Annette Desmarais's insider history of this worldwide peasants' and small farmers' organization is essential reading for all those who seek to understand the opposition to neoliberal globalization and the social and environmental destruction wrought by industrial agriculture. The hopes that have propelled peasants and small farmers to cross-border unity and action are on proud display in this moving account."
MARC EDELMAN, PROFESSOR OF ANTHROPOLOGY, HUNTER COLLEGE AND THE GRADUATE CENTER, CITY UNIVERSITY OF NEW YORK. AUTHOR OF *THE LOGIC OF THE LATIFUNDIO; PEASANTS AGAINST GLOBALIZATION*; AND CO-EDITOR OF *THE ANTHROPOLOGY OF DEVELOPMENT AND GLOBALIZATION*.

"Born from peasants' tenacious determination to continue being peasants ... la Vía Campesina has become a promoter of a 'modernization' which embraces everyone. This curious irony, for a class that classical analysts assigned a role in social transformation equivalent to a mere sack of potatoes, has been magisterially analyzed and explained by Annette Desmarais. Her book is an indispensable text to understand one of the most relevant actors in the new map of alternative social activism."
LUIS HERNÁNDEZ NAVARRO, OPINION PAGE EDITOR AND A COLUMNIST FOR LA JORNADA, ONE OF MEXICO'S NATIONAL DAILY NEWSPAPERS.

La Vía Campesina

La Vía Campesina

Globalization and the Power of Peasants

Annette Aurélie Desmarais

Fernwood Publishing • Halifax
Pluto Press • London • Ann Arbor, MI

Editing: Robert Clarke
Cover Photos: La Minga Informativa de Movimientos Sociales and William Kramer
Cover Design: John van der Woude
Printed and bound in Canada by Hignell Book Printing

Published in Canada by Fernwood Publishing
Site 2A, Box 5, 32 Oceanvista Lane, Black Point, Nova Scotia, B0J 1B0
and 324 Clare Avenue, Winnipeg, Manitoba, R3L 1S3
www.fernwoodpublishing.ca

Published in the rest of the world by Pluto Press
345 Archway Road, London N6 5AA and 839 Greene Street, Ann Arbor, MI 48106
www.plutobooks.com

Pluto Press: Hardback ISBN-13 978-0-7453-2705-1; ISBN-10 0-7453-2705-2
Paperback ISBN-13 978-0-7453-2704-4; ISBN-10 0-7453-2704-4

Parts of this book first appeared as "The Vía Campesina: Consolidating an International Peasant
and Farm Movement," *Journal of Peasant Studies* 29 (2) 2002: 91–124 (for the journal website,
see <http://www.tandf.co.uk/journals>); "The Vía Campesina: Women on the Frontiers of Food
Sovereignty," *Canadian Woman Studies/les cahiers de la femme* 23 (1) January 2004; and "United in
the Vía Campesina," *FoodFirst Backgrounder* 11 (4) 2005. An earlier version of chapter 4 was originally published by the North-South Institute as "'The WTO... Will Meet Somewhere, Sometime. And
We Will Be There!'" as part of its project "Civil Society Voices and the Multilateral Organizations"
<http://www.nsi-ins.ca/english/pdf/Voices_WTO_Desmarais.pdf>, Ottawa, September 2003. An
earlier version of sections of chapters 5 and 7 will appear in *The Journal of Rural Studies* in 2007.
We thank the Taylor & Francis Group, North-South Institute, and Foodfirst Institute for Food
and Development Policy for granting us permission to incorporate these publications into this book.

Fernwood Publishing Company Limited gratefully acknowledges the financial support
of the Government of Canada through the Book Publishing Industry Development
Program (BPDIP), the Canada Council for the Arts and the Nova Scotia
Department of Tourism and Culture for our publishing program.

A catalogue record for this book is available from the British Library
Library of Congress Cataloging in Publication Data applied for

Library and Archives Canada Cataloguing in Publication

Desmarais, Annette Aurélie
La Vía Campesina : globalization and the power of
peasants / Annette Aurélie Desmarais.

Includes bibliographical references.
ISBN 978-1-55266-225-0

1. Vía Campesina (Organization) 2. Farmers—Political activity.
3. Peasantry—Political activity. 4. Anti-globalization movement.
5. Rural development—International cooperation. 6. Farms, Small.
7. Social movements—Case studies. I. Title.

HD1415.D48 2006   306.3'49   C2006-906739-2

Contents

Tables and Figures

Acronyms

ANEC	Asociación Nacional de Empresas Comercializadoras de Productores del Campo
AoA	Agreement on Agriculture (WTO)
ASOCODE	Asociación de Organizaciones Campesinas Centroamericanas para la Cooperación y el Desarrollo
CAFTA	Canadian Agri-Food Trade Alliance
CAP	Common Agriculture Policy
CCAEP	Canadian-Caribbean Agricultural Exchange Program
CEDPA	Centre for Development and Population Activities
CGIAR	Consultative Group on International Agriculture Research
CLOC	Coordinadora Latinoamericana de Organizaciones del Campo
CNSTP	Confédération Nationale des Syndicats de Travailleurs Paysans
COPA	Comité des Organisations Professionnelles Agricoles de l'Union Européenne
CPE	Coordination Paysanne Européenne
CSOs	Civil Society Organizations
dKMP	Demokratikong Kilusang Magbubukid ng Pilipinas (Democratic Peasant Movement of the Philippines)
ECODEM	Coordinating Team for the Managua Declaration
EHNE	Enskal Herriko Nekazarien—Unión de Ganaderos y Agricultures Vascos
EU	European Union
FAO	United Nations Food and Agriculture Organization
FIAN	Food and Information Action Network
FSPI	Federation of Indonesian Peasant Unions
FTAA	Free Trade Agreement of the Americas
GATT	General Agreement on Tariffs and Trade
GFAR	Global Forum on Agricultural Research
GM	Genetically modified
GMOs	Genetically modified organisms
ICC	International Co-ordinating Commission of the Vía Campesina
ICESCR	International Covenant on Economic, Social and Cultural Rights

IFAD	International Fund for Agricultural Development
IFAP	International Federation of Agricultural Producers
IMF	International Monetary Fund
IPRs	Intellectual Property Rights
IPC	International Program Committee of the NFU
KMP	Kilusang Magbubukid ng Pilipinas (Peasant Movement of the Philippines)
KRRS	Karnataka Rajya Raitha Sangha (Karnataka State Farmers Association)
MMC	Movimento dos Mulheres la Camponesa
MST	Movimento dos Trabalhadores Rurais Sem Terra
NAFTA	North American Free Trade Agreement
NFFC	National Family Farm Coalition
NFU	National Farmers Union of Canada
NGOs	Non-governmental organizations
NOUMINREN	Japanese Family Farmers' Movement
OECD	Organization for Economic Cooperation and Development
PAHO	Pan American Health Organization
PFS	Paulo Freire Stichting [Foundation]
POs	People's organizations or popular organizations
ROPPA	Reseau des Organisations Paysannes et de Producteurs Agricoles de l'Afrique de l'Ouest
SAPs	Structural Adjustment Programs
TNCs	Transnational corporations
TRIPs	Trade-Related Aspects of Intellectual Property Rights (WTO)
UNAG	Unión Nacional de Agricultores y Ganaderos
UNORCA	Unión Nacional de Organizaciones Regionales Campesinas Autónomas
UNCTAD	United Nations Conference on Trade and Development
UPANACIONAL	Unión Nacional de Pequeños y Medianos Productores Agropecuarios
U.S.	United States of America
WINFA	Windward Islands Farmers' Association
WFS	World Food Summit
WFS: fyl	World Food Summit: Five Years Later
WTO	World Trade Organization

This work is dedicated to La Vía Campesina for allowing me
to share a small portion of the lives and wisdom of the rural women,
peasants, farmers, farm workers and indigenous agrarian communities
whose visions, commitment to social justice, leadership and resilience
make the La Vía Campesina possible. These "people of the land"
— their experiences, thoughts, and actions — form the roots of this book.

Acknowledgements

When I think of all those who have been part of this long journey of learning, I find it difficult to know where to begin. I especially want to thank the International Co-ordinating Commission of La Vía Campesina for their constant support. I want especially to acknowledge Rafael Alegría, Paul Nicholson, Hege Nerland, Dena Hoff, Francisca Rodriguez, Egidio Brunetto, Marcella Harris, Maria del Carmen Barroso, Henry Saragih, Maria Helena Siqueira, Juana Ferrer, Badrul Alam, Diamantino Nhampossa, Nemesia Achacollo, and Alberto Gómez.

My deep appreciation goes to the Unión Nacional de Organizaciones Regionales Campesinas Autónomas (UNORCA), the women of the Asociación Mexicana de Mujeres Organizadas en Red (AMMOR), and Ana de Ita and Luis Hernández Navarro, who went out of their way to facilitate the research in Mexico and made me feel at home. The same goes for the National Farmers Union, which made me feel like I belonged when I was doing research in Canada. I want to acknowledge M.D. Nanjundaswamy (now deceased), whose support was indispensable while I was conducting interviews in Karnataka, India. Here, the generosity and compassion of Pratima, Chukki, and Roopa deserve special mention. Many thanks to the staff of the Vía Campesina Operational Secretariat, Doris Gutíerrez de Hernández and Wendy Cruz, for their constant support and wonderful hospitality, and to NFU staffers Carla Roppel and Joan Lange for resolving my computer issues.

Special thanks go to my sister, Marthe, for her constant support; Andrée Desmarais, Janelle Desmarais-Moen, and Buzz (Adrien) Desmarais, who bring such joy to my life; and Claire, who took a chance and agreed to farm with a younger sister. Special mention of appreciation goes to Nico Verhagen, Technical Asssistant to the Vía Campesina, for openly sharing his insights on how best to support farm organizations' efforts to internationalize, for his careful reading of earlier drafts, for taking the time to clarify numerous points, for being a colleague and a friend. I owe much of my learning of farm politics, leadership, and organizational dynamics to watching two women leaders of the National Farmers Union, Nettie Wiebe and Wendy Manson, in action. Much of our collective understanding of and commitment to international linkages grew out of exchanges that took us to agricultural co-operatives in Northern Nicaragua and brought Nicaraguan peasant women to Saskatchewan farms. I also want to give heartfelt thanks to Saturnino (Jun) Borras for confirming, by example, the important contributions that researchers can make to agrarian activism and for constantly pushing me to write more.

I would like to dedicate this journey to the memory of my mother, Thérèse, and my father, Antoine Desmarais, who provided me with the incomparably wonderful opportunity of growing up on a farm in Saskatchewan.

I also want to acknowledge a number of people at Fernwood Publishing: Wayne Antony, for believing that the story of La Vía Campesina should be told and providing me with important insights on how best to do this; Robert Clarke, for being such a respectful and insightful copy-editor; Beverley Rach for the thoughtful layout and design; Debbie Mathers for inputting the final changes to the text; and Brenda Conroy for proofreading.

Finally, my heartfelt gratitude goes to Jim Handy, for his love, encouragement, moral support, and generosity. Jim's intellectual breadth and curiosity make him a constant source of inspiration. He is my best critic and best friend, and for this, and so much more, I am deeply grateful.

Foreword

by Walden Bello

The two most dominant modernist ideologies of our time give short shrift to the peasantry. In classical socialism, peasants were viewed as relics of an obsolete mode of production and designated for transformation into a rural working class producing on collective farms owned and managed by the state. In the different varieties of capitalist ideology, efficiency in agricultural production could only be brought about with the radical reduction of the numbers of peasants and the substitution of labour by machines. In both visions, the peasant had no future.

These modernist visions, propagated by urban intellectuals, created tremendous social upheavals. In the North, in many parts of which agricultural labour has been reduced to 5 percent or less of the work force; giant agribusinesses dominate production, determine what is consumed, and completely control agro-technology. In almost all countries that industrialized, whether via capitalism or socialism, confiscation of the peasant surplus — either through onerous taxation or through the market — was the key mechanism for the rapid accumulation of capital, which was then invested in industry. In societies throughout the South today, the fatal combination of land consolidation, surplus dumping of agricultural goods by the rich countries, and the technologies of the Green Revolution and genetic engineering is driving many peasants to suicide and forcing great numbers to cities, where they are trapped in big shantytowns, forming a gigantic "reserve army" of the unemployed and underemployed.

Hand-in-hand with these social tragedies are ecological tragedies associated with chemical-intensive agro-technology, deforestation, and uncontrolled industrial pollution. Climate change is the end point of the arrogant modernist dream of creating an artificial environment based on an imperialistic industrialization process to supplant an ecology rooted in a more harmonious relationship between community and the biosphere based on smallholder agriculture.

The twentieth century was one of tragedy for the peasantry, and the twenty-first century promises more of the same modernist tragedy masquerading as progress. But not if the rising movements of peasants and farmers can help it. For too long peasants have been the objects of history.

Now they are stirring and stirring angrily. La Vía Campesina is probably the most effective of these movements of people who now want to be subjects of history. La Vía Campesina not only fights for farmers' rights and for land reform, it is also fighting for a way of life that has proved its worth for eons. It is fighting for a relationship between people and their environment that was snapped by short-sighted industry-first strategies, whether these came in socialist guise or in that of neoliberal capitalism.

This book by Annette Aurélie Desmarais is the best full-length study that has yet been done of a movement that has distinguished itself in the forefront of the struggle against the World Trade Organization and corporate-driven globalization. Herself a farm activist, Desmarais has the trust of the key leaders and participants in a rising movement, allowing her to produce this dynamic portrayal of a community forged in a struggle to preserve its way of life. Desmarais lets the people of La Vía Campesina speak in their own voices about their problems, dreams, and challenges. She situates these voices in an analysis that also looks very carefully at the causes and dynamics of the destabilization and dislocations spawned by agribusiness in the era of globalization. Marx was definitely on a bad modernist trip when he wrote about "the idiocy of rural life." But he was right about capitalism creating its own gravediggers. It was capital's overreaching in the era of globalization that made possible the coming together — based on the consciousness of a common condition and the realization that they either had to hang together or hang separately — of the groups that make up La Vía Campesina today.

In our common struggle against neoliberalism and the WTO, I had the privilege of coming into contact with many of the admirable and memorable activists of La Vía Campesina — people like Nettie Wiebbe, Rafael Alegría, José Bové, Henry Saragih, João Pedro Stédile, and Paul Nicholson. I was always very impressed by their politics, their dedication, and their analytical acuity. Annette Desmarais' book has helped me better understand these friends and comrades in the struggle. It has also convinced me that La Vía Campesina's vision of agriculturally rich and diverse societies based on the principle of food sovereignty is a future that is not only worth fighting for, but also one that may be our only way out of the massive social and ecological predicaments spawned by corporate-driven globalization.

Walden Bello
Manila
February 14, 2007
Recipient of the Right Livelihood Award for 2003, Walden Bello is executive director of Focus on the Global South and Professor of Sociology at the University of the Philippines.

1. "Where Have All the Peasants Gone? Long Time Passing"

> I think that what really unites us is a fundamental commitment to humanism, because the antithesis of this is individualism and materialism. For us in the Vía Campesina the human aspect is a fundamental principle, so we see the person, man and woman, as the centre of our reason for being and this is what we struggle for — for this family that is at the centre of all. Common problems unite us.... But what also unites us are great aspirations.... What unites us is a spirit of transformation and struggle.... We aspire to a better world, a more just world, a more humane world, a world where real equality and social justice exist. These aspirations and solidarity in rural struggles keep us united in the Vía Campesina. — Rafael Alegría, Operational Secretariat, La Vía Campesina, 1996–2004

These words, spoken by a peasant leader from Honduras, tell us a lot about what is perhaps the most significant and largest peasant and farm movement to have emerged in recent times: La Vía Campesina. Since the signing of the Uruguay Round of the General Agreement on Tariffs and Trade (GATT) in 1994, representatives of rural organizations from the North, South, East, and West, organized in the Vía Campesina, have walked together in the streets of Geneva, Paris, Seattle, Washington, Quebec City, Rome, Bangalore, Porto Alegre, Cancún, and Hong Kong, among other cities. Whenever and wherever international institutions like the World Trade Organization (WTO), World Bank, and the United Nations Food and Agriculture Organization (FAO) meet to discuss agricultural and food issues, the Vía Campesina is there. La Vía Campesina is also there in local communities when peasants and farm families in locales as diverse as Honduras, Mexico, Brazil, Guatemala, Indonesia, Europe, and Canada are resisting the spread of genetically modified seeds or being evicted from their land to facilitate urban sprawl or the development of golf courses, intensive shrimp farms, large pig barns, or eucalyptus plantations.

For many onlookers this level of activity is surprising. For over a hundred years people who thought they knew what was happening in countrysides around the world have predicted the disappearance of the peasantry. Surely, by now they should all be gone! Instead, peasants, integrated into the Vía Campesina, are turning up everywhere, a troublesome and discordant voice

Table 1-1 Regional Distribution and Percentage
Increase of Vía Campesina Member Organizations

Vía Campesina Regions	Number of organizations 2000	Number of organizations that joined in 2004	Total number of organizations
Africa	1	4	5
Europe	22	1	23
Central America*	19	1	20
Caribbean	10	1	11
South America	20	10	30
North America	7	4	11
South Asia	3	17	20
East and South East Asia	19	4	23
Total	101	42	143

* Two months after the Fourth International Conference the Central American region formally dissolved ASOCODE and created a new regional entity, Vía Campesina Centroamericana, which now embraces twenty-six organizations.

amid the chorus extolling the praises of globalization.

The presence of the Vía Campesina has not gone unnoticed. It is a transnational movement embracing organizations of peasants, small and medium-scale farmers, rural women, farm workers, and indigenous agrarian communities in Asia, the Americas, Europe, and Africa. These groups are linked together through their intimate connections to the land. They use their own labour and the labour of their families in small-scale production. Wearing dark green caps, *pañuelos*, and white T-shirts, waving green flags embossed with a brightly coloured logo, and energetically chanting slogans, the Vía Campesina has become an increasingly visible and vocal voice of radical opposition to the globalization of a neo-liberal and corporate model of agriculture.

This resistance took an extreme turn on September 10, 2003 — the first day of the fifth Ministerial Conference of the WTO held in Cancún, Mexico — with the tragic death of Korean farm leader Lee Kyung Hae. Lee, along with another 120 Koreans, had joined the Vía Campesina delegation in Cancún in efforts to get the WTO out of agriculture. Wearing a sign — "WTO kills farmers" — Lee walked up to a high wire fence that had been build to "protect" trade negotiators from protesters and stabbed himself to death.

This act of resistance symbolized what the Vía Campesina had been saying all along: liberalization of agriculture is a war on peasants; it decimates rural communities and destroys farming families. Lee's desperate cry for change subsequently helped to strengthen the Vía Campesina; it has since declared September 10th an International Day of Protest Against the WTO. On that day organizations in many countries mobilize for food sovereignty. Clearly, Lee's death has not been in vain.

The growing visibility of the Vía Campesina as a key actor, strongly rooted in local communities while at the same time increasingly engaged and more skilful on the international stage, has attracted the attention of many rural organizations in search of alternatives. Between 2000 and 2004 the movement grew by over 41 percent. During the movement's Fourth International Conference held in Itaici, Brazil, in June 2004, forty-two organizations joined up (Table 1-1). The Vía Campesina now includes 149 organizations from fifty-six countries. Nearly half of these are peasant organizations based in Asia, where the majority of the world's peasants live. More recently another two organizations have initiated their integration into the Vía Campesina: the NOUMINREN (Japanese Family Farmers' Movement) and the Rural Coalition from the United States of America.

Situating La Vía Campesina

Amid the creeping corporate takeover of agriculture and food, increasing rural poverty, and growing hunger, peasants in the South and farmers in the North have clearly been able to coalesce around common concerns — flying in the face of the commonly held belief that rural peoples in the North and South could not possibly have much in common. As the Uruguay Round of GATT drew to a close in 1994, a group of scholars wondered how farmers would respond to the dramatic changes taking place in the countryside:

> Where should agriculture turn in crisis?... Can one envision a coalition of Belgian, Dutch, French, Italian, U.S., Uruguayan, Brazilian and New Zealand farmers marching on a GATT meeting in Punta del Este? And what could they demand to benefit them all, since they are all in competition with one another? (Bonanno et al. 1994: 8)

The authors argued that farmers and peasants did not have the organizational capacity to effectively pressure the WTO, FAO, and Organization for Economic Cooperation and Development (OECD) — the institutions that were increasingly responsible for determining agricultural and food policies. Rather, farmers' only recourse was to continue to negotiate with increasingly weakened national governments because these were the only political spaces available to them.

Yet in January 2001, when I was in Guatemala watching television coverage of the World Social Forum being held in Porto Alegre, Brazil, I observed that many of the protesters marching in the streets were sporting the green farm caps and *pañuelos* of the Vía Campesina. Here was a visual record of the extent of transnational peasant activism. Commentators like Bonanno and others had failed to see the decisive shift in peasant activism that was occurring. The activities of rural social movements in Latin America throughout the 1990s and into this new century provide clear evidence that peasant activism against the neo-liberal model of agricultural development is alive and strong. Then too, the regional peasant organizations that emerged in the early 1990s — for example, the Coordinadora Latinoamericana de Organizaciones del Campo (CLOC) and the Asociación de Organizaciones Campesinas Centroamericanas para la Cooperación y el Desarrollo (ASOCODE) — have been closely linked to, and working with, peasant organizations in other parts of the world, indicating the emergence of new structures of collective action and an alternative vision. Economic liberalization in the agricultural sector spurred farm and peasant leaders in both North and South to mobilize far beyond national borders and to reach across continents. On other words, their organizations became transnational, carving out new spaces for negotiation and collective action.

Maybe at one time it was difficult to imagine farmers from diverse countries marching together at a GATT meeting in Punta del Este in 1986, at the beginning of the Uruguay Round. But a few years later there was no need for imagining such a situation. In May 1993 farm leaders from around the world gathered together in Mons, Belgium, under the banner of a new global peasant movement, the Vía Campesina — Spanish for "Peasant Way" or "Peasant Road."

Just seven months after the Vía Campesina was formally constituted, over five thousand protesters, including peasants and farmers from Europe, Canada, the United States, Japan, India, and Latin America, marched together on the GATT in Geneva. Three years later, in November 1996, the Vía Campesina was an active and visible political actor at the World Food Summit (WFS), held in Rome and convened by the FAO. Its members challenged the FAO to recognize their legitimacy as representatives of peasants and small farmers organized in one of the largest farm movements in the world and requested to be given official delegate status at the WFS. Vía Campesina leaders also headed the anti-neo-liberal globalization marches at the various WTO ministerial conferences held in Geneva (1998), Seattle (1999), Cancun (2003), and Hong Kong (2005). They participated in the massive demonstrations in Prague, Washington, Quebec City, Quito, and Genoa in protest against the globalization of neo-liberalism, the International Monetary Fund (IMF), the World Bank, and the Group of Eight.

The Vía Campesina's international efforts have led to important shifts in the debate around food and agriculture. The Vía Campesina's concept of "food sovereignty" (a radical extension of the ideas surrounding food security) has spread widely and is now embraced by local, national, and international movements around the world. The concept is also being explored by global institutions such as the FAO, and recent reports to the United Nations Commission on Human Rights advocate food sovereignty as a means of ensuring the human right to food and food security. The concept of peasant rights re-entered the international arena when, in spring 2004, under the leadership of the Federation of Indonesian Peasant Unions (FSPI), the Vía Campesina petitioned the United Nations Commission on Human Rights for the development of a charter or convention on peasants' rights. After having all but disappeared from national government and international plans over the past twenty-five years, agrarian reform is now back on the agenda, and the World Bank's "market-assisted land reform program" is now in question. On March 10, 2006, 350 government delegates and 70 representatives of farmers' and non-governmental organizations (NGOs) gathered at the FAO's International Conference on Agrarian Reform and Rural Development and formally recognized the essential role of agrarian reform in eradicating hunger and poverty.

Clearly, La Vía Campesina is filling an important void. Its very existence is evidence of new structures of collective action in the countryside; its strategies defy traditional patterns of organizing in the rural sector; and the sheer magnitude of its international presence — its dynamic nature, cultural diversity, and wide geographical distribution — speaks to its transformatory potential. (See Figures 1.1 to 1.8.)

How were peasants and small farmers able to do this? Where did they find the organizational capacity and strength to challenge transnational agribusiness corporations and international institutions whose power and influence increasingly dictate national government policy? What has made the Vía Campesina so successful against seemingly impossible odds? This book explores the social and political significance of the Vía Campesina by addressing these questions. In doing so, I explore the main issues, strategies, and collective actions of this peasant movement and highlight its contributions to building alternatives to the powerful forces of neo-liberal economic globalization. In the process, I hope that by looking carefully at the first ten years of the Vía Campesina's existence we can better understand the role of rural social movements in reshaping rural development and how the role of agriculture in development might be rethought.

Looking at Peasant Movements from Within

This book offers an insider's account of the Vía Campesina by privileging the experiences, voices, and visions of the peasants, rural women, and farmers themselves. In the interests of shifting the centre of power and voice, I have filled the pages of this book with as many of their words as possible — and have done this directly, rather than paraphrasing them. In this way I am respecting peasants' and farmers' desires and concerted efforts to establish an international space in which they can articulate their needs, interests, and

Figure 1-1 Vía Campesina Organizations — North America

Canada
National Farmers Union (NFU)
Union Paysanne

USA

National Family Farm Coalition (NFFC)
Border Farm Workers Project

Mexico

Unión Nacional de Organizaciones Regionales Campesinas Autónomas (UNORCA)
Asociación Mexicana de Uniones de Crédito del Sector Social (AMUCSS)
Asociación Nacional de Empresas Comercializadoras de Productores del Campo (ANEC)
Central Independiente de Obreros Agrícolas y Campesinos (CIOAC)
Coordinadora Nacional Plan de Ayala (CNPA)
Frente Democrático Campesino de Chihauhau (FDCC)
Coalición de Organizaciones Democráticas de Uniones Campesinas (CODUC)

N

0   1,000   2,000   4,000 km

Map by Jessica Henderson

Figure 1-2 Vía Campesina Organizations — South America

Venezuela
Coordinadora Agraria Nacional Ezequiel Zamora (CANEZ)

Columbia
Asociación Nacional de Usuarios Campesinos (ANUC-UR)
Coordinador Nacional Agrario (CNA)
Federación Nacional de Cooperativas Agropecuarias (FENACOA)
Federación Nacional Sindical Unitaria Agropecuaria (FENSUAGRO-CUT)

Ecuador
Confederación Única Nacional de
    Afiliados Al Seguro Social
    Campesino (CONFEUNASSC)
Federación Nacional de
    Organizaciones Campesino-
    Indígenas (FENOC-I)

Brazil
Articulação Nacional de Mulheres
    Trabalhadoras Rurais do Sul (ANMTR)
Movimento de Atingidos por Barragens (MAB)
Movimento dos Trabalhadores sem Terra (MST)
Movimento dos Pequeños Agricultores (MPA)
Movimento dos Mulheres la Camponesa (MMC)

Peru
Confederación Nacional
    Agraria (CNA)
Confederación Campesina
    del Perú (CCP)

Bolivia
Federación Nacional de Mujeres Campesinas de
    Bolivia "Bartolina Sisa"
Confederación Sindical Unica de Trabajadores
    Campesinos de Bolivia (CSUTCB)
Consejo Andino de Productores de Coca
Movimiento de Trabajadores sin Tierra (MST)

Chile
Asociación Nacional de Mujeres
    Rurales e Indígenas (ANAMURI)
Confederación Campesina Nehuen
Confederación Nacional e Indígena
    "El Surco"

Paraguay
Movimiento Campesino Paraguayo (MCP)
Organizacion de Lucha por la Tierra (OLT)
Coprinadora Nacional de Organizaciones de
    Mujeres Trabajadoras Rurales e Indígenas
    (CONAMURI)
Mesa Coordinadora de Organizaciones
    Campesinas (MCNOC)

Argentina
Consejo Asesor Indígena (CAI)
Movimiento Campesino de Santiago del Estero
    (MOCASE)
Asociación de Pequeños productores del
    Noreste de Córdoba (APENOC)
Coordinadora de Campesinos, Indígena y
    Trabajadores Rurales (COCITRA)
Mesa Nacional

N

0   600   1,200   2,400 km

Map by Jessica Henderson

Figure 1-3 Vía Campesina Organizations — Central America

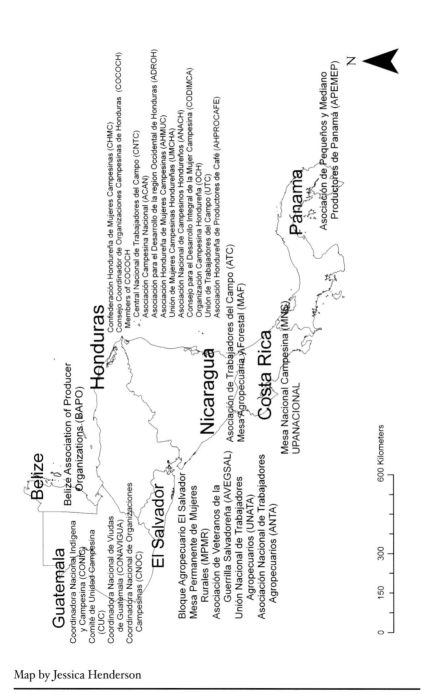

Map by Jessica Henderson

Figure 1-4 Vía Campesina Organizations — Caribbean

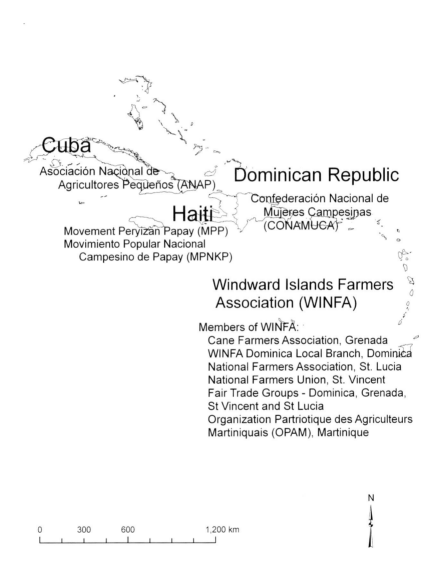

Cuba

Asociación Nacional de
Agricultores Pequeños (ANAP)

Dominican Republic

Confederación Nacional de
Mujeres Campesinas
(CONAMUCA)

Haiti

Movement Peryizan Papay (MPP)
Movimiento Popular Nacional
    Campesino de Papay (MPNKP)

**Windward Islands Farmers
Association (WINFA)**

Members of WINFA:
    Cane Farmers Association, Grenada
    WINFA Dominica Local Branch, Dominica
    National Farmers Association, St. Lucia
    National Farmers Union, St. Vincent
    Fair Trade Groups - Dominica, Grenada,
    St Vincent and St Lucia
    Organization Partriotique des Agriculteurs
    Martiniquais (OPAM), Martinique

N

| 0 | 300 | 600 | 1,200 km |

Map by Jessica Henderson

Figure 1-5 Vía Campesina Organizations — East and Southeast Asia

South Korea

Korean Women Farmers
Association (KWFA)
Korean Peasant League (KPL)

Thailand
Assembly of the Poor

Philippines

Demokratikong Kilusang
Magbubukid ng Pilipinas (dKMP)
Kilusang Magbubukid
ng Pilipinas (KMP)

Vietnam
Vietnamese National Farmers
Union (VNFU)

Malaysia
Panggau

Indonesia

Federation of Indonesian Peasant Unions (FSPI)
Members of FSPI
    Perhimpunan Masyarakat Tani Aceh (PERMATA)
    Serikat Petani Sumatera Utara (SPSU)
    Serikat Petani Sumatera Barat (SPSB)
    Persatuan Petani Jambi (PERTAJAM)
    Serikat Petani Sumatera Selatan (SPSS)
    Serikat Petani Lampung (SPL)
    Serikat Petani Jawa Barat (SPJB)
    Serikat Petani Jawa Tengah (SPJT)
    Serikat Petani Jawa Timur (SPJatim)
    Federasi Serikat Petani Jawa Timur (FSPJT)
    Serikat Petani Pasundan (SPP)
    Serikat Petani Banten (SP-Banten)
    Serikat Petani Kabupaten Sikka (SPKS-NTT)
    Serikat Petani Nusa Tenggara Barat (Serta-NTB)

East Timor
Hasatil-East Timor

N

0   500   1,000   2,000 km

Map by Jessica Henderson

Figure 1-6 Vía Campesina Organizations — South Asia

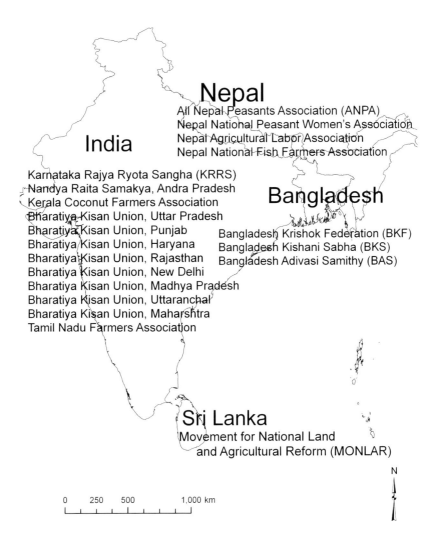

Nepal
All Nepal Peasants Association (ANPA)
Nepal National Peasant Women's Association
Nepal Agricultural Labor Association
Nepal National Fish Farmers Association

India
Karnataka Rajya Ryota Sangha (KRRS)
Nandya Raita Samakya, Andra Pradesh
Kerala Coconut Farmers Association
Bharatiya Kisan Union, Uttar Pradesh
Bharatiya Kisan Union, Punjab
Bharatiya Kisan Union, Haryana
Bharatiya Kisan Union, Rajasthan
Bharatiya Kisan Union, New Delhi
Bharatiya Kisan Union, Madhya Pradesh
Bharatiya Kisan Union, Uttaranchal
Bharatiya Kisan Union, Maharshtra
Tamil Nadu Farmers Association

Bangladesh
Bangladesh Krishok Federation (BKF)
Bangladesh Kishani Sabha (BKS)
Bangladesh Adivasi Samithy (BAS)

Sri Lanka
Movement for National Land
and Agricultural Reform (MONLAR)

N

0   250   500   1,000 km

Map by Jessica Henderson

Figure 1-7 Vía Campesina Organizations — Europe

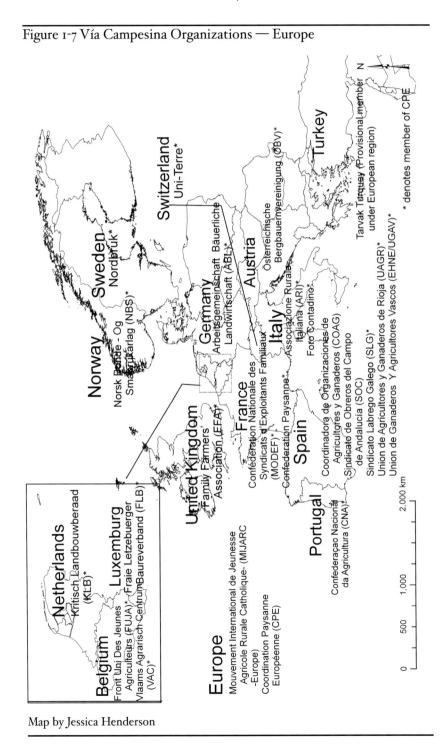

Map by Jessica Henderson

Figure 1-8 Vía Campesina Organizations — Africa

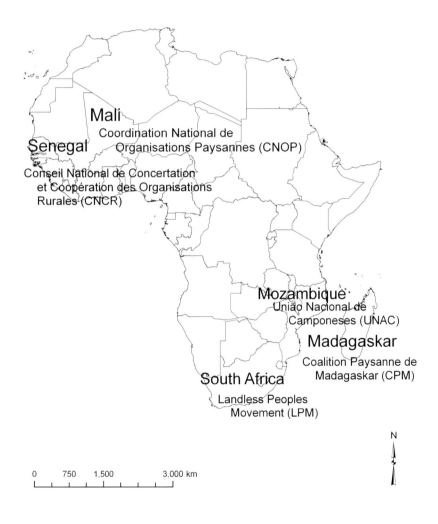

Mali
Coordination National de
Organisations Paysannes (CNOP)

Senegal
Conseil National de Concertation
et Coopération des Organisations
Rurales (CNCR)

Mozambique
União Nacional de
Camponeses (UNAC)

Madagaskar
Coalition Paysanne de
Madagaskar (CPM)

South Africa
Landless Peoples
Movement (LPM)

0   750   1,500   3,000 km

N

Map by Jessica Henderson

demands in their own voice. In the following pages, then, quotations not otherwise credited come from interviews I conducted (mostly in person, with a few by phone or e-mail) in the period 2000–02. I've translated the interviews conducted in Spanish, while in India I worked with a translator.

In many ways I was in quite a privileged position while doing this research, because I have worked as technical support to the Vía Campesina since its inception in 1993. This position has provided me with access both to numerous farm leaders around the world and to all kinds of meetings, conferences, discussions, and documents. More importantly, over the years I was able to gain a truly important resource, the trust of Vía Campesina leaders.

In the interest of revealing peasants' and farmers' visions for social change, this book is based on various sources. To understand the debates and logic behind the particular positions that the Vía Campesina ultimately voiced in the international arena, I looked at both its public and internal documents. The press releases, position statements, proceedings of meetings, and internal communication among participating organizations provide glimpses into the numerous activities and actions of the movement, and the different levels (local, national, international) on which it works. They also allowed me to witness the extent of congruence or disagreement within the Vía Campesina itself. As a participant in many Vía Campesina meetings and mobilizations, I saw first-hand the issues that came to the forefront, as well as how these issues were articulated and debated, and how decisions were ultimately made.

Interviews with locally based leaders in Mexico, Canada, and India highlighted numerous examples of just how the local, national, and international connect within the Vía Campesina. Interviews with national farm organizations in these three countries gave me critical insights into the reasons why farm organizations opt to "go global," the factors that contribute to their success or failure in doing so, and the conditions and resources necessary to pursue this kind of work further. I also talked with most members of the movement's International Co-ordinating Commission (ICC) and technical support staff to record their experiences in consolidating an international peasant and farm movement.

If one of the main purposes of this book is to better understand rural development in the context of globalization, then why focus on a peasant movement? My interest is both personal and political. I was a grain and cattle farmer — with my sister — for fourteen years in the province of Saskatchewan, Canada. We started as conventional farmers and used most of the chemicals recommended to us as good farming practices by the extension services of the Saskatchewan Department of Agriculture. We gradually sold off our cattle, became vegetarians, and switched to organic production. As a farmer I had the privilege of participating in the Oxfam Canada Farmers Brigade, a project that sent Canadian farmers to teach preventative maintenance of farm machinery in agricultural co-operatives in Nicaragua. It was when I was in Nicaragua that I began to understand the importance of farmers being organized. One of my key mentors in this process was Martha H. Valle, who was at the time a regional leader of the Women's Section of the Unión Nacional de Agricultores y Ganaderos (UNAG).

When I returned to Canada I found myself increasingly interested in the politics of food. Eventually, I made the difficult choice to leave farming to work as co-ordinator of the Oxfam Global Agriculture Project, which facilitated the building of linkages between the National Farmers Union (NFU) of Canada and its counterparts around the world. It was in that position — which I held from 1989 to 1998 — that I eventually began working as technical support to the Vía Campesina, which the NFU helped found in 1993.

Around 1997 the international development agency that had from the beginning supported the Global Agriculture Project suddenly changed course. This kind of political grassroots work was no longer a priority, and I was given a new job description that involved considerable campaigning and fundraising — none of which I saw as contributing directly to the urgent need for social change in rural areas. Faced with the question of how I could continue to support the Vía Campesina I approached the movement with the idea of doing doctoral research on and with the movement. At the time the Vía Campesina was going into its fifth year, and its leadership agreed that research focused on the movement might be useful in determining its strengths and weaknesses and possibly signalling ideas for future directions.

Most interestingly, in my search for an appropriate graduate school I had a discussion with an anthropologist who, after hearing about my intent to do research with a global peasant movement, looked at me askance and said, "But peasants no longer exist!" She then proceeded to provide me with numerous academic sources indicating just that.[1] It was a particularly ironic moment because by that point I had been working for about ten years with people from around the world who called themselves peasants. Indeed, for years I had been hearing comments quite to the contrary — comments like that of Marcel Carreon Mundo, a Mexican peasant leader. One time, as we were driving together down the back roads of Quintana Roo on the way to a local meeting, he said to me: "A campesino comes from the countryside. There have always been campesinos. What did not exist before were investors, industrialists, political parties, etc. Campesinos have always existed and they will always exist. They will never be abolished."

If we think broadly about politics as a struggle for power — that is, power to be, to define, to speak, and to act — then focusing on a social movement can be a deep political act. This is especially true in the case of peasant movements — whose participants, as some suggest, no longer exist. Peasants have been described as a *"species* made nearly *extinct* by globalization" (Feder

1978 quoted in Welch 2001: 1). Gerardo Otero (1998), writing on Mexico, argue that peasants are now "semiproletarians." Some writers document a consistent process of *depeasantization* (Araghi 1995), while others, as Marc Edelman (2001a: 2) suggests, "have been too busy *reconceptualizing* peasants out of existence."[2] Orin Starn (1992), an anthropologist who worked with Peruvian peasant communities, says that it is almost as if researchers now consider peasants to be remnants of a distant past with little to contribute to any current analysis of collective action. This could be because, as Mexican scholar Roger Bartra (1992: 17) states, "Peasants are in the habit of casting a long shadow of nostalgia and melancholy over modern society."

Others have examined changes in peasant survival strategies, highlight peasants' stubborn refusal to disappear, and stress the need for "rethinking peasantries" (Bryceson. Kay and Mooij 2000). Edelman (1999) demonstrates how Costa Rican peasants are resisting globalization by engaging in a cultural struggle as they rearticulate a peasant identity, give new meanings to their "peasant-ness," and redefine development. Cliff Welch's (2001) work in Latin America confirms the persistence of a "somewhat abused and transformed" peasantry. Indeed, he notes that in the teeth of globalization an active process of "re-peasantization" is going on as the absolute number of peasants grows, as peasant movements engage in new forms of resistance, and as they build on-the-ground alternatives. In discussing the flight of Mexican peasants across the U.S. border in search of work, Richard Rodriguez invites us not to ignore peasant wisdom: "The illegal immigrant is the bravest among us. The most modern among us. The prophet... The peasant knows the reality of our world decades before the California suburbanite will ever get the point" (quoted in Urrea 1996: 2).

Given the significant shifts taking place in the countryside through the restructuring of agriculture as a result of Structural Adjustment Programs (SAPs), regional free-trade agreements, the WTO's Agreement on Agriculture (AoA) and Trade-Related Aspects of Intellectual Property Rights (TRIPs), and the decisions made at the 1996 World Food Summit and the World Food Summit: Five Years Later (2002), we need to understand better the dynamics of organizing in the countryside. Traditional actors such as peasant organizations continue to play a critical role in advocating change. Indeed, in many countries in Asia, Africa, and the Americas, peasant organizations are at the forefront of struggles against neo-liberalism, not only as part of their efforts to gain greater access to and control over productive resources but also as key actors defending community and diversity.[3] As important as these national struggles are, I believe that in an increasingly international agricultural economy it is necessary to explore the ways in which agrarian activism has reached across national borders — doing exactly what some analysts suggested peasants and farmers were incapable of doing.

Perhaps more importantly, if globalization has now become the essential framework of "development" as we know it, and if three-quarters of the world's poor live in the countryside and depend on agriculture for survival, we need to consider carefully the demands of rural organizations and their ideas about what is important for development. Furthermore, if rural women are the poorest of the poor living in rural areas, it is also critical to look at how rural women are organizing for change.

La Vía Campesina and Civil Society

The Vía Campesina did not appear, nor does it operate, in a vacuum. Its collective identity, positions, and strategies were further defined through its opposition to the WTO and interactions with other civil society organizations, namely, the International Federation of Agricultural Producers (IFAP) and international development NGOs. Distinguishing between movements that are more closely tied to or dependent on existing structures — those on the "inside" — and those whose modes of existence are threatened by globalization — those on the "outside" — helps us to understand the limitations and/or possibilities for social change. Doing so can shed light on the meaning of social change: whether it accommodates and reinforces existing realities or whether it represents radical reimagining or re-envisioning (Pollack 2001).

When they refer to non-state actors, many international institutions, national governments, and writers now favour all-encompassing terms like "civil society," and more recently "global civil society." These terms confuse more than clarify. They lump into one category all non-state actors — NGOs, professional organizations, research institutions, ethnic movements, human rights groups, peasant organizations, feminist organizations, and urban community self-help groups, among others. Catherine Eschle (2001b: 71) points out that what this does is effectively blind us "to the hierarchical and oppressive relations that exist *within* civil society." She argues that in the absence of any analysis of exactly who the various actors are and what interests they represent, the inherent class differences and power imbalances therein are completely obscured. This is deeply problematic because it masks the very real world in which peasant movements function, and it systematically undermines their efforts in bringing about social change.

A close look at the Vía Campesina experience allows glimpses into the unequal distribution of power and resources within civil society and the power struggles therein. It also highlights the very real limitations of participating in negotiations with powerful multilateral agencies. In certain strategic instances, when it is clear that no good can come from negotiation with the powerful, the Vía Campesina has also demonstrated the importance of a delegitimization that stems from disengagement — a strategy first articulated by Gandhi almost a century ago.

Therefore, I intend to make a clear distinction between two very different components of civil society: NGOs and peasant organizations or people's organizations. In general, NGOs have different aims, purposes, interests,

NGOs: A Neo-Comprador Class?

NGOs have garnered harsh (and remarkably similar) criticisms from the far right to the far left around the contentious issues of their legitimacy and accountability. *The Economist*, a staunch supporter of neo-liberalism, announced in 1999 that NGOs had become big business and could "represent a dangerous shift of power to unelected and unaccountable special-interest groups" (1999b: 18). In a publication on the ravages of globalization, James Petras and Henry Veltmeyer (2001: 129) argued that NGOs had come to form a "neo-comprador class":

> Today, thousands of NGO directors drive $40,000 four-wheel-drive sports utility vehicles from their fashionable suburban homes or apartments to their well-furnished offices and building complexes, leaving the children and domestic chores in the hands of servants and their yards to be tended by gardeners. They are more familiar with and spend more time at the overseas sites of their international conferences on poverty (Washington, Bangkok, Tokyo, Brussels, Rome, etc.) than the muddy villages of their own country. They are more adept at writing up new proposals to bring in hard currency for "deserving professionals" than risking a rap on the head from police attacking a demonstration of underpaid rural school teachers. NGO leaders are a new class not based on property ownership or government resources but derived from imperial funding and their own capacity to control significant popular groups. The NGO leaders can be conceived of as a kind of neo-comprador group that doesn't produce any useful commodity but does function to produce services for the donor countries, trading in domestic poverty for individual perks.

Other critics recognize that NGOs are a diverse lot with different aims, ideological orientations, mechanisms for representation, and organizational practices. Some NGOs are more progressive and "concerned" than others and can play an important role in supporting — but not directing — the work of people's organizations (Tadem 1996). But as Elizabeth Jelin (1998: 412) warns:

> Cases of "authoritarian technocracy" *on behalf of* the poor (*we know what is good for you and will make sure that you comply*) are innumerable.... The fact is that NGOs... do not have a built-in mechanism of accountability. They do not have a constituency or membership composed of their "sovereign citizens." They are financially accountable to those who provide funds and to their own ideology and consciousness, hopefully (but *only* hopefully) based on "good" values, solidarity, compassion, and commitment. Given this relative absence of institutional and societal accountability, there is always the danger of arbitrary action, of manipulation, of lack of transparency in objectives and practices.

organizational cultures and structures, and mechanisms for decision-making and accountability than peasant organizations. At the risk of simplification, I use the term NGO when referring to development non-profit organizations that channel funds — received from private donations, governments, corporations, and international institutions — for development projects (presumably) in support of mass-based organizations. Also included in this category are organizations that capture significant resources to conduct research on issues concerning the marginalized. NGOs, by and large, are staffed by well-educated, middle-class professionals; they are project-driven in that their existence depends largely on their ability to secure funds from national and international funders for specific development projects or campaigns directed towards the marginalized and disadvantaged.

Dieter Rucht (1999: 218–20) demonstrates that NGOs working at an international level play different roles: some are "problem detectors, critics, challengers and accusers" while others act as "allies," "advisor[s]," and/or "administrator[s]" to dominant forces. He argues that as international NGOs experience rapid growth, professionalization, and institutionalization, they tend to "soften the challenging nature of their claims" and there is greater opportunity for co-optation and deradicalization as the NGOs become increasingly dependent on state and/or multilateral funding. This shift can then seriously limit the imagined alternatives as it becomes very difficult, if not impossible, for these organizations to think outside of existing structures (Pollack 2001: 197). In the international arena this can lead to what Aaron Pollack calls the "epistemological hegemony of modernity," because there appears to be little space to explore alternative perspectives. For another group of writers (Amoore et al. 2002: 19), "Such 'tinkering at the margins' of globalization… has the unintended effect of helping the globalization project to consolidate itself."

NGOs were created, at least partially, to speak for those without a voice. Part of their mandate has always been to help these mute actors find an effective voice. Unfortunately, having done so, many NGOs have not been comfortable with what the "formerly voiceless" have to say. Many NGOs have not learned how to keep quiet when appropriate.

Peasant organizations, on the other hand, can best be categorized as people's organizations or popular organizations, mass organizations, community-based organizations, or social movements that include, among others, trade unions, fisherfolk organizations, urban poor organizations, and women's organizations. People's organizations are community- or sector-based, grassroots organizations of volunteers that function to further the interests of their mass membership; many have democratically elected leaderships, and are directly and immediately accountable to their membership or constituency.

These peasant organizations are part of a stream of "critical" or "radical" social movements that by definition struggle for a radical transformation of the existing structures of political, social, and economic power; their vision is based on principles of social and economic justice, which includes ethnic and gender equality. Mobilization and public protest remain the most important strategies that critical social movements use in their struggle for greater access to and control over productive resources.

Of course, not all social movements have adopted horizontal structures and democratic or inclusive practices. But, as Walden Bello, an activist from Focus on the Global South, based in Thailand, says, "How we organize reflects our goal" (quoted in Bell 2002: 5). The exclusionary nature of the neo-liberal model of development (promoted since the early 1980s) has led to a continuous decline in the living standards of the lower strata of society in many countries, and to increasing disparities between the rich and poor. However, those who have been disenfranchised, dispossessed, and excluded by global capitalism are not passive victims. The brutal force of globalization contributed to the emergence of a great variety of new social actors. It also led to new structures of collective action among traditional social actors, including peasant organizations. From urban and rural women's organizations, indigenous communities, environmental groups, and collective kitchens to human rights groups and peasant organizations, all are trying to establish a presence and carve out alternative political spaces in which their concerns and demands can be articulated, negotiated, and accommodated in the context of a contested globalization and a continuing debate about development.

What is happening is a struggle between two different visions of the world. On the one hand, the forces of neo-liberal economic globalization work to obliterate diversity, to homogenize, and to create one global economy and one global culture based on consumerism and the adoption of Western science and technology. This process involves the "commodification of everything" via the consolidation of an omnipotent global marketplace built on the framework of what John Kenneth Galbraith calls "socially barren" trade policy. The forces of social resistance, on the other hand, assert difference and embrace diversity. They want to "bring people back in," to "redefine community" and development using a different vision of the world based on a whole set of different values (Gills 2000: 3, 6). Some of the slogans used by the Vía Campesina and other social movements clearly express this alternative vision: for example, the World Social Forum's insistence that "another world is possible," and the anti-WTO coalition Our World Is Not for Sale.

The struggle contests the very meaning of development and who should be involved in defining and implementing it. It is a struggle in which radical social movements are key agents of change as they envision alternatives that question every aspect of neo-liberalism, as they work to shift the terms of debate and influence multilateral policy processes by introducing new norms and discourses, and as they move resistance to a place in which it can build concrete alternatives in the here and now.

In doing so, radical social movements, as many have argued, are involved in cultural politics as they create alternative identities, new solidarities, alternative social spaces, and alternative political cultures (Eschle 2001a). Around the world, radical social movements are not working for "inclusion" in existing political structures and the dominant culture; instead, they strive to "transform the very political order in which they operate" (Alvarez, Dagnino, and Escobar 1998: 8). Simultaneously, critical social movements are seeking new meanings and ways of being in the world. They seek to democratize sites and structures of power, and to limit the power of those sites and structures, and their vision for social change often encompasses developing a political culture that is based on the principles and practices of inclusion and social justice (Stammers 1999: 86).

This is not to suggest that all social movements around the globe have these same goals. But the Vía Campesina is one such radical movement that engages in this kind of cultural politics. The Vía Campesina struggles for inclusion and greater participation in defining a *different* world order as it strives for greater access to and control over productive resources for farming families everywhere. Whether or not it is succeeding in embodying the various principles of a radical social movement is an important measure of success or failure.

As such, the Vía Campesina differs considerably from the more reformist or conformist farm movement, the International Federation of Agricultural Producers (IFAP). The two movements function from fundamentally different ideological frameworks, represent different constituencies and interests, and use different strategies.

A number of commentators have explored how social movements and NGOs interact with major multilateral economic institutions such as the World Bank, the IMF, and the WTO, which manage and extend the process of globalization. In relations with these institutions, not all social movements are created equal. According to Robert O'Brien and his co-authors (2000: 224), certain types of global social movements are able and willing "to engage multilateral economic institutions on an ongoing basis." Moreover, they suggest, "The factors that determine who is in and who is out can vary according to ideology, location, expertise and influence."

Those social movements that gain and maintain access to the WTO are those that are more ideologically inclined to accept the basic premise of globalization, although they may disagree with the scope, speed, and intensity of liberalization. That is, conformist or reformist views are more likely to be accepted within the WTO, while grassroots social movements with more critical views have had little if any access (Scholte et al. 1998: 19). Being close to the centres of power (Geneva and Washington) has also facilitated greater access and engagement, as has having influence in the political system of powerful states like those of the European Union or the United States. As O'Brien et al. (2000: 225) point out: "The degree to which a movement can

---

NGOs and the WTO

The multilateral economic institutions themselves also actively seek out and select the civil society organizations with which they want to consult and develop ongoing relations. The institutions are more apt to engage in dialogue with social movements that "speak the same language" as they do, especially ones that understand economics and trade law or have expertise that they themselves lack (O'Brien et al. 2000: 224). For instance, in its analysis of the debacle of the WTO Ministerial Conference in Seattle, *The Economist* (1999b: 19) suggested that the WTO had much to learn from the World Bank's largely successful strategy of co-opting NGOs:

> The Fifty Years is Enough campaign of 1994 [directed at the World Bank] was a prototype of Seattle (complete with activists invading the meeting halls). Now the NGOs are surprisingly quiet about the World Bank. The reason is that the Bank has made a huge effort to co-opt them....
>
> James Wolfensohn, the Bank's boss, has made "dialogue" with NGOs a central component of the institution's work. More than 70 NGO specialists work in the Bank's field offices. More than half of World Bank projects last year involved NGOs. Mr. Wolfensohn has built alliances with everyone, from religious groups to environmentalists. His efforts have diluted the strength of "mobilisation networks" and increased the relative power of technical NGOs (for it is mostly these that the Bank has co-opted)....
>
> The WTO will not evolve in the same way.... But it could still try to weaken the broad coalition that attacked it in Seattle by reaching out to mainstream and technical NGOs.

---

put pressure upon key states and the degree to which its concerns can be accommodated without challenging the most powerful interests are key to determining its relationship with multilateral economic institutions."

The IFAP is well equipped and well situated to engage in dialogue with multilateral economic institutions; this is one of its main strategies in efforts to reform trade agreements and development approaches to better serve farmers' interests. This helps us understand why Vía Campesina's opposition to the WTO is so implacable: the IFAP and Vía Campesina do not speak the same language — indeed, they profess diametrically opposed visions of the future. The peasant and farm organizations that formed the Vía Campesina are convinced that more radical strategies and positions are urgently needed to address the crisis in the countryside. In forming the Vía Campesina, they effectively created a progressive alternative to the IFAP.

The main goal of the Vía Campesina is to build a radically different model of agriculture, one based on the concept of food sovereignty. The peasant movement believes that this can only be done by building unity and solidarity among the great diversity of peasants and farm organizations around the world. Through solidarity and unity, the Vía Campesina has consolidated a collective peasant identity as "people of the land," mounted radical opposition to multilateral institutions, defined alternative policies on key issues of concern to rural communities, and engaged in collective action in efforts to build food sovereignty.

"Building Unity within Diversity"

Bonanno and others were sceptical of peasants' ability to organize internationally because of their diversity. The Vía Campesina turned what some saw as an obstacle to international organization — diversity — into one of its key strengths. The transnational movement brings together organizations representing different constituencies. While most of its geographically far-flung member organizations are strictly rural-based, some of them are actively working in urban settings. Brazil's Movimento dos Trabalhadores Rurais Sem Terra (MST), for example, works primarily with the landless in the countryside, but also has started to form "rurban" settlements (*assentamentos rurbanos*) in the *favelas*, setting up urban-based families on small plots of land close to, or within, city limits (*New Left Review* 2002: 92). The thrust of the work of the Unión Nacional de Organizaciones Regionales Campesinas Autónomas (UNORCA) in Puebla, Mexico, is organizing *comerciantes ambulantes* (street vendors) in urban settings, and in Vera Cruz UNORCA played a significant role in organizing transport carriers (*transportistas*). The newly formed Union Paysanne in Quebec brings together farmers with — among others — researchers, students, consumer groups, and eco-tourism businesses — sectors that are all committed to building an alternative to "*malbouffe*" and industrial agriculture.

The region with the fewest Vía Campesina members is Africa, but that may be just a matter of time. In November 1998 the movement's International Coordinating Committee (ICC) was invited to an All-African Farmers Conference held in Dakar, where the African representatives decided that rather than joining as individual organizations they would organize and consolidate themselves first at the regional level in Africa and join the Vía Campesina later as a united region.

The Vía Campesina also represents diversity in how farm and peasant organizations are organized. Although they might well engage in actions at the national and international levels, some organizations, like the Karnataka State Farmers Association (KRRS), are organized only at the state level. Canada's National Farmers Union is a national organization while UNORCA in Mexico is a national federation that works in twenty-three of the Mexican states. Still others, like the Coordination Paysanne Européenne (CPE) or ASOCODE, are regional entities that bring together national organizations. Each of these different organizational structures demands particular skills, experience, and knowledge in negotiating among its defined membership.

> ### "Food from Nowhere"
>
> *Malbouffe* (meaning "bad food" but usually translated as junk food) is a concept developed by the Confédération Paysanne in France in its struggle against the globalization of industrial agriculture. *Malbouffe* gained worldwide recognition through José Bové, the Confédération Paysanne's charismatic leader, who was imprisoned for leading a protest that dismantled a McDonald's outlet still under construction in the small town of Millau in 1999.
>
> As Bové explains, *malbouffe* is "food from nowhere." It has, he says "the same taste from one end of the world to the other"; it has been stripped of "taste, health and cultural and geographical identity. Junk food is the result of the intensive exploitation of the land to maximize yield and profit" (Bové and Dufour 2001: 54–55).
>
> Shortly after the Union Paysanne was formed in May 2001, a progressive alternative to the mainstream and dominant Union de Producteurs du Québec, Bové travelled to Quebec and met with the leaders of the new organization to discuss French farm politics and exchange ideas about organizing strategies. As a result of the visit the Quebec organization integrated a rejection of *malbouffe* into its vision for change. The Union Paysanne emphasizes a peasant agriculture that involves "a human-scale agriculture and vibrant rural communities" (Union Paysanne, n.d.).
>
> The new organization certainly struck a chord with the public's growing distrust of the food system. In the first year of its existence, the Union Paysanne gained over three thousand members. It is action-driven; it was a vocal and visible actor in the struggle over intensive livestock operations and is one of the reasons that the Quebec Government issued a moratorium on the building of large hog operations. The Union Paysanne formally joined the Vía Campesina in 2004.

Consequently, each of them has its own unique organizational culture, which can assist or hinder its ability to function well in a multicultural and diverse international movement.

One of the Vía Campesina's main strengths is how it weaves together organizations embedded in their own particular political, economic, social, and cultural contexts — but still manages to establish unity within this diversity. In doing this it depends on well-defined constituencies and a process of strict accountability to the numerous peasant and farm organizations that make up its membership. In representing millions of farming families around the world, it employs a horizontal structure. According to Paul Nicholson, a founding member of the Vía Campesina from the Basque Country, whose organization would become the Vía Campesina's regional co-ordinator for Europe, the structure makes decision-making an extended, time-consuming, and sometimes long-winded affair. Consultation and accountability are the key, facilitated by the well-defined structure and processes for representation and democratic decision-making. The Vía Campesina is divided into

The Movement in Africa and the Middle East

Over the years a number of exchanges have taken place among Vía Campesina organizations and their African counterparts. The Vía Campesina has worked together with the Réseau des Organisations Paysannes et de Producteurs Agricoles de l'Afrique de l'Ouest (ROPPA) on various food sovereignty issues, and African representatives have participated in the international conferences of the Vía Campesina.

In the events surrounding the World Food Summit: Five Years Later held in Rome in June 2002, the Vía Campesina and ROPPA worked closely together as members of the International Planning Committee of the NGO/Civil Society Organizations' Forum on Food Sovereignty. As part of the Forum on Food Sovereignty they also co-organized a workshop on agriculture and market access. More recently ties between African organizations and the Vía Campesina were further strengthened and consolidated as a result of meetings and joint actions carried out in the framework of the World Summit on Sustainable Development, held in Johannesburg in late August 2002. The Vía Campesina delegation of thirty-six representatives from all regions included twelve representatives from the União Nacional de Camponesas (UNAC) of Mozambique.

In South Africa, Vía Campesina delegates participated in a series of events — including the first official National Assembly of South Africa's Landless People's Movement, a Day of Solidarity that included visits to communities confronting forced removals, a major demonstration (March of the Landless), and a Landless People's concert — organized by the Landless People's Movement and the National Land Committee of South Africa (Vía Campesina 2002g). A whole day was set aside for exchanges between Vía Campesina delegates and representatives of various small farmers and landless African organizations to enable them to come to a better understanding of each other's realities and to pursue avenues of further collaboration.

This collaboration is yielding some important results. For example, the Vía Campesina worked with a number of other social movements and locally based African peasant organizations to organize a major international event on food sovereignty in Mali in February 2007. The Nyeleni Forum for Food Sovereignty brought together representatives of social movements and NGOs from around the world, as well as some key government leaders, to further define the meaning and practical policy implications of food sovereignty. This event and the surrounding activities have, no doubt, strengthened the African presence in the Vía Campesina.

Interest among Arab organizations in future collaboration surfaced when the Vía Campesina sent a four-person delegation — Paul Nicholson (CPE), Doris Gutierrez de Hernandez (Vía Campesina Operational Secretariat), Mário Lill (MST), and José Bové (Confédération Paysanne and CPE) — to Palestine in early spring 2002. The Vía Campesina sought to establish contacts with farmers' organizations and to better understand the situation of Arab and Israeli farming peoples, aiming also to develop a long-term strategy for joint work to protect the rights of farming families. On March 30, International Earth Day, the delegation visited a Bedouin community and participated with about five thousand people in a huge protest against Palestinian farmers being driven off their land and the continued violence in the region.

A few days later two members of the Vía Campesina delegation joined a group of forty international pacifist militants to act as a human shield in the headquarters of the Palestinian leader, in the besieged city of Ramallah, in efforts to stop Israeli attacks. Over the next four weeks the Vía Campesina issued numerous press releases describing the devastating situation of Palestinian farm families, demanding that the principle of food sovereignty be respected and that Palestinians be granted the right to remain on their land to produce food. The Vía Campesina denounced the Israeli attacks and called for international mobilization to insist that governments and the United Nations demand an end to the Israeli violence.

eight regions: East and Southeast Asia, South Asia, North America, Central America, South America, the Caribbean, Europe, and Africa. Delegates from all regions gather together every three or four years in the Women's Assembly and the International Conference of the Vía Campesina to determine overall direction, policies, and strategies. Regional conferences are held prior to the International Conference to ensure that the Vía Campesina's work is grounded in local realities. The sixteen-member International Co-ordinating Commission — with two representatives (one man and one woman) from each of its eight regions — is the most important link among the various peasant organizations (see Figure 1-9). Outside of the International Conference, the ICC is the key decision-making and co-ordinating body of the Vía Campesina. All major decisions are made in consultation with its sixteen members.

On key issues the consultation process goes beyond the ICC, because each regional co-ordinator must reflect the needs, concerns, and decisions of the organizations within his or her region. It is only through extended communication and consultation that the regional co-ordinators gain a regional mandate to present positions and resolutions to the ICC. For Vía Campesina organizations, the regions are the key points of intersection between communities and national and international struggles.

Since its inception the Vía Campesina has organized four international congresses and a number of regional meetings and women's workshops in different parts of the world. Also, the Vía Campesina delegations represented a significant presence and force at a long list of important gatherings including, among others: the Global Assembly on Food Security in Quebec City (1995) in celebration of the Food and Agriculture Organization's 50th anniversary; the world food summits held in Rome; events surrounding the WTO Ministerial Conferences in Geneva, Seattle, Doha, Cancún, and Hong Kong; the Global Forum on Agricultural Research (GFAR) held in Dresden

Figure 1-9 International Co-ordination Committee

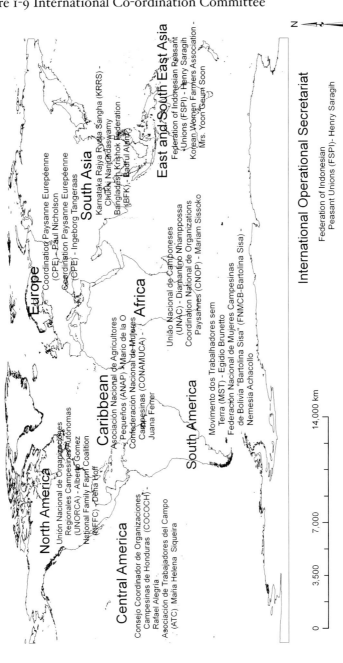

Map by Jessica Henderson

(2000); the World Social Forum in Porto Alegre (2001–03 and 2005); and the World Summit on Sustainable Development in Johannesburg (2002). These gatherings enable the Vía Campesina to pursue one of its main objectives: "to build unity within the diversity of organizations" (Vía Campesina, n.d.). At these events, peasant and farm leaders acknowledge differences, move on to establish some common ground, solidify a collective identity, and arrive at a consensus on strategies and actions.

This collective identity and sense of common purpose were clearly expressed at the Second International Conference of the Vía Campesina, held in Tlaxcala, Mexico, April 18–21, 1996. As Nettie Wiebe, NFU president (1995–98), told the delegates:

> And here we are at Tlaxcala, Mexico, a large, diverse and wonderful gathering committed to a common purpose.... We understand that our differences are real differences but that they can be overcome, and what is really important is that we appreciate the richness of our diversity.
>
> We come from our particular places. And we as women are acutely aware of a long history, in many of our cultures, of having been subservient and auxiliary to the main purposes.... [W]e have shown a great deal of good will in trying to overcome and move forward on this point. I feel very confident that we will work, women and men together, equally and freely in this movement....
>
> We have enormous strengths. For the first time in the world, we, the people of the land, are collecting ourselves around some common purposes and committing ourselves to work in solidarity with each other to achieve those goals.
>
> It is as if we have planted some seeds. I come from a place where the winter is long and cold, and I feel that we have planted some seeds and this is our spring. Some of our seeds are still buried deeply, but I am seeing that many have sprouted. And we, the people of the land who know the seasons, are seeing growth and feeling hope. (Vía Campesina 1996b: 51–52)

While peasant and farm organizations would certainly continue to actively resist globalization at the national level, by forming the Vía Campesina they were now internationalizing their efforts. Rafael Alegría, the Vía Campesina's Operational Secretariat from 1996 to 2004, stressed:

> From the Vía Campesina's point of view, the neo-liberal model is causing the collapse of this... peasant economy. It is destroying natural resources, and the environment. It is also undermining our own peasant movements around the world. For this reason, it is very important that we have an international organisation like the

> Vía Campesina, so we can come together on the issues we are facing and bring together our ideals and aspirations that have not yet disappeared from this world.... Those of us in the Vía Campesina believe we need to find a global solution for the peasants of the world. Creating a global response is the very reason for the Vía Campesina's existence. (Vía Campesina 1996b: 8–9)

In closing the Second International Conference, Alegría went on to say: "We have been brought together through daily confrontation with the international capitalist system. We are still confronting this system, but today we also have the capability to negotiate at all levels. There is no doubt that this is a great achievement at the international level" (Vía Campesina 1996b: 53).

Much of the Vía Campesina's success is due to how it balances — with great care and effort — the diverse interests of its membership as it openly deals with issues such as gender, race, class, culture, and North/South relations — matters that could potentially cause divisions. Reflecting on his experience as a member of the Vía Campesina delegation in events surrounding the WTO Ministerial conference in Seattle, François Dufour, a leader of the Confédération Paysanne and member of the CPE, says:

> You can't talk about factions within Vía Campesina, which is a worldwide farmers' organization defending what it considers to be the most crucial issues of the day. What holds for Santiago or Bamako, doesn't necessarily hold for Rome or Paris. The exchange of opinions and experiences makes this a wonderful network for training and debate. The delegations to the Vía Campesina don't negotiate in terms of conquering the market but to promote, above all, development of mutual respect. This "farmers' Internationale" represents a living example of a new relationship between the Northern and Southern states. (quoted in Bové and Dufour 2001: 158)

According to the Vía Campesina the conflict is not between farmers of the North and peasants in the South. Rather, the struggle is over two competing — and in many ways diametrically opposed — models of social and economic development: on the one hand, a globalized, neo-liberal, corporate-driven model in which agriculture is seen exclusively as a profit-making venture and productive resources are increasingly concentrated into the hands of agro-industry; and, on the other, a very different, more humane, rural model based on a "rediscovered ethic of development" stemming from the "productive culture" and "productive vocation" of farming families (Managua Declaration 1992). In the second model, agriculture is farmer-driven and based on peasant production. It uses local resources and is geared to domestic markets. Agriculture not only plays an important social function but is also economically viable and ecologically sustainable.

Food Sovereignty — Alternative Traditions, Differing Modernities

The idea of food sovereignty is at the heart of the Vía Campesina's alternative model of agriculture. The Vía Campesina (1996c) originally defined food sovereignty as "the right of each nation to maintain and develop its own capacity to produce its basic foods, respecting cultural and productive diversity" and "the right to produce our own food in our own territory." Subsequently the Vía Campesina (2000e) further elaborated the concept to include the "right of peoples to define their agricultural and food policy."

According to the Vía Campesina, food sovereignty is to be distinguished from food security; it is not only a question of ensuring that a sufficient amount of food is produced nationally and made accessible to everyone. Equally important is the issue of what food is produced, how it is produced, and at what scale. For the Vía Campesina (2000e), food sovereignty means:

- Placing priority on the production of healthy, good quality and culturally appropriate food primarily for the domestic market. It is fundamental to maintain a food production capacity based on a system of diversified farmer-based production — one that respects biodiversity, production capacity of the land, cultural values, preservation of natural resources — to guarantee the independence and the food sovereignty of populations.
- Providing remunerative prices for farmers (men and women) which requires the power to protect internal markets against imports at low prices.
- Regulating production on the internal market in order to avoid the creation of surpluses.
- Stopping the process of industrialization of production methods and developing family farm based sustainable production.
- Abolishing all direct and indirect export aids.

In today's world of global, liberalized trade the Vía Campesina's concept of food sovereignty is nothing less than revolutionary. As João Pedro Stédile, a leader with the MST, the Vía Campesina regional co-ordinator for South America, said:

This [concept] brings us into head-on collision with international capital, which wants free markets. We maintain that every people, no matter how small, has the right to produce their own food. Agricultural trade should be subordinated to this greater right. Only the surplus should be traded, and that only bilaterally. We are against the WTO and against the monopolization of world agricultural trade by the multinational corporations. As José Marti would say: a people that cannot produce its own food are slaves;

they don't have the slightest freedom. If a society doesn't produce what it eats, it will always be dependent on someone else. (quoted in *New Left Review* 2002: 100)

José Bové reinforced this approach by pointing out:

> Our concept of sovereignty enables people to think for themselves, without any imposed model for agriculture or society, and to live in solidarity with each other. This sovereignty means independent access to food: to be self-sufficient and to be able to choose what we eat.... We welcome fair trade, cultural exchange and solidarity: we stand for a dignified and free life under real democracy. (Bové and Dufour 2001: 159)

Reaching the goal of food sovereignty also requires a broadly conceived agrarian reform. For the Vía Campesina, agrarian reform goes far beyond the redistribution of land; it involves a comprehensive reform of agricultural systems to favour small-farm production and marketing. For some Vía Campesina organizations, agrarian reform means taking land and other productive resources off the market and practising the principle of social ownership of land, whereby families who work the land have usufruct rights. Stédile explained:

> In Vía Campesina, we're building a platform independent of the particular tendencies of the farmers' movements within each country. One plank on which we agree, at the international level, is that there must be the sort of agrarian reform that would democratize the land — both as a basis for political democracy, and for building an agriculture of another kind. This has major implications. From the time of Zapata in Mexico, or of Julio in Brazil, the inspiration for agrarian reform was the idea that the land belonged to those who worked it. Today we need to go beyond this. It's not enough to argue that if you work the land, you have proprietary rights over it. The Vietnamese and Indian farmers have contributed a lot to our debates on this. They have a different view of agriculture, and of nature — one that we've tried to synthesize in Vía Campesina. We want an agrarian practice that transforms farmers into guardians of the land, and a different way of farming, that ensures an ecological equilibrium and also guarantees that land is not seen as private property. (quoted in *New Left Review* 2002: 100)

Consuelo Cabrera Rosales, a Mayan indigenous woman leader from Guatemala, told me that some indigenous groups within the Vía Campesina envision a broader concept of territorial autonomy that includes more holistic approaches to the land and what the land can contain and sustain. The issue

of what exactly land redistribution entails — whether land would be expropri-
ated, what compensation would be offered, who would get land, and under
what tenure — is of major concern to many peasant and farm organizations.
The Vía Campesina seeks to support the efforts of its members' local and
national constituencies rather than impose a centralized vision of an ideal
land redistribution program.

Concurrently, the Vía Campesina has reached a collective position
whereby agrarian reform "is an instrument to eliminate poverty and social
differences and to promote... development of our communities." For the Vía
Campesina (2000d):

> Land is a good of nature that needs to be used for the welfare of all.
> Land is not, and cannot be a marketable good that can be obtained
> in whatever quantity by those that have financial means. We defend
> the principle of the maximum size of the social ownership of the
> land per family in relation to the reality in each country.
>
> Access to the land by peasants has to be understood as a
> guarantee for survival and the valorization of their culture, the au-
> tonomy of their communities and a new vision on the preservation
> of natural resources for humanity and future generations. The land
> is patrimony of the family and land titles only in the name of men
> have to be avoided.

In addition to the distribution of land, agrarian reform also entails the
democratic access to and control over all productive resources such as water,
seeds, credit, and training; it also entails supply management and regulated
markets to ensure fair prices to those who produce food (Vía Campesina
2000d:1–4).

Moreover, food sovereignty is only possible in combination with the
democratic control of the food system and a recognition that "cultural heritage and genetic resources belong to all humanity" (Vía Campesina 1996b:
22). This means that all life forms — including plant and animal — must be
protected from patenting. For the Vía Campesina (2000g: 2–4), "Seeds are
the fourth resource that generates wealth for us from nature, after land, water
and air. " Seeds are the primary means of production and until recently have
to a large extent remained in the hands of farmers:

> Patenting of plants, animals and their components means that
> peasant and indigenous communities lose control of the resources
> that we have traditionally used and known. This means limited and
> controlled access to genetic resources which no doubt will impose
> new forms of control over nations and their human populations.
> Use of patented material by farmers can mean that purchased seed
> comes with a technological package which leads to a lack of sustain-

ability in the agricultural ecosystems and in the family economy. That is not all, it also breaks rural traditions like the keeping of seed for later cycles of cultivation, exchange of seeds among farmers and communities, and the development of knowledge linked to practice in the management of natural resources. (Vía Campesina 2000g: 2–4)

In recognition of the key role that peasant and farm communities play in conserving and enhancing biodiversity, the Vía Campesina adamantly rejects the concept of intellectual property as defined by the WTO's TRIPs in favour of a well-defined proposal for internationally recognized collective peasants' rights. Peasants' rights include, among other things:

- the right to the means to conserve biodiversity;
- the right to resources and their associated knowledge;
- the right to decide the future of genetic resources;
- the right to define the control and use of benefits derived from the use, preservation and management of the resources; and
- the right to use, choose, store and freely exchange genetic resources. (Vía Campesina 2000g: 3)

These rights fit well into the Vía Campesina's broad vision of biodiversity:

Biodiversity has as a fundamental base the recognition of human diversity, the acceptance that we are different and that every people and each individual has the freedom to think and to be. Seen in this way, biodiversity is not only flora, fauna, earth, water and ecosystems; it is also cultures, systems of production, human and economic relations, forms of government: in essence it is freedom. (Vía Campesina 2000g: 3)

As such, the Vía Campesina's concept of food sovereignty places peasants' and small-scale farmers' interests and roles at the centre. The movement argues for a fundamental shift in who defines and determines the purpose and terms of knowledge, research, technology, science, production, and trade related to food. What the Vía Campesina (1996b) is talking about is the need to build peasant cultures and economies based on principles that "have not yet completely disappeared," such as moral imperatives and obligations, fairness, social justice, human rights, and social responsibility. This, according to the Vía Campesina, is what building rural community and culture is all about.

Is the Vía Campesina in danger of reifying community — engaging in a romanticized notion of its roots and rejecting modernity — at the cost of proposing concrete social alternatives? I do not think so. Communities should be seen as sites of diversity, differences, conflicts, and divisions most often expressed along gender, class, and ethnic lines and characterized by competing claims and interests. Here, David Warren Sabean's notion of "community as discourse," drawn from his work in early German communities, is illuminating:

> What makes community possible is the fact that it involves a series of mediated relationships.... By emphasizing relationships, it can be seen that community includes both negative and positive elements, both sharing and conflict.... Community exists where not just love but also frustration and anger exist.... What is common in community is not shared values or common understanding so much as the fact that members of a community are engaged in the same argument, the same raisonnement... the same discourse, in which alternative strategies, misunderstandings, conflicting goals and values are threshed out.... What makes community is the discourse. (Sabean 1984: 28–30)

Sabean argues that culture then becomes a "series of arguments among people about the common things in their everyday lives" (95). This captures the process that the Vía Campesina is involved in as it struggles to define the nature and substance of its alternative peasant model. As Alegría explained:

> We cannot have, nor aspire to have, only one way of thinking because we are so many, we are too big. What is important is to discuss, engage in debate and agree on some ways forward, not to detain ourselves. If there are contradictions or differences this is normal. What we need to do in the Vía Campesina is to ensure that we always have the capacity to listen to each other and always act with deep respect for the way of thinking of each of the organizations and to always discuss in an open and transparent way and then move forward. The day that the Vía Campesina attempts to impose ways of thinking or vertical lines, then we will have ceased to be a distinct social movement truly committed to building an alternative model.

The peasant model advocated by the Vía Campesina does not entail a rejection of modernity, or of technology and trade, accompanied by a romanticized return to an archaic past steeped in rustic traditions. Rather, the Vía Campesina insists that an alternative model must be based on certain ethics and values in which culture and social justice count for something and concrete mechanisms are put in place to ensure a future without hunger. The Vía Campesina's alternative model entails recapturing aspects of traditional, local, or farmers knowledge, and combining that knowledge with new technology when and where it is appropriate to do so. The movement rejects a tradition of modernity in which everything is privatized and local

---

Traditional Ways of Growing Basic Food

The tradition of *traspatio*, best translated as a backyard garden, involves growing fruit, vegetables, and medicinal plants and raising a small number of animals for domestic consumption. *Milpa* has no translation but refers to traditional Meso-American indigenous peasant agriculture based on a polyculture using corn, beans, and squash. Although the concept of *milpa mejorada* (improved *milpa*) certainly has a longer history, here I am referring specifically to a production system used by Mayan peasants in the state of Quintana Roo in Mexico, where the *milpa Maya mejorada* involves polyculture and agro-forestry in which about 25 percent of the small plots of land are used to grow food and the remaining 75 percent are planted to trees (UNORCA 2000a).

---

knowledge has no place; it insists that this vision of modernity can and must be contested. Quite obviously, the Vía Campesina is engaged in a process of exploring new ways of living in the contemporary world, building different concepts of modernity from its members' own alternative and deeply rooted traditions.

By integrating careful borrowings with traditional practice, peasants and small-scale farmers everywhere are reaffirming the lessons from *their* histories and reshaping the rural landscape to benefit those who work the land as they collectively redefine what food is produced, how it is produced, and where and for whom. We have only to look, for example, at the practices of Mexican farm organizations that work to ensure food for self-sufficiency through the peasant tradition of the *traspatio* combined with the government-sponsored *milpa Maya mejorada* (which involves using hybrid seeds and some chemical inputs) while at the same time seeking to establish direct farmer-to-farmer trade links with Canadian and European farm organizations.

The Vía Campesina formed in the North and South around common objectives: an explicit rejection of the neo-liberal model of rural development, an outright refusal to be excluded from agricultural policy development, and a firm determination to work together to empower a peasant voice. Through its strategy of "building unity within diversity" and its concept of food sovereignty, peasant and farmers' organizations around the world are working together to ensure the well-being of rural communities — in particular by working to establish an alternative model of rural development, a model based on small-scale family farms and peasant agriculture.

2. Modernization and Globalization: The Enclosure of Agriculture

> Globalization is affecting us in distinct ways, our lives and our patrimony. Globalization is a global offensive against the countryside; it is a global offensive against small producers and family farmers that are not in the logic of an "efficient" countryside, an industrialized countryside. It is a global advancement against peasants' and small producers' visions for resource management, conservation of biodiversity and all of these issues.... We are all facing the same enemies in this globalization. And, all of these have names and last names, they are the big companies, the transnationals. So, there are different circumstances but we are facing the same global tendency driven by the governments of the richest countries for the benefit of the large transnationals. —Alberto Gomez Flores, 2000, executive co-ordinator, UNORCA

La Vía Campesina emerged in a particular economic, political, and social context that was undermining the ability of farmers and peasants around the world to maintain control over land and seeds. It emerged during a time when a particular model of rural development was altering rural landscapes, threatening to make local knowledge irrelevant and denigrating rural cultures. Key elements in this phenomenon were the encroaching globalization of a modern industrial model of agriculture, on the one hand, and the search for an alternative development approach among those most harmed by the epidemic of dislocation left in its wake.

As early as 1974, heads of states and agricultural ministers from around the world had gathered together in Rome for the U.N. World Food Conference. At the time world grain prices were high and observers expressed growing concerns about impending food shortages. The 1974 conference declared that freedom from hunger and malnutrition was a fundamental human right and that within ten years "no child will go to bed hungry [and] that no family will fear for its next day's bread" (FAO 1974). To reach this goal, governments agreed to a number of strategies, including an increase in production via an intensification of the Green Revolution; support for rural development by investing in rural infrastructure and creating equitable land tenure, credit, and marketing systems; and abolishing obstacles to, and liberalizing, trade.

Twenty-two years later, in November 1996, government representatives met once again in Rome at the U.N. World Food Summit. The problem at hand: how to deal with increasing levels of food insecurity. Interestingly, several of the strategies advocated this time around were remarkably similar to those mentioned two decades earlier. The WFS reiterated the need to increase production through a "new Green Revolution," this time involving more extensive use of agro-biotechnology, especially genetic engineering. It also advocated more equitable access to, and distribution of, resources and further liberalization and increasing trade as "key element[s] to achieving food security" (FAO 1996). While the official WFS documents clearly specified existing structures and mechanisms — such as the WTO and Trade Related Aspects of Intellectual Property Rights (TRIPs) — to reach the goal of increasing global trade and supporting agro-biotechnological advances, it did not identify mechanisms for the equitable distribution of resources.

In June 2002, heads of state reconvened in Rome at the WFS: Five Years Later, to assess their progress in reaching the goals established in the WFS Rome Declaration on World Food Security and World Food Summit Plan of Action. Little headway, if any, had been made in resolving worldwide hunger and poverty. According to the FAO, in 2001 over 815 million people were undernourished, and "in most developing countries the number of hungry even increased" in the preceding decade. In the months leading up to the WFS: Five Years Later, Jacques Diouf, director general of the FAO (2001a, 2001b), desperately pleaded for a shift in political action stating that the "scandal" and "tragedy" of hunger could no longer be tolerated. Yet the WFS: Five Years Later did not question or revisit the basic foundations and assumptions of decisions made five years earlier. Instead, it reiterated commitments to intensify production and increase trade, while placing less emphasis on inequitable rural social structures.

Much had changed between the first World Food Conference in 1974 and the Summit of 2002. Perhaps most importantly, over the twenty-eight-year span a significant shift occurred in how we "value" food (Goodman and Watts 1997). In 1974 food was considered a basic human right, and governments were committed to eradicating hunger within a decade; in 1996 the WFS opted to "reduce" hunger by half, and one of the most powerful nations in the world, the United States, disagreed with the concept of food as a right. Rather than seeing food as a basic human right that nation-states would be obliged to ensure, the U.S. position considered the right to adequate food as a "goal" or "aspiration," and it impeded efforts to improve international obligations in this area. The U.S. position probably stems from a fear of economic retaliation should any aspect of any free-trade agreement undermine an individual's or community's access to food. Indeed, at the 2002 WFS the world's commitment to the right to food was reduced from a Code of Conduct to developing a set of "voluntary guidelines" that would assist governments to realize the right to "access" adequate food. The Declaration of the World Food Summit: Five Years Later goes on to clarify that the voluntary guidelines are not meant to be international; instead, they are restricted to issues of national food security (FAO 2002, Article 10).

Modernization of Agriculture

In the Western world the modernization of agriculture has fundamentally altered how we value food and agriculture. At the turn of the twentieth century most production and consumption was closely linked, with farmers supplying their own input needs from on-farm resources. Farmers controlled virtually all stages of production. They engaged in some on-farm processing and had more direct ties to consumers. Their engagement with the market was restricted, by and large, to when they brought their products to be sold in local markets. In the modern industrial food system, however, production has been delinked from consumption, allowing new players to insert themselves and take control of different stages of production.

The best way of understanding these conditions is to imagine the agro-food system as a long horizontal chain — which over the years has been lengthened significantly. In the modernization or industrialization of agriculture, production became more and more distanced from consumption, and agribusiness corporations usurped different stages of production. New off-farm stages and sectors of production — such as the provision of inputs, food processing, transportation, marketing — were created and expanded (Boyd and Watts 1997).

In the West, a main force behind the modernization of agriculture was the private corporate sector, which made concerted efforts, often through state-sponsored scientific research and development, to control or refashion "nature" through technological innovations that involved projects of appropriation and substitution (Goodman and Redclift 1991: 87–132). David Goodman (1991: 40) describes appropriation as the "transformation of discrete activities into sectors of agro-industrial accumulation and their re-incorporation into agriculture as agricultural inputs." For example, the tractor replaced on-farm horsepower, synthetic chemicals replaced manure, and hybrid seeds replaced farmers' seeds. Substitution involves processes whereby "agricultural products are reduced to an industrial input and then replaced by fabricated or synthetic non-agricultural components in food manufacturing" (Whatmore 1995: 42). In other words, to give a couple of examples, margarine replaced butter, and high fructose corn syrup replaced sugar cane.

The development of an industrial model of agriculture fit well with governments' interests in fashioning a cheap food policy that would support industrial growth. In the process the autonomy of farmers was undermined, if not destroyed, as they became dependent on their connections with agribusiness corporations. The history of the development of high-yielding seed varieties provides a good example of this shift. Studies conducted in the 1950s clearly demonstrated that farmers' centuries-old practices of open pollination and recurrent selection produced yields comparable to those produced in laboratories (Marglin 1996). However, rather than pursuing these farmer-controlled methods, seed companies inserted themselves directly into the production process by developing scientifically produced high-yielding seed varieties tied to a whole technological package, including inputs, mechanization, and irrigation. This involvement represented a significant coup for agri-business corporations in that it effectively took seeds out of the hands of farmers and boosted the accumulation of industrial capital.

Two agricultural economists, Douglas Allen and Dean Lueck (1998), suggest that agri-business corporations and investors have been most successful in areas where they have succeeded in "taking nature out" of agriculture, or at least controlling it better. Scientific developments in animal-disease control, nutrition, and genetics, for example, led to a technique of total confinement and the construction of factory farms for hogs and chickens. They also led to the entry of a multitude of new business actors in the food chain, tied farmers to production contracts, and facilitated the dominance of agribusiness in the various food sectors. In the late 1990s the U.S. Department of Agriculture reported that 89 percent of U.S. poultry farms were tied to production contracts, and about 86 percent of the total value of poultry production similarly fell under production contracts (USDA 1998: 61). By 2002, production contracts accounted for a full 98 percent of broilers (young chickens raised for broiling or roasting). Furthermore, the U.S. broiler industry became highly concentrated, with only four firms producing 56 percent of the chickens (Hendrickson and Heffernan 2005). Under these conditions farmers lose their autonomy because they have little (if any) say over production decisions. Yet farmers continue to assume a disproportionate share of the risks.

James C. Scott (1998), director of the Program in Agrarian Studies at Yale University, says that agricultural change has often been driven largely by an ideology of "high modernism," which he characterizes as having a "muscle-bound" belief in science and technology and exhibiting a zealous self-confidence in the linear process of progress. High modernism is future-oriented, demanding a radical break from tradition and the past. It focuses on expanding and intensifying production, and on exercising greater control over nature. Scott argues that this trajectory — whether it is called high-modernist agriculture, high-tech agriculture, or high-input agriculture — is a story of the domination of the *episteme* of scientific knowledge over the *mētis* of local farmers.

The concept of *episteme* can be traced to the French philosopher René Descartes (1595–1650), who equated uncertainty and doubt with disorder. *Episteme* seeks to bring about a rational order by applying a science-based knowledge system that is cerebral, impersonal, analytic, articulate, and theoretical. It involves abstraction, logical deduction, verification, simplification, standardization, aggregation, and codification. *Episteme* claims objectivity and universality. *Mētis* refers to practical, local knowledge; it is "savoire faire" or just plain common sense that is arrived at through practical experience and an intimate understanding of the local environment. *Mētis* is grounded in diversity and pluralism and makes no claims to universality. As nature and environments are by definition localized and complex, a universalizing *episteme* in agriculture required the application of the systematic taming of nature and the denigration and suppression of *mētis*. *Episteme* also claims superiority in that it is considered to be the only legitimate form of knowledge; anything that cannot be explained or verified by scientific means is discarded as "superstition," "tradition," "backward," and "primitive" (Scott 1998: 262–306).

High modernist agriculture thus assigned scientific institutions a privileged place as the sites responsible for defining and disseminating knowledge. In this scheme, farmers are no longer considered producers of knowledge. Instead, as Mary Beckie's (2000: 35) comparison of the role of knowledge systems in zero tillage and organic farming found, in conventional agriculture "farmers are seen as recipients of this expert knowledge," and the practice of agriculture then becomes "a technical exercise in production that can be modified and improved through scientific and technological innovations." Robert Stirling (1999: 10), an academic who spent years establishing links between academia and farm organizations, argues that high-input agriculture creates such a dependency on industrial inputs that farmers become "consumers rather than producers. Their range of farming options is circumscribed by the input options and commodity markets made available to them by multinational agribusiness and the state."

Laura Rance (2002: 9), a reporter with *Farmers' Independent Weekly*, published in rural Manitoba, highlights this loss of farmers' knowledge: "Understanding why things happen the way they do, has been slipping from farmers' collective consciousness — replaced by cookie-cutter farming systems and one-stop shopping solutions." Rance interviewed a crop nutrition consultant who found that the knowledge of field husbandry, which uses a wide range of cultural and management practices, has all but disappeared on the Canadian prairies. The consultant observed: "This process of figuring out farm-based solutions is actively discouraged by 'system-based' approaches. There is a negative attitude out there towards people who think."

The modernization of agriculture, then, involved industrialization, mechanization, monoculture, intensive capitalization, and specialization. In the interests of corporate profits, farmers' crops disappear from fields; they are deconstructed and reconstituted by food manufacturers, emerging on grocery shelves in hermetically sealed brightly coloured packages with a label claiming "may contain...." In this modern agriculture, nature is altered to better fit machines, and so-called "scientific" knowledge replaces farmers' on-the-ground knowledge and local practice. Increased penetration and concentration of corporate interests into agriculture mean that farmers' autonomy — that is, their ability to make production decisions — is broken as they became increasingly dependent on industrial inputs and as family farms become responsible only for those stages of production that are closest to nature.

One of the most visible consequences of the modernization of agriculture has been the substantial decline in the role of primary production — that is, the portion of agriculture that is carried out "on the farm" — accompanied by a steep decline in the farming population. For example, in 1920 the United States had 6.5 million farms; by 2002 the number had fallen to 2.13 million (USDA 1998). There are now more prisoners in the United States than there are farmers. In the early 1940s Canada had 731,000 family farms; by 1966 only 430,522. From 1996 to 2001 the number of Canadian farms decreased yet again, from 276,548 to 246,923 (Statistics Canada 2001).

Globalization of High Modernist Agriculture

This modern model of agriculture was exported throughout the world in the guise of a "development" aimed at ridding the world of poverty. Many critics argue that the current mainstream understanding of poverty is rooted in the concept of "underdevelopment," which President Harry Truman elaborated in point four of his inaugural speech on January 20, 1949. Truman defined a bipolar world divided between "developed" countries, characterized by a certain level of affluence and growth, and "underdeveloped" countries and peoples, seen as "backward" and "poor" since they had not yet reached "adequate" standards of living (Rist 1997: 76). Rather than explaining poverty as a result of the historical dynamics inherent in highly skewed power relations largely defined by particular economic interests, such thinking saw it simply as a function of "not having" — which meant a lack of sufficient income, consumption, and production. This unidimensional view of poverty meant that only one possible solution existed: poverty would be alleviated by increasing production, consumption, and economic growth — with economic growth measured by Gross National Product — via the transfer of Western science and technology, and the creation of desire for Western consumer goods. Through development, then, the South would "catch up" with the North via a further integration into the market. Furthermore, because the underdeveloped and poor were seen as incapable of defining their own interests, needs, and solutions, there was (and remains) an assumption that economic and social progress could best be achieved through the intervention of development "experts," people considered to have the necessary experience and knowledge and who were thus better equipped to identify the needs of local populations.

The goal of catching up (envisioned as material, economic progress) through the creation, integration, and expansion of markets was used to justify colonial economic policies and was at the heart of the historical processes of modernization. More recently the same goal has been central to the argument for increased liberalization and globalization (Rist 1997: 25). Although slight shifts in rural development strategies have occurred over the past fifty years, the fundamental aim of modernization has remained constant. That is, rural development has involved attempts to reduce rural poverty by extending the benefits of development through programs aimed at improving technology, increasing productivity and production — thereby increasing the incomes of rural people — and increasing consumption power (Barraclough, Ghimire, and Meliczek 1997: 10). Using this definition of poverty, development policy — concerned with prompting "poor" economies (and thus primarily rural) to produce and consume more — has focused on two linked ideas: the transfer of excess population from rural areas to the cities and industry, and the modernization of agriculture.

These very ideas were reflected in a best-selling book that purports to trace the roots of European prosperity. William J. Bernstein (2004: 21) warns, "Those who romanticize farm life should bear in mind that in the modern world, the percentage of population engaged in agriculture is a powerful marker of poverty." Indeed, Bernstein argues that when the vast majority of a country's population is engaged in farming and when the country does not export a substantial amount of its product, that society lives in a subsistence economy equivalent to that of Burkina Faso, one of the poorest countries in the world.

Some writers argue that development can best be understood as an exercise in political, economic, and cultural domination in which the local knowledge, cultures, and social systems are completely devalued (Apffel-Marglin and Marglin 1990, 1996). J.D. Sadie, writing over forty years ago, described the prerequisites for development:

> Economic development of an underdeveloped people by themselves is not compatible with the maintenance of their traditional customs and mores. A break with the latter is a prerequisite to economic progress. What is needed is a revolution in the totality of social, cultural and religious institutions and habits, and thus in their psychological attitude, their philosophy and way of life. What is, therefore, required amounts in reality to social disorganization. Unhappiness and discontentment in the sense of wanting more than is obtainable at any moment is to be generated. The suffering and dislocation that may be caused in the process may be objectionable, but it appears to be the price that has to be paid for economic development; the condition of economic progress. (quoted in Berthoud 1992: 72-73)

The modernization of agriculture is a major tool in creating the "suffering and dislocations" considered necessary for development. It is deeply political and can best be understood as the imposition of a Western model of agricultural development on other cultures — and in the West as well.

The Perils of Structural Development

Structural Adjustment Programs (SAPs), often accompanied by economic stabilization plans aimed at controlling inflation, forced governments to restructure their economies by: 1) reforming the public sector through reductions in the size of the government and severe limitations on the government's involvement in the economy, privatization of state enterprises, and cutbacks in public spending on health, education, and other social programs; 2) creating an outward-looking economy through focusing on increasing production for export, liberalizing trade, and increasing foreign investment; and 3) deregulating key aspects of financial, labour, and environmental controls. Industrialized nations experienced similar processes through economic restructuring.

While SAPs did succeed (for the most part) in controlling inflation, studies demonstrate that in many developing countries the programs also contributed to greater impoverishment, higher rates of unemployment, and a phenomenal growth of the informal market (Mohan et al. 2000). For ordinary people — and especially marginalized sectors of the population living in the countryside — these changes proved to be devastating.

It represents, as Lakshman Yapa (1996: 69) says, "a particular way of seeing food, technology, nature, culture and society," in which agriculture is almost exclusively concerned with increasing production for profit. This worldview was exported to other cultures, most notably in the form of the Green Revolution, and was the hallmark of U.S. foreign policy for decades. Around the world the Green Revolution was presented as a modern and scientific solution to the "backward" and "primitive" practices of peasant communities (Yapa 1996: 80). This so-called revolution was essentially a technological package that included high-yielding seed varieties and industrial inputs such as fertilizers, herbicides, pesticides, irrigation, mechanization, and monoculture — all designed to increase production and consumption at the same time.

In effect, the modernization of agriculture is a "war on subsistence" seeking to break subsistence farmers' autonomy (Robert 1992: 185). It completely devalues traditional farming practices based on local culture and local knowledge; and it "helps" peasants shift from subsistence to commercial agriculture by making them increasingly dependent both on Western technology and knowledge and on imported industrial inputs and goods (Marglin 1996: 234). Thus the Green Revolution was cultural, not just technological.

The spread of industrial agriculture was abetted by Structural Adjustment Programs and new trade regulations in agriculture. Throughout the 1980s, faced with an unprecedented debt crisis, governments in the North and South implemented SAPs aimed at generating economic growth and much-needed foreign exchange, which would ostensibly enable countries to pay off their debts. These austerity programs were based on policies, primarily designed by the IMF and World Bank, that centred on neo-liberal principles of modernization, capitalization, deregulation, and liberalization.

SAPs and economic restructuring in the agricultural sector emphasized the diversification of export crops and the production of non-traditional agro-exports at the expense of production for national consumption. Another key was the creation of an environment conducive to foreign investment. They also included — and this is perhaps the most pernicious aspect of structurally adjusted agriculture — the systematic dismantling of supportive infrastructure — state-led programs and mechanisms (such as subsidies and price controls) geared to support and reinforce domestic agricultural markets and farmers' livelihoods. One of the most obvious consequences of the SAPs was the integration of debtor countries' economies into a highly competitive global economy.

After the Second World War, with the backing of the World Bank, the IMF, and the GATT, many governments around the world promoted a market ideology in the context of "development." But the signing of the Uruguay Round of the GATT in 1994, along with a number of regional trade agreements in combination with the SAPs, represented a significant shift in the conditions that nations were prepared to place in the hands of market forces.[1]

Prior to the Uruguay Round, GATT rules applied mostly to manufactured and industrial goods, with governments expressing little interest in liberalizing agriculture and food. Protectionism in agriculture was strong, and nation-states proudly defended national programs and state-run institutions — such as agrarian reform, supply management, and orderly marketing systems — that farmers' organizations had won after long years of struggle. Agricultural development policies, including Green Revolution technologies, were designed primarily to strengthen national agricultural sectors, increase production, and ensure national food self-sufficiency. Hence agriculture received special treatment in the GATT through important exemptions (enshrined in Articles XI and XVI) that allowed countries to support and protect their farm sectors through a combination of subsidies, import quotas, and tariff quotas.

By the late 1980s Europe and the United States, along with a number of other countries, had become export-dependent as a result of increased production, rising stockpiles, and corporate interests seeking to expand their markets. Consequently, when the Uruguay Round opened in 1986, the liberalization of agricultural trade was the rallying cry of the European Union (EU), the United States, and the newly formed Cairns Group.[2] Still, major differences between the United States and EU positions on agricultural trade effectively stalled the talks for years. In November 1992 the European Union and United States resolved their differences with the signing of the Blair House Accord, which then quickly led to the Agreement on Agriculture.

Decisions made at the Marrakesh meeting of the GATT in April 1994 had a profound impact on the everyday lives of the world's population. Effectively bringing the eight-year-long Uruguay Round to a close, heads of state signed the GATT Final Act and agreed to establish a supra-state legal and independent entity, the World Trade Organization. The WTO, established on January 1, 1995, was to be responsible for the implementation of twenty-two agreements ranging from agriculture and services to intellectual property rights and genetic resources. The Marrakesh decisions signalled a pronounced shift away from more controlled to almost exclusively market-driven economies. With the creation of the WTO, world leaders embarked on a globalizing mission of market liberalization.

The three pillars of the WTO's AoA are market access, export competition, and the reduction of domestic support. The aims of the agreement are threefold: to increase market access by reducing tariffs and imposing an import food requirement for national consumption; to increase market access by reducing export subsidies; and to reduce direct and indirect government supports.

The inclusion of agriculture in SAPs, regional trade agreements, and the WTO clearly demonstrates a move to treat agriculture and food no differently than other industries. David Goodman and Michael Watts (1997: 1) stress that the 1990s were:

> a moment of unprecedented deregulation of agriculture (a shift from aid to trade), the hegemony (the so-called "new realism") of export-oriented neo-liberal development strategies, and a recognition that globalisation (a word not even part of the lexicon of the earlier Rome summit) of the world agro-food economy was proceeding apace.

The move to promoting exclusive market solutions to public policy issues was also facilitated by the collapse of socialism in Eastern Europe, an event that ushered in a "new world order" and opened the flood gates for the expansion of unfettered capitalism, creating conditions in which only liberal democracies were expected to flourish. In the words of French scholar Gerald Berthoud (1992: 73), neo-liberalism marks a significant shift to a time when the state is no longer seen as the regulator or benefactor; instead, "the market itself is increasingly viewed as the only means to promote development."

Agriculture and Biotechnology

> We've just started and I think that we will be very successful in the future.... It is the start of a nice time to be a farmer — it really is! —Dr. Fred Perlak, co-director responsible for all cotton projects, Monsanto[3]

Advances in genetic engineering and biotechnology are perhaps the most important developments affecting agriculture today. They offer the greatest opportunity for corporations to gain more control of the food system and to reap huge profits. R.C. Lewontin (1998: 79) points out that if corporations want to succeed in gaining greater control over agricultural production through biotechnology, they must meet three conditions: 1) research and development must be cost-effective; 2) the developments must be politically and socially acceptable; and perhaps most importantly, 3) *"ownership and control over the product of biotechnology must not pass into the hands of the farmer but must remain with the commercial provider of the input"* (Lewontin's emphasis). Transnational corporations are striving to meet these conditions, as is clearly evident in their struggle for ownership of genetically modified seeds through the WTO's Trade-Related Aspects of Intellectual Property Rights.

Given that seeds are the primary means of production in agriculture, as the old adage goes, "Whoever controls the seed, controls the farmer." Not surprisingly, since the 1990s a whole series of mergers and acquisitions have occurred among chemical, plant biotechnology, and seed companies. A study prepared by the United Nations Conference on Trade and Development (UNCTAD) demonstrates an unprecedented consolidation and concentration in the agro-chemical industry: three corporations (Bayer, Syngenta, and BASF) account for about half of the global market; in 2004–05 the seed industry experienced yet another shakedown as the world's largest biotech and pesticide companies — Monsanto, DuPont and Syngenta — raced to buy out seed companies. Only a handful of conglomerates — Monsanto, DuPont, Syngenta, Dow, and Bayer — own the great majority of agricultural patents (UNCTAD 2006: 1, 9, 26).

The importance of seeds to the industry also explains why much of the research and development in biotechnology has focused on the genetic engineering of seeds designed to fit into "technological packages" that effectively link farmers directly to corporations from the seeds through to the final product. For example, most of the research and development in the agri-biotech industry has been directed towards developing herbicide-resistant seeds, such as Monsanto's Roundup, Ready canola, soybeans, and cotton — Roundup is a herbicide also owned by Monsanto — or insect-killing plants such as Bt potatoes, cotton, and corn. This work places transnational corporations in a much better position to offer farmers "a bundled package of brand products, each tied to another" (UNCTAD 2006: 7).

Intellectual Property Rights (IPRs) are promoted by international institutions and governments as the most effective mechanism to protect and enhance plant biological resource conservation and genetic diversity. If we consider knowledge as a "commons" and genetic diversity as "common heritage," then the IPR regime is essentially about the privatization and commodification of what were once public resources. Much of current development thinking and policy development regarding the protection and control of common property, the environment, and cultural and social resources can be traced back to Garrett Hardin's (1968) nearly four-decade-old and tragically flawed discussion of the "tragedy of the commons." Indeed, in conventional development circles, locally based common property systems are still viewed as "backward" and as "impeding development" (Vivian 1992: 60). In mainstream development the commons continue to be misinterpreted (in true Hardinesque fashion) as open-access or "free-for-all" and viewed as inefficient, unproductive, and the major cause of environmental degradation. Consequently, the development industry focuses on dismantling and redefining local property systems via privatization and/or state ownership. More recently we have seen a concerted effort to promote the idea that local commons are subsumed by the global commons, which can then best be managed by global managers and global institutions such as the WTO (Goldman 1998). This position leads to the disempowering of the local and has serious implications for the environment.

The use of market mechanisms for the management of plant genetic resources is based on the same rather dubious assumptions. The critics of the common heritage approach to genetic resources argue, like Hardin, that without private ownership and control (either in the form of sovereignty or IPRs) the loss of biological resources is inevitable because of the inherent element of overexploitation in such an "open and unregulated" system. They assume that common heritage means open access and hence a complete absence of any norms, rules, and regulations. This leads the critics of the common heritage approach to present only two clear-cut ways of managing biological resources: the open access/no control model, or the sovereignty/ market approach. As well, the critics assume that poor communities equal overexploitation of local natural resources equal loss of genetic diversity. They expect that when patents are secured through IPRs, communities will be adequately compensated, leading to the alleviation of poverty and enhanced protection and cultivation of genetic resources (Dove 1996: 46). They also assume that the rightful owners of genetic resources can be easily identified (Brush 1996b: 145–47).

These assumptions raise a whole range of issues. For one thing, it is highly unlikely that IPR legislation as it is now will benefit poor indigenous and rural communities and lead to the conservation of genetic diversity. Michael Flitner (1998: 155), a well-known researcher on this issue, believes that, to the contrary, it opens the way for an "accelerated expansion of the commodification of nature" and will lead to the "expropriation of the essential means of production from millions of farmers." The IPRs solution, coupled with the Convention on Biodiversity introduced at the United Nations Conference on the Environment and Development in Rio de Janeiro in 1992, are couched in the argument that poverty is the cause of the loss of genetic diversity, just as poverty was erroneously considered to be the greatest threat to the environment both at Rio and in *Our Common Future,* the report of the World Commission on Development and the Environment. Consequently, the advocates of this approach argue, financial compensation and the integration of indigenous and rural communities into national and international markets are the keys to ensuring stewardship and conservation of biodiversity (Brush 1996b). This, of course, ignores that the loss of biodiversity is the direct result of an environmentally and culturally destructive development model, a model that persistently strives to control and manipulate nature to facilitate the accumulation of profit. In this light, perhaps the real goal of the IPRs mechanism is to facilitate industry's (rather than communities') access to and control over genetic resources; IPRs reinforce state control while mandating that states need to introduce legal mechanisms for corporate exploitation of genetic resources. While the international community cloaks this aspiration in a discourse focused on the protection and enhancement of biological resources, it has not yet addressed what is perhaps a much more important question — how to protect and enhance cultural knowledge and diversity.

Nowhere are the links between local knowledge, cultural diversity and traditional resource management systems stronger than in the cultivation and protection of biological genetic resources. Biological diversity is completely dependent on cultural diversity, and cultural diversity depends on diverse local knowledge systems. Many communities that depend on the environment for their livelihoods and sustenance have developed highly complex locally based institutional arrangements geared to ensure the sustainable use and management of common property systems (Baden and Noonan 1998; Kothari and Parajuli 1993). Traditional resource management systems include a wide range of institutional arrangements that often include social and religious practices, strict systems of controls and regulations governing resource access and use, and the transmission of local knowledge. Fikret Berkes and M. Taghi Farvar (1989: 12) stress that how the commons are managed is as diverse a matter as is the cultural, social, political, economic, and ecological context in which they are found. They also stress that local control is central to the effective management of common property systems:

> Common property systems are an integral part of the local culture....
> [They are] a way of life rather than merely a means of earning a living.... Community members share a common culture, knowledge of the resource and knowledge of resource-use rules, facilitated by the simple rule "you must live in this community to use this resource."

Local control is central to the effective management of common property systems. Local sustainable management of the commons is based on communities' intimate knowledge of local ecological systems, and it also rests on their continued ability to maintain authority over their territories and community members. Essentially, a key to the success of commons regimes depends largely on their ability to limit the power of the community's elite

Pigs and Local Disempowerment in the Canadian West

The case of the province of Alberta provides a good example of local disempowerment over common resources.

Canada's hog industry is expanding rapidly, with a number of provincial governments fully supporting the construction of industrial-scale hog barns. Like the U.S. broiler industry, large hog production units effectively drive out small pig farms and the industry becomes highly concentrated. For example, by 1996, the top 5 percent of pig farms were responsible for 64 percent of production in Canada (Stirling 1999: 9).

In 2001 the Alberta provincial government removed decision-making authority regarding intensive livestock operations from local municipalities and placed it in its own hands. This move was justified partly with claims that it would help resolve the rising number of community conflicts over the issue and also by arguments that local communities simply did not have the expertise to make decisions on such "highly technical" issues requiring sophisticated knowledge of engineering and hydrology (Duckworth 2001: 3). Those living in the countryside who opposed the installation of intensive livestock operations in their communities, however, argued that this new legislation effectively took away their "local right to protest or to set standards that protect a community's environment." As Jack Hayden, president of the Alberta Association of Municipal Districts and Counties, stated: "Land-use decisions are properly decided at the local level and the community that have to live with those decisions" (quoted in Duckworth 2001: 3).

In Alberta, decisions governing intensive livestock operations will now be made by people not living in the community, people who will not have to deal with the devastating environmental consequences characteristic of intensive livestock operations — water and soil contamination, health endangering fumes, and oppressive odour — and who are also protected from the financial and social impacts of these intensive production units on rural communities. The industry's response to the serious environmental problem created by the phosphorus-polluting, large intensive hog farms is the "EnviropigTM" developed by researchers working at Canada's University of Guelph. These transgenic pigs are genetically engineered with a combined mouse and bacterial gene to make them use phosphorous more efficiently, cutting the level of phosphorus in pig manure by up to 60 percent (University of Guelph). A major challenge now is how to convince a sceptical public on the merits and safety of eating genetically modified pork chops. Essentially, rather than focusing on the production model (intensive livestock operations) as *the* problem, industry fixates on biotech solutions to environmental problems that the model itself created.

Sources: Qualman 2001 and Ervin et al. 2003 for excellent discussions on the growth of the hog industry and its impact on the Canadian prairies; Yakabuski 2002 for Canada as a whole; and Page 1997 for the case of the U.S. state of Iowa.

and on the continuing bargaining power of any person within the community. It is "the breakdown of a community with the associated collapse in concepts of joint ownership and responsibility [that] can set the path for the degradation of common resources" (Berkes and Feeny, quoted in the *Ecologist* 1992: 129–30).

There is growing evidence that rather than halting environmental degradation, this development approach — primarily concerned with increasing corporate profit through extensive and intensive resource extraction — is actually one of the major contributors to that destruction (Vivian 1992; Shiva 1997a, 1997b). Natural-resource depletion and environmental degradation are not primarily caused by mismanagement on the part of local communities. Frequently, the decline of common property resources occurs as a direct result of external pressures, of the increasing encroachment of outsiders whose interests do not lie in the long-term well-being of the community or of the environment, and the subsequent dismantling of locally based and culturally specific community structures and social relations (Vivian 1992: 72; Gibbs and Bromley 1989: 30).

Mainstream development's deep and long-standing attachment to Hardin's concept arises from a well-established, basic predisposition to some of the values reflected in his argument.[4] His idea, for example, of the self-seeking individual who will take advantage of communal resources to the detriment of the community as a whole fits well with a long history of literature, particularly British, going back to the misapplication of Darwin's notion of competition (explained as the struggle for "survival of the fittest") to social and human spheres — as well as to Adam Smith, who emphasized the merits of "rational" individualism and self-interest, and Jeremy Bentham, who argued for the superiority of private property. Current development thinking may also be influenced by the historical experience, or at least the predominant explanations of the historical experience, of Britain. According to conventional interpretation, British agriculture "modernized" and became dramatically more efficient with the privatization of the commons through the enclosures of the seventeenth and nineteenth centuries. These enclosures not only permitted greater efficiencies in agriculture but also provided a pool of rural migrants who provided a base for English industrialization. This history is often contrasted with that of France, where the increased political support garnered by French peasants ensured their continued possession of land and access to commons, thus contributing to the continued inefficiency and poverty of French agriculture (Aston and Philpin 1985). This range of ideas is central to the aspects of Western modernity and the role of the state that have driven the process of development over the last century.

Agents and Winners of Globalization

> Behind the obfuscation of such terms as "market access," "domestic support," "sanitary and phytosanitary measures" and "intellectual property rights" in the final draft of the GATT agreement, is a raw restructuring of power around food: taking it away from people and concentrating it in the hands of a handful of agro-industrial interests. The conflict is not between farmers of the North and those of the South, but between small farmers everywhere and multinationals. (Shiva 1993a: 231)

When the Vía Campesina entered the global scene in 1993 the international space, of course, was not empty. Indeed, it was largely dominated by business; transnational corporations (TNCs) are the motorforce of globalization. No one can deny the prominent role that the business community played in pushing for the Uruguay Round and ultimately reshaping the international trade regime with the creation of the WTO. Corporate interests, largely represented by TNCs, continue to be an active and dominant actor in continuing trade negotiations.

TNCs influence international agricultural trade deliberations in two main ways. First, it is TNCs that trade and not governments. That a select few TNCs control the great majority of the world's agricultural trade gives them overwhelming market power. For example, 90 percent of the global trade in wheat, maize, coffee, and pineapple and 70 percent of banana and rice markets are controlled by only a handful of TNCs; five agribusiness corporations control 75 percent of the world's trade in grains (Torres et al. 2000: 14, 40). Research compiled by the ETC Group (2001, 2005) clearly demonstrates the increasingly concentrated nature of agriculture and food markets today

The high levels of concentration evident at the global level are also found at the national level. For example, Filemon Torres and his co-authors (2000: 14–15) report that in Costa Rica one company monopolizes more than 50 percent of the vegetable business, and the largest three businesses together control 70 percent; Honduras follows the same pattern, with one company controlling 40 percent of production and the biggest three companies controlling 80 percent of the market. (See Table 2-1, which clearly indicates that a similar situation exists in the United States.)

Liberalization of the agricultural trade combined with the TRIPs agreement spurred waves of mergers and acquisitions throughout the 1990s among agro-chemical, seed and pharmaceutical companies, agri-food corporations, and food retailers. Pat Mooney (1999: 90), head of the ETC Group, found that of the world's largest 180 food and beverage companies doing business in 1980, nearly twenty years later only sixty remained. To ensure higher profits, corporations and investors strive to own as much of the production

---

Concentration in Corporate Power

Animal pharma: The top ten companies control 55 percent of the world veterinary pharmaceutical market.

Biotechnology: The top ten publicly traded biotech companies account for almost three-quarters of the global biotech market.

Seeds: The top ten seed companies control almost half of the commercial seed market.

Genetically modified (GM) seeds: Monsanto's seeds accounted for 88 percent of the world's total area sown to genetically modified crops in 2004. Monsanto accounted for 91 percent of the worldwide area sown in GM soybean, 97 percent of GM corn, 63.5 percent of GM cotton, and 59 percent of the area planted to GM canola.

Pesticides: The top ten firms control 84 percent of the global pesticide market.

Food retail: In 2004 the top ten global food retailers accounted for 24 percent of the estimated $3.5 trillion global market.

Food and beverage processing: The top ten companies account for 24 percent of the global market for packaged foods; they also account for 36 percent of the revenues earned by the world's top 100 food and beverage companies.

Sources: ETC Group (Action Group on Erosion, Technology and Concentration), "Globalization, Inc: Concentration in Corporate Power: The Unmentioned Agenda," *ETC Group Communiqué* 71 (2001); and "Oligopoly, Inc. 2005: Concentration in Corporate Power," *ETC Group Communiqué* 91 (November/ December 2005).

---

and marketing stages in the food chain as possible. Market power is reached by increasing market share through a combination of corporate strategies, including horizontal and vertical integration, consolidation and concentration, production and marketing contracts, and globalization (Heffernan and Constance 1994; Heffernan 1998). These strategies facilitate the globalization of an industrialized model of agriculture, with agribusiness corporations "value-adding" their way to a greater market share of the consumer food dollar by gaining increasing ownership and control over almost all upstream and downstream stages of the food chain — from provision of inputs, transportation, and food processing to marketing.[5] Even *The Economist* (2000b: 1, 6), a staunch supporter of globalization, admits that agribusiness integration, consolidation, and concentration are effectively "transforming the industry from a chain to a complex web" or into "food clusters" that "control the passage of food from soil to supper." Essentially, liberalization has enabled a small group of TNCs to extend their reach around the world; they are now better positioned to determine what food is produced where, by whom, and at what price. In the process farmers' level of decision-making power has fallen considerably. Rural sociologists at the University of Missouri put it like this:

Table 2-1 Concentration in U.S. Agricultural Markets

Concentration levels are best expressed by the concentration ratio (CR) relative to 100 percent of the top firms. The concentration ratio of the top four companies is stated as CR4; of the top five companies it is CR5; and so on.

Beef packers: CR4 = 83.5 percent
Tyson, Cargill, Swift and Co., National Beef Packing Co.

Historical CR4:	1990	1995	1998	2000
	72%	76%	79%	81%

Pork packers: CR4 = 64 percent
Smithfield Foods, Tyson Food, Swift and Co., Hormel Foods

Historical CR4:	1987	1989	1990	1992	2001
	36%	34%	40%	44%	59%

Broilers: CR4 = 56 percent
Tyson Foods, Pilgrim's Pride, Gold Kist, Perdue

Historical CR4:	1986	1990	1994	1998	2001
	35%	44%	46%	49%	50%

Flour milling: CR4 = 63 percent
Cargill/CHS, ADM, ConAgra, Cereal Food Processors

Historical CR4:	1982	1987	1990
	40%	44%	61%

Food retailing: CR5 = 46 percent.
Wal-Mart Stores, Kroger Co., Albertsons, Inc., Safeway, Inc., Ahold USA, Inc.

Historical CR4:	1997	2001
	24%	38%

Source: Mary Hendrickson and William Heffernan, "Concentration of Agricultural Markets," Department of Rural Sociology, University of Missouri, Columbia, Mo., 2005.

In a food chain cluster, the food product is passed along from stage to stage, but ownership never changes and neither does the location of the decision-making. Starting with the intellectual property rights that governments give to the biotechnology firms, the food product always remains the property of a firm or cluster of firms. The farmer becomes a grower, providing the labor and often some of the capital, but never owning the product as it moves through the food system and never making the major management decisions. (Heffernan, Hendrickson, and Gronski 1999: 3)

Farmers' profits, such as they are, are also undercut. The successful pursuits of TNCs — which flourish in the fertile liberalized environment created by governments through the WTO — have led to oligopolistic structures and what economists, in their own unique sanitized language, call "imperfect" markets that lead to market failures for farmers. In this scenario TNCs wield tremendous market power and boast record-high profits while farmers around the world face a severe financial crisis. The NFU (2000a, iii–iv), compared the return on equity rates for Canadian farmers and corporations and found a "startling picture of relative profitability":

> While farmers earned just 0.3 percent return on equity in 1998, agribusiness corporations earned 5 percent, 20 percent, 50 percent, and even higher rates…. While the farmers growing cereal grains — wheat, oats, corn — earn negative returns and are pushed close to bankruptcy, the companies that make breakfast cereals reap huge profits. In 1998, cereal companies Kellogg's, Quaker Oats, and General Mills enjoyed return on equity rates of 56 percent, 165 percent, and 222 percent respectively. While a bushel of corn sold for less than $4, a bushel of corn flakes sold for $133. In 1998, the cereal companies were 186 to 740 times more profitable than the farms. Maybe farmers are making too little because others are taking too much.

The enormous market power of TNCs has been matched by considerable political power. The conventional model of agriculture was politically engineered; it evolved as a result of very close links between business interests and state support in the form of extensive research and development and favourable policies that facilitated the growth and expansion of corporate interests (Goodman and Redclift 1991). These links were clearly visible when the industrial model of agriculture, rather than an ecological approach, was exported around the world through the Green Revolution as international development institutions and governments wholeheartedly promoted the model. Also, the history of international trade negotiations clearly demonstrates how business interests influenced, for example, French and U.S. trade policies (Milner 1988). Those practices continue today.

In the United States, one of the most powerful players in the WTO, the business community has direct links to U.S. trade negotiators through their Washington-based lobbyists and their prominent representation at the Advisory Committee for Trade Policy and Negotiations (Korten 1995: 177–81). In addition, corporate interests are especially well represented in the official trade delegations. For example, one report pointed out that in the final negotiations of the TRIPs, "96 out of the 111 members of the U.S. delegation were from the private sector" (Green 2001: 4). Similarly, in the official Canadian delegation to the fourth WTO Ministerial conference in Doha, the interests of agri-industry (meat packers and processors, oilseed

---

Canadian Delegates to a WTO Meeting

At the Fourth Ministerial Meeting of the WTO, held in Doha, Qaatar, the non-government members of the official Canadian delegation were:

1. Liam McCreery, president of the Canadian Agri-Food Trade Alliance (CAFTA). According to information provided on its website, CAFTA is "a national coalition of associations, organizations and companies that advocates the liberalization of agri-food markets. CAFTA was created to ensure that the interests of its members are effectively represented in international trade negotiations through co-operation with federal, provincial and international governments and international industry." CAFTA's board members include, among others, representatives from Cargill, Agricore, Canadian Meat Council (packers/processors), Canada Beef Export, Canadian Cattlemen's Association, Canadian Sugar Institute (manufacturers), Malting Industry Association of Canada, and Canadian Oilseed Processors Association (crushers and processors). CAFTA is a strong advocate of a completely liberalized trade regime.

2. Don Knoerr, former president of the Canadian Federation of Agriculture (CFA) and chair of the Agriculture, Food and Beverage Sectoral Advisory Group on International Trade (SAGIT), a private-sector advisory committee with representation from bulk commodity and value-added product sectors. It provides advice on international trade and business development to the minister of agriculture and agri-food and the minister of international trade.

3. William Dymond, executive director of the Centre for Trade Policy and Law. Two of Dymond's important achievements are his involvement as senior advisor to the Trade Negotiations Office for the Canada-U.S. Free-Trade Agreement and his role as chief negotiator for Canada for the OECD Multilateral Agreement on Investment (MAI).

4. Peter Clark, president of Grey Clark Shish and Associates, a law firm specializing in international trade.

5. Brian Oleson, senior economist with the Canadian Wheat Board, a state trading enterprise in the business of selling grain on the international market on behalf of farm interests.

6. Ann Weston, vice-president of the North-South Institute, an independent research body (a civil society voice).

7. Bob Friesen, president of the CFA, a pro-liberalization (but with caveats) farm organization.

---

crushers, manufacturers, grain companies, malting companies) were overwhelmingly represented.

The agri-food multinational Cargill provides a stark example of the great corporate influence that can be wielded in international trade negotiations. William Pearce, a vice-president of the company, served as President

Nixon's trade advisor. Daniel Amstutz, another Cargill executive, essentially wrote the Reagan administration's proposal to the GATT in 1987 and was subsequently hired as the U.S. government's chief negotiator on agriculture. Cargill's president and CEO were on the GATT Advisory Committee to the U.S. government throughout the Reagan, Bush, and Clinton administrations (Kneen 1995: 69).

At the first WTO Ministerial conference, held in Singapore, 65 percent of the non-governmental organizations that received accreditation represented business interests (Scholte, O'Brien, and Williams 1998: 17). The significant presence of commercial interests at the WTO was confirmed further by the presence of numerous corporate lobbyists, Chambers of Commerce, technical trade advisory committees, and insurance companies and industry groups that attended the WTO Ministerial meetings in Geneva, Seattle, and Doha.

The attendance record at these meetings, however, provides only a super-ficial view of the role and enormous influence of TNCs in trade negotiations. In many ways — and this certainly works to their advantage — TNCs remain invisible in the discourse on trade negotiations, which are framed in the context of nations trading with one another. The trade rules are directed at national policies that have an impact on international markets. But as Sophia Murphy (2002: 19), a researcher with the U.S.-based Institute for Agriculture and Trade Policy points out, individual nations are not competing against each other for a greater share of the world market. Instead, countries are competing for investment by the large TNCs. Murphy argues that by not recognizing TNCs (and their strategies) as the real drivers of trade, the WTO rules conveniently ignore the real problem: the tremendous concentration of market power in agricultural markets.

Impact of the Globalization of Agriculture

> A large percentage of [the] world population, and specially the rural poor have not benefited from globalisation and in many cases they have been negatively affected, as the specialization normally associated with globalisation weakens a community's control over its livelihood, and reduces the range of choices on ways for people to make a living. (Torres et al. 2000: 3)

With the implementation of SAPs, regional and bilateral trade agreements, and the WTO's Agreement on Agriculture, rural landscapes in the North and South are undergoing rapid and profound change as national governments redefine agricultural policies and legislation to facilitate integration into an international market-driven economy. Existing agricultural and marketing structures are being dismantled, while new agrarian laws aimed at restructur-ing land tenure, land use, and marketing systems are being promulgated to increase production, especially for export, and to industrialize and further liberalize the agricultural sector.

Examples of such laws in Latin America, to mention just a few, are the Law of Modernization and Development of the Agriculture Sector in Honduras, changes to Article 27 of the Mexican Constitution approved in 1992 (designed primarily to privatize the *ejido*), and Ecuador's Agrarian Development Law of 1994. Examples in India include, at the national level, the Land Acquisition (Amendment) Bill passed in 1998, which facilitates access to land for the corporate sector (domestic and foreign) for investment and "development." At the state level, the Land Amendment Act promulgated in 1995 in Karnataka moves land use away from agriculture to industry, raises the land ceiling, and allows the ownership and rental of land by non-farmers. In Canada, in the summer of 2002 the Saskatchewan provincial government passed new legislation, the Saskatchewan Farm Security Amendment Act, which effectively removed restrictions for out-of-province, foreign, and corporate ownership of farm land. These laws emphasize "modernization" and the creation of a more "investor friendly," "market responsive," and "dynamic" agricultural sector.

Regional free-trade agreements and the WTO have promised economic growth and prosperity for all — including those living in the countryside. The three pillars of the WTO's Agreement on Agriculture — market access, domestic support, and export subsidies — sought to increase trade and level the playing field so that all of the world's producers could compete more effectively in the international marketplace. That at least was the theory. Liberalization and the creation of a global competitive agricultural economy were promoted as *the* solution to the high levels of poverty and food insecurity that had plagued rural areas for decades. Yet a growing number of studies clearly indicate that rural impoverishment is on the rise.

For example, a study of 113 countries conducted by the International Fund for Agricultural Development (IFAD) found that between 1965 and 1988 — a period during which many countries initiated SAPs and pushed for modernization in agriculture — the "level of rural poverty (in terms of both a share of population, and absolute population size) has increased significantly" (Jazairy, Alamgir, and Panuccio 1992: 2–3). The study stated that 97 percent of the rural population of Bolivia lived in extreme poverty while in Honduras the figure was 93.4 percent (ibid.: 17). In Brazil, during the period from 1960 to 1980, a time of intense modernization in the countryside, 29 million people migrated to the cities in search of work (ibid.: 72).

More recent findings counter the prediction that increased liberalization will bring prosperity to the countryside. A comprehensive study on rural poverty stated: "Overall there has been no global correction since the late 1970s of the urban biases that sentence rural people to more widespread and deeper poverty, illiteracy and ill-health" (IFAD 2001: 3). Evidence also shows that since the 1980s a number of transitional countries have experienced sharp rises in rural poverty, and that by the turn of the century 1.2 billion people were living in extreme poverty — with 75 percent of these people living and working in rural areas (Jazairy, Alamgir, and Panuccio 1992: 3, 15–16). Throughout the 1990s aid to agriculture fell by two-thirds; and during the late 1990s rural poverty increased by 10 to 20 percent in a number of Latin American countries (Gonzalez 2000: 2). Across the board rural poverty had persisted and often included more than 50 percent of the population (Torres et al. 2000: 12). The FAO's *The State of Food Insecurity in the World 2004* reports that in 2000–02 a staggering 852 million people around the world were undernourished — an increase of 10 million from the previous year.

The globalization of agriculture has also had the perverse effect of globalizing obesity. The number of obese people in the world is now equal to those who are malnourished, and the recent worldwide increase in obesity has been linked directly to changes in agriculture and the greater availability and consumption of mass-produced, industrialized foodstuffs (Picard 2002: A12). Studies conducted in 2002 by the Pan American Health Organization (PAHO) found a growing trend towards obesity in lower-income areas of Brazil and Argentina. Quoting a representative from Argentina's Ministry of Health and Social Action, a PAHO (2002) press release stated: "The poor do not eat what they want, nor what they know that they should eat, but what they can get.... The food industry favors those consumption patterns by segmenting and mass-marketing products of poor quality and higher fat and sugar content to sectors with less purchasing power."

In another study examining the links between the AoA and food security in fourteen developing countries, the FAO (2000: 13) observed "a general trend towards the consolidation of farms as competitive pressure began to build up following trade liberalization." In the context of few safety nets, if any, this trend led to an increased displacement and marginalization of farming peoples (ibid.: 14). Of the countries that the FAO examined, only a few demonstrated an increase in food exports, while the majority experienced sharp rises in food imports. For instance, in a comparison of the value of food imports between 1990–94 and 1995–98, India's imports grew by 168.4 percent, Brazil's by 106.7 percent, and Peru's by 57.3 percent. This influx of cheap imports undermined the ability of small producers to compete. In a country such as India, where over 70 percent of the population's livelihoods depend on agriculture, this was a recipe for disaster. While India did experience economic growth after it embarked on the path to liberalization in 1991, poverty did not decline (FAO 2000). Other studies also clearly link the trade liberalization of agriculture to increased food insecurity (Murphy 1999; Madeley 2000).

Mexico is perhaps one of the best examples of agricultural economic liberalization: it now boasts eight free-trade agreements encompassing twenty-four countries in three continents (*El Financiero* 2000). The most devastating of these deals for the Mexican peasantry are the agriculture provisions in the

North American Free Trade Agreement (NAFTA), which came into effect in January 1994. Once self-sufficient in basic grains, Mexico became increasingly import-dependent. Between 1992 and 1996 food imports rose from 20 to 43 percent of total internal consumption; imports of rice, one of Mexico's basic grains, went from one-half million tonnes to seven million tonnes (*Third World Resurgence* 1996b: 29–30). By 1999, 25 percent of the country's beans and 97 percent of its soy were imported (Comisión de Agricultura 2000: 181). Liberalization included the dismantling of guaranteed prices for producers and a substantial reduction in subsidized inputs. High levels of corn imports led to a 45 percent drop in the price paid to farmers (Nadal 2000: 36); between 1993 and 1998 wheat prices paid to farmers fell by 32 percent and bean prices by 51 percent (Public Citizen's Global Trade Watch 2001: 15). Increased food imports at prices that peasants, struggling with the collapse of support programs, could not match led to farmers being pushed off the land and to increasing poverty. Heightened levels of poverty and the abandonment of basic food subsidies led to decreased food consumption. While corn prices fell, the cost of tortillas increased by 179 percent (Nadal 2000: 36).

In 1996 Víctor Suárez, at the time co-ordinator of the Asociación Nacional de Empresas Comercializadoras de Productores del Campo (ANEC), a member organization of the Vía Campesina, said: "Eating more cheaply on imports is not eating at all for the poor in Mexico.... One out of every two peasants is not getting enough to eat. In the eighteen months since NAFTA, the intake of food has dropped by 29 percent" (quoted in *Third World Resurgence* 1996b: 30).

It is not just farming people in the South who felt the brunt of trade liberalization in agriculture. The Coordination Paysanne Européenne reported in 1995 that every two minutes one farm in the European Union is "disappeared" (CPE: 1995). Since 1978 half of the farming population in France and Germany has left agriculture. In the OECD countries, by 2000 the number of farms was falling at a rate of 1.5 percent per year, and only 8 percent of the labour force was now working in agriculture (*The Economist* 2000b: 6). Food First reported that in the United States in just two years between 1994 and 1996, about "25 percent of all US hog farmers, 10 percent of all grain farmers, and 10 percent of all dairy farmers went out of business" (Mittal and Kawaai 2001: 4). The U.S. Department of Labor predicted a continuing decline in rural America — that over the next ten years more than 270,000 farmers would lose their jobs (NFU-USA 2002). While U.S. farmers' expected a 20 percent drop in net income in 2002, Cargill experienced a 51 percent increase in profits and ConAgra Foods reported a 48 percent increase in net earnings (NFU-USA 2002; *Reuters* 2002).

Canadian farmers too — considered to be among the world's most "competitive" and "efficient" producers — have been forced off the land in considerable number because farming is no longer economically viable. Darrin Qualman (2002: 1–3), executive secretary of the NFU, argued:

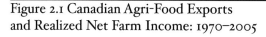

Figure 2.1 Canadian Agri-Food Exports
and Realized Net Farm Income: 1970–2005

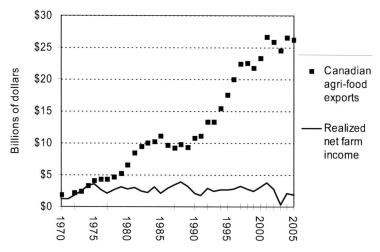

Sources: National Farmers Union, compiled from data in Realized Net Farm Income: Statistics Canada, online publications, #21-010-X, at http://www.statcan.ca/cgi-bin/downpub/freepub.cgi?subject=920#920, and from data provided in Agriculture and Agri-Food Canada, Markets and Trade Team

Since 1988 — the year Canada signed the Canada-U.S. Trade Agreement — Canadian agri-food exports have nearly tripled. Canadian farmers and exporters have been very successful in increasing exports, in gaining "market access." The result, however, has not been the farm prosperity that politicians, economists, and trade negotiators predicted. Since 1988 net farm incomes have remained stagnant — or fallen dramatically if inflation is taken into account.

Clearly, rising exports have not translated into economic benefits for Canadian farmers (see Figure 2-1). Statistics in the agro-export-based province of Saskatchewan illustrate just how acute the farm crisis is: realized net farm incomes in 2006 were worse than the levels that farmers had experienced in the 1930s (see Figure 2-2).

Farmers are caught in a cost-price squeeze in which profit margins shrink as input costs rise, while farm prices drop steeply. According to the latest Canadian Agriculture Census, between 1996 and 2001 farm prices dropped by 27 percent while input costs increased by 8.5 percent (Lang: 2002). During the 1990s farm debt grew substantially, from $23.5 billion to a record high of $38 billion in 2000 (Wilson 2001: 5).

Falling farm incomes lead to rural depopulation and the abandonment of

Figure 2.2 Saskatchewan Realized Net Farm Income,
net of government payments, per farm: 1926-2006

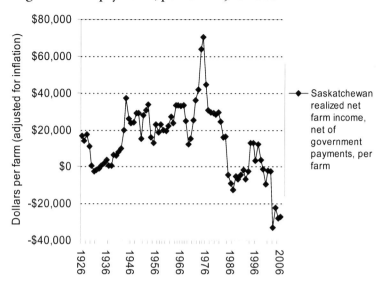

Sources: National Farmers Union, compiled from data in Realized Net Farm Income:
Statistics Canada, online publications, #21-010-X, at http://www.statcan.ca/cgi-bin/
downpub/freepub.cgi?subject=920#920

whole communities. Between 1971 and 1996 the number of Canadian farms
fell by 25 percent (Stirling 1999: 8), and from 1996 to 2001 the number of
farms declined by another 10.7 percent. The number of Canadians working in
agriculture also fell at unprecedented rates. According to Statistics Canada,
from 1996 to 2001 there was a 26.4 percent drop in Canada as a whole, while
in some provinces the figure was much higher: Alberta saw a 37.6 percent
decline; Saskatchewan 36.2 percent; and Ontario 31.5 percent (Lang 2002:
3). As the number of farmers declined, the remaining farms were getting
larger.

Free-trade proponents argue that farmers benefit from increasing
production for export and increasing levels of agricultural trade. Yet, as the
numbers indicate, this is clearly not the case. Instead, neo-liberal agricultural
policies benefit agribusiness TNCs. As the NFU (2002b: 4) argues:

> For farmers, so-called "free trade" agreements do two things si-
> multaneously:
>
> • By removing tariffs, quotas, and duties, these agreements erase
> the economic borders between nations and force the world's one
> billion farmers into a single, hyper-competitive market.
> • At the same time, these agreements facilitate waves of agri-

business mergers that nearly eliminate competition for these corporations....

> "Free trade" agreements may increase trade but, much more importantly, *they dramatically alter the relative size and market power of the players in the agri-food production chain*. For farmers and their net incomes, increased exports may be one of the least significant effects of trade agreements and globalization. Much more significant — perhaps completely overwhelming any potential benefits from increased exports — may be the effect these agreements have on the balance of market power between farmers and agribusiness corporations, *because this balance of market power determines the distribution of profits within the agri-food production chain*. (emphasis in original)

Farm policies largely ignore the highly skewed power relations in the modern food system to the detriment of farmers around the world. As the NFU's Nettie Wiebe said in an interview:

> It is worth noting that the Canadian government has adhered diligently to the WTO rules by withdrawing agriculture supports, deregulating and privatizing the infrastructure such as transportation and inspection. Canadian farmers are the "poster boys" of the WTO, rigorously following the prescriptions to invest, industrialize, diversify, maximize production, and focus on exports. For that we are rewarded with record losses of income, people and communities. If we're the "winners" in the WTO game, what must the losers be experiencing?

The extent of the agricultural crisis elsewhere was initially captured by the tragic suicide of over four hundred farmers during in the 1997–98 agricultural season in the districts bordering the states of Andhra Pradesh, Karnataka, and Maharashtra in India (Shameem 1998; Vasavi 1999). These suicides clearly demonstrated the extreme difficulties faced by farmers as they shift from the low-cost, low-risk growing of traditional basic grains to a high-cost, high-risk model of production for the market in a context where there is little (if any) institutional support. Most of the farmers who committed suicide were involved in commercial market-oriented agriculture, doing exactly what current agricultural policy advocated: embarking on the prescribed path to modernization and liberalization. Yet their lives ended in desperation and tragedy. Making the links even more graphic, to kill themselves these farmers employed one of the tools of agricultural modernization: chemical pesticides.

In recent years "suicide by pesticide" has become an epidemic in India, a harvest of death.[6] Since 1997 more than 25,000 Indian farmers have committed suicide by drinking chemicals designed to "improve" agricultural production (Frontline/World 2005). During the summer of 2004 in the state of Andhra Pradesh alone, seven farmers committed suicide every day. For Chad Heeter, a freelance filmmaker who produced a documentary called *Seeds of Suicide* on the subject, "This is the other side of globalization." Although India's new prime minister, Manmohan Singh, travelled to the area in the middle of the epidemic and announced a relief program to the families of those who had committed suicide, the tragedy persists (BBC News 2004). More than an aid package will be necessary to reverse years of policies so devastating to peasants and small farmers.

The implementation of SAPs in the North and South, the signing of this particular GATT agreement, and the latest round of WTO trade negotiations clearly reflect the globalization of a worldview that sees market forces as key determinants of the economic, political, and social aspects of our societies. Jerry Mander (1996: 5), a founding member of the International Forum on Globalization, stresses that the principles of this global economy focus exclusively on "the primacy of economic growth; the need for free trade to stimulate growth; the unrestricted 'free market'; the absence of government regulation; and voracious consumerism combined with an aggressive advocacy of a uniform worldwide development model."

Some critics suggest that this development model should be seen as an "enclosure of the commons" whereby all resources needed for sustenance are entrapped by the market (Shiva 1997b). In saying this they are broadening the concept of the commons beyond the notion of property to include resources needed for sustenance and well-being, such as — among others — health, air, food, a defensible life-space, and community (*Ecologist* 1992: 123–24).

In Search of Alternative Development

Growing poverty levels — accompanied by environmental degradation — in the face of modernization and globalization have led to questions about the links between "development" and poverty reduction. Indian scholar Rajni Kothari (1995: 2) sees poverty as a "consequence of 'development'" and argues that "societies that adopted the path of capitalist development 'grew into poverty'" and they "are now desperately trying to 'grow out'" of that poverty by expanding their economies. The Indian activist and writer Vandana Shiva (1993c: 71–73) argues that very often what is perceived as poverty by outsiders is simply a preference for using local resources to meet locally perceived "needs" in an efficient but non-market-oriented, non-Western manner. Others emphasize that poor people's own perceptions of deprivation and poverty are often non-economic — focusing instead, perhaps, on issues related to social well-being, vulnerability, stability, insecurity, defenselessness, and exposure to risks. They sometimes see poverty as a matter of social exclusion. These approaches tend to stress the multidimensional nature of poverty — the social and political as well as economic aspects. Perhaps most importantly they focus on the processes, including the mechanisms, institutions, and actors, that lead to social exclusion.

Alternative definitions of poverty inevitably lead to alternative visions of development. The goal of these new approaches — whether it is called people-centred, another, alternative, or autonomous development, or the more radical alternative to, anti-development or post-development — is equitable, sustainable, and participatory development. All reject the top-down, simple transfer of Western technology and, for the most part, are geared to structural transformation. They advocate, to varying degrees, principles of self-reliance, environmental and ecological sustainability, community-based endogenous strategies. They stress the need for people-led, social equity, and bottom-up participatory methods and processes. While they are varied, they share key concepts: respecting the local environment, and the value of empowerment — especially in the context of valuing local knowledge and customs, and in allowing marginalized peoples to define their own needs.

John Friedmann (1992: 68) argues that among the marginalized people he worked with in Latin American communities, the most precious need is a "defensible life space" that includes "a supportive neighbourhood or community." He says this condition represents "the most highly prized social power of all, and households are prepared to make almost any kind of sacrifice to obtain it." In adopting this alternative vision of poverty, alternative rural development policy would focus much less on production and consumption and much more on the need to foster or protect a social space defined as a home and a shared moral community.

Just possibly, these two conditions — increased modernization, production, and consumption on the one side and a moral community on the other — are fundamentally in opposition. For example, in his study of ecological struggles in India, Pramod Parajuli (1996) asserts that the demise of community is integral to the expansion of capitalism. Consequently, in the case of India, the history of the developmentalist state has involved persistent attempts to dismantle self-sustaining and self-governing communities. The ensuing struggles become conflicts between a "political economy of profit" and the "moral economy of provision," and resistance centres on reclaiming and strengthening community (Parajuli 1996: 39). Resistance also includes claims for autonomy, governance, alternative models of development, strengthening of ethnic identities, and the forging of what Parajuli calls "ecological ethnicities."

Defining poverty as social exclusion and disempowerment, and the processes therein, leads to alternative development policies and programs geared to participation and empowerment. In the context of rural development, resistance to modern industrial agriculture is often referred to as *alternative* or *traditional* versus *conventional* agriculture. These terms are not without problems, because "alternative" agriculture often refers to peasant-based or small-scale farming done in the context of complex social and cultural relations, often integrating new ideas and crops with long-held traditional practices and knowledge, and this combination remains the most common

Table 2-2 Comparison of Conventional and Alternative Agriculture

Dominant/Conventional Agricultural Paradigm	Alternative Agricultural Paradigm
Centralization • centralized control over production, processing, and marketing • concentrated production, fewer and larger farms, therefore fewer farmers and rural communities	*Decentralization* • more local/regional production, processing, and marketing • dispersed production (more farms and farmers), control of land, resources, and capital
Dependence • scientific and technological approach to production, dependence on experts • reliance on external sources of energy, inputs, and credit • predominant reliance on long-distance markets	*Independence* • smaller, lower input production units, less reliance on external sources of knowledge, energy, and credit • more personal and community self-sufficiency • primary emphasis on personal values, knowledge, skills
Competitive • competitive self-interest • farming is a business • emphasis on efficiency, flexibility, quantity, and increasing profit margins • emphasis on keeping up with latest technologies, and increasing size of operation • no commitment to the traditional family farm and rural communities as an important "way of life"	*Community* • increased co-operation • farming is a way of life and a business • emphasis on a holistic approach to production, optimizing all parts of the agro-ecosystem • emphasis on appropriate technology and scale of production • commitment to traditional family farm and rural community as an important "way of life"
Domination of nature • humans are separate from and superior to nature • nature consists mainly of resources to be used for economic growth • imposition of human time frames and systems on natural cycles • productivity maximized through industrial inputs and scientific modifications • appropriation and substitution of natural processes and products with scientific and industrial processes and products	*Harmony with nature* • humans are part of and dependent on nature • nature provides resources but is also valued for its own sake • working with natural nutrient and energy cycles • working with an ecological/closed system approach — developing a diversified and balanced system • incorporating more natural products and processes • using cultural methods to build soil health

Dominant/Conventional Agricultural Paradigm	Alternative Agricultural Paradigm
Specialization	*Diversity*
• limited genetic base used in production	• broad genetic base
• most crops grown in monocultures	• incorporation of polycultures, complex rotations
• separation of crops and livestock production	• integration of crops and livestock
• standardized production systems	• heterogeneity of farming systems
• predominance of a specialized, discipline-oriented scientific approach	• interdisciplinary (natural and social sciences), participatory (inclusion of farmers), systems-oriented
Exploitation	*Restraint*
• external costs (environmental, social) often ignored as short-term benefits outweigh long-term consequences	• full-cost accounting
• reliance on non-renewable resources	• short- and long-term outcomes equally important
• high consumption/materialism propels economic growth	• greater use of renewable resources, conservation of non-renewable resources
• hegemony of scientific knowledge and industrial approach results in loss of indigenous/local knowledge and cultures	• sustainable consumption, simpler lifestyles
	• equitable access to basic needs
	• recognition and incorporation of other knowledge and ways of doing, allowing for a more heterogeneous knowledge base

Source: Beckie 2000, adaptation of Beus 1995: 60.

form of agriculture around the world. Conventional agriculture is often only "conventional" for a small group of industrialized farmers.[7]

Although modern/conventional agriculture dominates the landscape in most industrialized countries, this is not necessarily the case in many developing countries. Modern agriculture has admittedly made incursions into the rural South, but as *The Economist* (2000b: 11) states, in many parts of the world conventional agriculture "sits uncomfortably alongside traditional farming practices." Even within developed countries there is growing resistance to conventional agriculture and a concerted shift to ecologically based agriculture, as evidenced by the exponential growth in organic production and the marketing of organic products (ibid.: 8).

In alternative agriculture practices, polyculture replaces monoculture, and diversity overcomes uniformity. Natural fertilizers and biological pest control give farmers greater independence and autonomy. Farmers interact with nature rather than dominating or controlling it, and community wins over competition. (See Table 2-2.)

The Enduring Family Farm

According to statistics gathered by the U.S. government in 1992, more than 85 percent of farms are organized as family farms, while corporate farms account for only 0.4 percent of all farms and 6 percent of all sales receipts, and cover only 1.3 percent of farm acreage (Allen and Lueck 1998: 344). The situation is similar in Canada, where 63.5 percent of farms are family-owned and corporate ownership accounts for 1.4 percent of all farms (ibid.: 3). The same pattern is seen in many parts of the world, and especially in developing countries, where peasant or smallholder agricultural production persists (Netting 1993; Rosset 1999). According to a Cristobal Kay, a researcher with the Institute of Social Studies, based in the Hague, peasant agriculture remains significant throughout Latin America. Kay's (1995: 35–36) research demonstrates that throughout the 1980s, peasant agriculture:

> comprised four-fifths of all farm units and accounted for one-fifth of total agricultural land.... The peasant economy accounted for almost two-thirds of the total agricultural labour force.... The peasant economy made a particularly large contribution to agricultural production in Bolivia (80 percent), Peru (55 percent), Mexico (47 percent), Colombia (44 percent), Brazil (40 percent), and Chile (38 percent).

The restructuring of the food economy necessarily involves changes in consumption, production, and distribution. Some critics argue that the further consolidation of the industrial model of agriculture through globalization and liberalization will lead inevitably to the demise of smallholder production everywhere (Lappé, Collins, and Rosset 1998). Yet the family farm remains a prominent structure in agricultural production around the world.

Why is it that family farms continue to be such a significant part of agriculture despite the acute crisis in the countryside? One of the main arguments for the persistence of family farms is that agriculture is not like other industries in that agribusiness is severely constrained by the biological processes of nature inherent in the production of food (Allen and Lueck 1998). There is also growing evidence that small farms are more "efficient" than large corporate farms (Rosset 1999: 8). Others argue that the numbers of small family farms remain stable because they are more sustainable (Ahearn, Korb, and Banker 2005). Finally, the persistence of family farms may rest outside the purview of economics and entail a number of social goals. That is, for many farm families the commitment to agriculture may reflect a desire for community and social well-being as much as the need to earn a fair return on labour and investment. For example, in a study focused on the United States researchers Nola Reinhardt and Peggy Barlett (1989: 216–21) found that farming may represent a strong connection to land and places inhabited by ancestors and be rooted in ideas of ethnic identity, moral lives, and religion. They stressed that many of the goals of family farmers might best be expressed as "dimensions of intangible wealth" that include, among other things, "pride of ownership, continuity of family, freedom of choice in work time and pace, ability to identify effort and reward." While the objective may be to earn a livelihood, this goal does not necessarily mean the need "to obtain the highest rate of return on their resources."

When asked, "What keeps you connected to farming?" in a series of workshops across the country, Canadian farm women ranked an attachment to beauty and nature very highly. The workshop report stated:

> There is a sense of rootedness — a deep connection to and passion for the land — that women value, both for themselves and their children. Farming is deep in their spirit, heart and blood and, for many, farming is all they have ever wanted to do.
>
> The smell of the soil in the spring, the quiet and peace of living in a serenely beautiful landscape untainted by the sounds of traffic and sirens are powerful connections, as is the open space and isolated backyards, and the opportunity for time to think. There is beauty in the darkness and moonlight on their farms, and women take great pleasure in staring at stars in a night sky unpolluted by artificial illumination. Farm women are attached to the acts of farming, garnering deep satisfaction from planting, growing and harvesting crops and gardens, being outside and experiencing all the seasons. Caring for animals keeps women connected with farming, the joy and satisfaction of seeing animals born and then grow through their life cycles. There is a passionate commitment to farming and to nature that is intensely spiritual. (Roppel, Desmarais, and Martz 2006: 32–33)

While these descriptions refer to North American farm families, peasant families in many parts of the world share an equally strong, if not stronger, commitment to maintaining their connection to the land as a necessary component of being part of a rural community (Racine 1997; Handy 1994). This condition is exactly what Friedmann means by a "defensible life space."

The idea that agriculture, especially in the context of small farms, is not just about production and maximizing profit is gaining increasing legitimacy in the international community. The FAO (1999) is exploring the "multifunctionality" of agriculture, and some countries are increasingly using the concept in attempts to change the WTO Agreement on Agriculture. The United States Department of Agriculture (USDA 1998), the bastion of industrialized agriculture, has stressed the "public value" of small farms as including diversity, environmental benefits, self-empowerment, and community responsibility. These farms are, it says, places for families, providing a personal connection to food and solid economic foundations. It is perhaps idealistic and naïve to suggest that these ways of thinking represent a significant shift away from the more exclusive production-oriented model to an inclusive view of the role and purpose of agriculture. But they do suggest the existence of two competing and highly contested models of agriculture: on the one hand the locally centred, farmer-driven alternative model; and, on the other, the corporate-driven global industrial model.

In rejecting the idea of globalization as universal and inevitable we need to reconceptualize the restructuring of agriculture as a "highly contested" process. We need to recognize that the production of food remains locally based and that social agency plays a critical role in shaping the nature of that production (Whatmore and Thorne 1997). As Sarah Whatmore (1995: 45) argues, production occurs in a particular place with particular people embedded in historically defined "local social relations, cultures, political identities, economic strategies, [and local] land use practices." This kind of analysis points to the numerous "spaces" and forms of resistance to the industrial model that are being created at the local, national, and international levels. Perhaps most important is a recognition that social agency and resistance also involve the active construction or defence of alternative models of agriculture in which primary production and decision-making about the social relations of that production remain in the hands of family farms. It is in this context, and to these ends, that the international farm and peasant movement, the Vía Campesina, emerged and took action.

3. Peasants and Farmers Going Global

> The Vía Campesina is committed to changing the unjust, unsustainable models of production and trade. Peasants and farmers are suffering a financial, social and cultural crisis everywhere, north and south. And we are everywhere committed to working in solidarity to build more just, sustainable peasant societies. We, the peasant and small-scale farming societies, are not defeated. We are strong and determined and we are the majority in the world. We are proud of our work, which is to produce safe foods for our families and humankind. We cherish our diversity, both biological and cultural. The future belongs to us. —Bangalore Declaration, Vía Campesina, Oct. 3, 2000

As the Uruguay Round of the GATT drew to a close in 1994, peasant and farm organizations clearly understood that international trade agreements would result in fundamental changes to the structure of agricultural economies and the social fabric of rural communities. Perhaps most disturbing, the creation of the WTO would fundamentally alter the relationship between farmers' organizations and the state. The WTO's power would reach far into what had been until then the business of national governments — formulation of national agriculture policies. By signing international agreements, national governments and politicians could forsake domestic programs, asserting that such things were all beyond their control. Their hands were tied — all policies and programs must comply with the decisions of the WTO.

Still, peasant and farm families would not be compliant accomplices during this process of economic restructuring, nor would they prove to be passive victims in the face of increasing poverty and marginalization. Economic liberalization and the globalization of an industrialized model of agriculture spurred farm and peasant leaders in the North and South to mobilize far beyond national borders, to reach across continents. As João Pedro Stédile of the MST explained:

> It is very striking that it is only now that farmers are starting to achieve a degree of worldwide coordination, after five hundred years of capitalist development. Workers have had an international day for over a century, and women for not much less, but farmers have only just agreed to mark one — 17 April, a source of pride to us: a tribute to Carajás. As long as capitalism meant only industrialization, those who worked on the land limited their struggle to the local level. But as the realities of neoliberal internationalization

have been imposed on us, we've begun to hear stories from farmers in the Philippines, Malaysia, South Africa, Mexico, France, all facing the same problems — and the same exploiters. The Indians are up against Monsanto, just as we are in Brazil, and Mexico, and France. It's the same handful of companies — seven groups, in total, worldwide — that monopolize agricultural trade, and control research and biotechnology, and are tightening their ownership of the planet's seeds. The new phase of capitalism has itself created the conditions for farmers to unite against the neoliberal model. (quoted in *New Left Review* 2002: 99)

La Vía Campesina emerged as an anti-corporate, peasant, and farmer-driven international movement as a result of a long history of exchanges between farmers from the North and peasant organizations in the South. In the context of an agricultural economy increasingly globalized through the mechanism of the GATT/WTO, peasant and farm organizations established even more common ground as they identified common interests, consolidated a collective identity as "people of the land," and developed a collective analysis that identified transnational corporations as the enemy. The Vía Campesina's identity, vision for change — best captured in the concept of food sovereignty — and collective will were elaborated further and strengthened as a result of interactions with two other key elements of civil society in the international arena: the International Federation of Agricultural Producers and non-governmental organizations.

Establishing Common Ground as "People of the Land"

The immediate roots of the Vía Campesina can be traced to discussions among representatives of eight farm organizations from Central America, the Caribbean, Europe, Canada, and the United States who had gathered to participate in the second congress of the Unión Nacional de Agricultores y Ganaderos held in Managua, Nicaragua, in May 1992. At that conference peasants and farmers established the common ground shared by farming families in the North and South.

Farm leaders also vowed to strengthen ties among their organizations and to forge international links with farm organizations from around the world. The Managua Declaration clearly captured this desire to engage in a collective endeavour to develop alternatives to neo-liberalism. It was a clear and forceful call for peasants and farmers everywhere to work together. As the Declaration stated, "Through our unity we will find the means to have our voice and our propositions heard by those who would usurp our right to cultivate the land and assure our families' dignity."

As a follow-up to the Managua meeting, just one year later on May 15–16, 1993, forty-six farm leaders (20 percent of them women) from around the world — including representatives from most of the organizations that had

---

Excerpts from the Managua Declaration

Neoliberal policies represent a dramatic constraint on farmers throughout the world, bringing us to the brink of irredeemable extinction and further aggravating the irreparable damage which has been caused to our rural environs....

We note that the GATT affects farmers in poor countries and as well impoverishes farmers in rich countries to the benefit of monopolies and transnational corporations.

Trade and international exchange should have as their fundamental goal, justice, and cooperation rather than competition and the survival of the fittest.

We as producers need to be guaranteed sufficient income to cover as a minimum our costs of production. This, to date, has not been a concern of the negotiators of the GATT. We reject policies which promote low prices, liberalized markets, the export of surpluses, dumping and export subsidies.

Sustainable agricultural production is fundamental and strategic to social life and cannot be reduced to a simple question of trade. Farmers demand direct participation in the GATT negotiations.

The Managua Declaration was signed by ASOCODE, Windward Islands Farmers Association (WINFA), Canadian National Farmers Union (NFU), National Farmers Union (NFU-USA), Coordination Paysanne Européenne (CPE), Coordinadora de Organizaciones de Agricultores y Ganaderos (COAG-Spain), National Farmers Union (Norway), and the Dutch Farm Delegation (Netherlands).

Source: Managua Declaration 1992: 1–2.

---

signed the Managua Declaration — gathered in Mons, Belgium, and formally constituted the Vía Campesina. The farm leaders had been brought together under the auspices of a Dutch NGO, Paulo Freire Stichting (PFS), which was aiming primarily to establish an international farmer-driven research project on alternative agricultural policies. The farm leaders arrived at Mons with a broader and more pressing agenda. Most importantly, they sought to forge progressive organizations into an international peasant and farm movement.

Farm leaders defined five regions and elected a five-person Co-ordinating Commission made up of representatives from the five areas: MST for South America; ASOCODE for Central America, the Caribbean, and North America; Peasant Solidarnosc (Poland) for Eastern Europe; the Peasant Movement of the Philippines (Kilusang Magbubukid ng Pilipinas: KMP) for Asia; and CPE (Europe) for Western Europe. The Vía Campesina also expanded on agreements reached in Managua by further defining basic elements of a progressive agricultural policy. All major points of agreement were reflected in a formal declaration that closed the conference on May 16. The Mons Declaration stressed:

As a response to the current irrational and irresponsible logic of production and to the political decisions which support it, we propose the following basic conditions in order to bring about an agricultural development which is ecologically sustainable, socially just and which allows the producer real access to the wealth s/he generates day in [and] day out:

1. The right of small farmers to a living [in the] countryside; this implies the full right of farmers to their own autonomous organizations and the recognition of their social importance in the definition and implementation of development in general, and rural development in particular.
2. The right to a diversified agriculture which guarantees, as a matter of priority, a supply of healthy, high quality food for all peoples in the world, based on a profound respect for the environment, for a balanced society and for effective access to the land.
3. The right of every country to define its own agricultural policy according to the nation's interest and in *concertación* with the peasant and indigenous organizations, guaranteeing their real participation. (Vía Campesina 1993a: 2)

The Vía Campesina emerged in explicit rejection of neo-liberal agricultural policies and as a direct response to the GATT negotiations' exclusion of the concerns, needs, and interests of people who actually work the land and produce the world's food. Peasants and small-scale farmers in the North and South were determined to work together on the urgent task of developing alternatives to neo-liberalism and to make their voices heard in future deliberations on agriculture and food. As Paul Nicholson explained at the Second International Conference of the Vía Campesina in 1996:

To date, in all the global debates on agrarian policy, the peasant movement has been absent; we have not had a voice. The main reason for the very existence of the Vía Campesina is to be that voice and to speak out for the creation of a more just society.... What is involved here is [a threat to] our regional identity and our traditions around food and our own regional economy.... As those responsible for taking care of nature and life, we have a fundamental role to play.... The Vía Campesina must defend the "peasant way" of rural peoples. (Vía Campesina 1996a: 10–11)

Certainly, arriving at this collective "we" was not easy. As farm policy was increasingly transferred from national to regional and global levels, farm organizations sought to form international links and alliances with like-minded progressive organizations. Throughout the mid-1980s and early 1990s many of the organizations that participated in the Managua and Mons meetings

— most of them founding members of the Vía Campesina — had engaged in exchanges and dialogue with their counterparts in the North and South. These activities had enabled farm leaders to jointly contemplate their place in an increasingly globalized world. They were able to develop a collective analysis of the changes taking place in the countryside everywhere, share experiences and strategies of organizing in the countryside, and discuss possible responses and collective actions.

Farm Organizations Forge International Links

The National Farmers Union in Canada was among these organizations working to form links. Throughout the 1970s the NFU had led a number of farmers' study tours geared towards building a better understanding of how different countries were dealing with production and rural issues. NFU delegations travelled to China, Mozambique, and Cuba. In the 1980s NFU members participated in Oxfam Farmers Brigades and agricultural study tours to Nicaragua aimed at providing Nicaraguan farmers organized in the Unión Nacional de Agricultores y Ganaderos with much-needed agricultural tools and machinery parts. They worked at repairing farm machinery, teaching preventative maintenance, and raising public awareness in the Canadian rural constituency about the Nicaraguan revolutionary effort, as well as establishing solidarity ties with Nicaraguan popular organizations.

In December 1988, only two years after the Uruguay Round had begun, the NFU met with other progressive farm leaders at the International Trade and GATT Conference held in Montreal. At this event the NFU established contact with — among others — the KMP from the Philippines, whose leader Jaime Tadeo voiced many of the same concerns as the NFU. Both organizations believed that the exclusive free-market ideology advocated by the Cairns Group in the GATT negotiations would lead to the further marginalization of rural peoples in the North and South (KMP 1988). The KMP, like the NFU, argued for a fair and just agricultural trade agreement that would fully respect each nation's right to self-determination — that is, each nation's right to define policies, programs, and mechanisms to ensure the well-being of its populations while not harming the food security of other countries. The KMP also expressed hope that the ties farm organizations had established during the conference would endure: "Let this be the beginning of a lasting friendship and unity among us in our common fight to build a better world for poor and small farmers and farm workers the world over."

Through these international experiences, the NFU focused on defining more concrete goals for its international work, which included a commitment to form institutional linkages with its counterparts in developing countries. This approach was driven primarily by the youth and women within the NFU who saw international linkages as an effective way of building leadership capacity within the organization. For example, in the mid-1980s the NFU and

---

NFU Women: Defining Solidarity and Partnership

Real solidarity is a two-way relationship between parties who share a commitment to some common goals. Solidarity, in contrast with charity, is only possible where both parties are working in ways that are mutually recognized as being essential to a shared agenda. This goes beyond the sometimes romantic and semi-condescending "we ended up receiving more than we gave" to something more like "we supported each other along the path we were both travelling."

Solidarity with Nicaraguan agricultural producers... means that Canadians must identify in concrete terms not only how we can support them in pursuing the revolutionary agenda for social justice there but, just as importantly, how that agenda can be pursued with farming people here in Canada and how Nicaraguans can support us as well. That is, solidarity demands that Canadians wishing to support the process of social change there must be equally able and willing to support and promote those goals here in Canada. This involves working in an organized way in Canada to change unjust structures with as much commitment and courage as is shown in support for that goal in Nicaragua. Solidarity is a two-way street. It demands that both parties reach an understanding and respect for each others' struggles and alternatives.

The concept and concrete expressions of solidarity are closely connected to that of partnership. There can be no partnership between unequals. True partners in mutual projects will make equal contribution in terms of giving, avoiding the giver/receiver model of charity. Partnership is the mutual exchange of experiences, skills and resources for mutual benefit. The equality of such a relationship requires that the design, goals and implementation of joint projects must be worked out together and there must be a mutual evaluation process.
Source: Excerpts from NFU-UNAG Women's Linkage Project Committee 1990: 1.

---

the Windward Islands Farmers' Association (WINFA) — with the support of two Canadian development NGOs, Interpares and Crossroads — established the Canadian-Caribbean Agricultural Exchange Program, involving six-week-long leadership capacity-building and agricultural work stints with Canadian and Caribbean farm youth linked to both organizations.

The women of the NFU too began working on international linkages. In March 1989 a number of them participated in a two-week Women in Agriculture Study Tour to Nicaragua hosted by the Women's Section of the UNAG and organized by the Oxfam Farmers Brigade. Tour participants realized that to engage in solidarity meant understanding each other's realities. (See Appendix A.)

After their return to Canada, NFU tour participants began working on building an institutional linkage between the women of the NFU in Region Six (Saskatchewan) and the Region Six (Matagalpa) Women's Section of UNAG. NFU members believed that solidarity and partnership were the key building blocks of the linkage. The NFU's subsequent work in the Vía Campesina was

> **Women in the Canadian NFU**
> The NFU's international exchanges — among other things — contributed significantly to developing leadership capacity among NFU women, as evidenced by the occupancy, by 1996, of four of the six top national leadership positions in the NFU by women who had all been involved in the Canadian-Caribbean Agricultural Exchange Program as a youth or through the NFU-UNAG Women's Linkage.

largely shaped by the concepts of solidarity and partnership as defined by the NFU women.

The NFU-UNAG Women's Linkage Project involved leadership capacity-building and helped consolidate solidarity and partnership ties between the two organizations through biannual delegation visits between Canada and Nicaragua. It also involved regular communication and exchange of information, ideas, and experiences about organizing in the countryside. When UNAG delegations came to Canada, the majority of their time was spent in farm communities in meetings in church basements, town halls, and farmers' kitchens and staying on the farms of NFU members. These face-to-face encounters helped broaden the NFU's outward-looking or international perspective beyond the national leadership of the NFU to include the grassroots membership. As NFU and UNAG women learned more about each other's daily realities, they deepened their analysis of the commonalities and differences that the earlier Women's Study Tour participants had observed. In this process, the NFU and UNAG women went beyond understanding differences and recognizing common ground to identifying a "shared gender struggle" (NFU-UNAG Women's Linkage, n.d.). (See Appendix B.)

The NFU women's experience in the NFU-UNAG Women's Linkage greatly influenced the organization's future approach to international work. As Shannon Storey (1997: 56-57), Women's President of the NFU (1999–2002) explains:

> The NFU looks to farm organizations in developing countries less as people needing help than as partners in the fight to empower farmers in an international economic arena dominated by multinational companies and neo-liberal ideas. Without women's... involvement at the international level, the NFU might still have become involved in the Vía Campesina, but perhaps not with the same strong sense of the Vía Campesina as an international partnership between farmers with common needs, problems and goals.

In the early 1990s, prior to the formation of the Vía Campesina, the NFU also strengthened ties with the National Family Farm Coalition (NFFC) in the United States and farm organizations in Mexico — such as the Unión

Nacional de Organizaciones Regionales Campesinas Autónomas and the Asociación Nacional de Empresas Comercializadoras de Productores del Campo — in a common struggle to oppose NAFTA. For example, in November 1991 the NFU participated in a three-day Tri-National Conference on Agriculture, the Environment, and the Free Trade Agreement held in Mexico City. This extremely important conference marked the first time in history that participants, mainly farmers, from all three countries gathered to share information and experiences about the structure and operation of the agriculture sector in each country, and about the winners and losers under national agricultural policies. Farmers and peasants from Mexico, Canada, and the United States identified common problems they faced as producers and began to seek ways to solve those problems together.

During the same period, in France, the Confédération Nationale des Syndicats de Travailleurs Paysans (CNSTP), known today as the Confédération Paysanne, established bilateral relations with organizations in the Americas, including the NFFC, UNORCA, Confederación Campesina del Peru, and UNAG in Nicaragua. According to Gérard Choplin, CPE co-ordinator, these links enabled the CNSTP to further explore the detrimental effects of the Common Agriculture Policy on farming communities in different countries. Subsequently the various organizations formed a special commission, Solidarité et Luttes Paysannes Internationales, to consolidate their ties with other peasant organizations. European farm organizations went on to establish ties with their counterparts in South America, Asia, and Africa.

Many rural social movements throughout Latin America also engaged in a similar process of organizational exchanges within and beyond their own regions, all of which successfully contributed to the formation of the Coordinadora Latinoamericana de Organizaciones del Campo (CLOC), which held its first congress in February 1994, nine months after the formation of the Vía Campesina. Exchanges focused on sharing knowledge of sustainable practices — such as the Campesino a Campesino project — were also key to bringing together Central American and Mexican peasant organizations (Holt-Giménez 2006). In his work on the transnationalization of Central American peasants, Edelman found that other factors, such as the expansion of the fair trade movement combined with peasant and farm organizations' involvement in value-adding, provided new opportunities for international engagement and contributed to expanding peasants' perspectives beyond the local and national levels.

Through these exchanges — which lasted anywhere from one to six weeks and sometimes longer — farm leaders would spend time in each other's countries, learning about the changes taking place in the agriculture sector, analyzing the responses of peasant organizations, examining various resistance strategies, and looking carefully at the alternatives that organizations were putting into place. The exchanges were instrumental in enabling peasants and farmers to close the North/South divide and establish common ground. Pedro Magaña, a leader with UNORCA, explains the importance of his visits with Canadian and U.S. farmers:

> Well, an important conclusion for me was that the model and conditions in which the family farmers of the United States find themselves is not a future that we want for ourselves. Then, we turn around and see our own situation and we don't want that either. It really had an impact on me. I believed that American farmers were super producers, that they were doing really well, they had the best, an organized development superior to ours. Now I know this is not the case.... They have lost the quality of life. Today a farmer must work 14–15 hours a day... they are living on credit. Often they lose the land. Their children do not work the land, they have to leave. They've lost the community life. The quality of food is seriously questioned because of the high use of chemicals and hormones. The suicides of American and European farmers is a daily occurrence. We do not want to go there. This was one of my first big learnings and experiences from my visit to the United States.
>
> We also had the opportunity to host Canadian farmers. They went to Guanajuato and were shocked to see how small our land-holdings are, how backward our technology is, the differences in costs of production, and how high our interest rates are.... But, in the end... we face the same transnational strategy, a strategy of capital accumulation with a devastating consequence on people's economy. Our enemy is the same. The strategies may be different. But, as farmers, our objective is the same: give to society adequate and healthy food. But the governments do not recognize the social function of the production of food. And, this is the common objective of the global struggle, that the social function of agriculture be recognized, that the farmers' rights to produce... be recognized.

Stuart Thiesson, secretary treasurer of the Saskatchewan Farmers Union (1951–68) and executive secretary of the NFU (1969–92), commented:

> The thing that maybe tied you together, or the commonality of it, was the role of the multinational corporations in all of these areas.... Being able to bring back [the experiences] and have people understand the role of the multinationals was an important aspect of those exchanges because it didn't matter whether you were a peasant or whether you had a 1,600-acre farm, the multinationals had their influence in terms of your business. And now, of course, the encroachment of multinationals in terms of farmers is getting closer to home all the time.

Simon Alexander, a Caribbean farm leader, spent six weeks with NFU members in Saskatchewan as part of the Canadian-Caribbean Agricultural Exchange Project. He found more similarities than differences between Canadian and Caribbean farmers.

> Things are not all rosy up here.... When I first arrived here, I saw all the big machinery and thought the farmers here must be very rich. But that's not the case. There are a lot of poor farmers in Canada.... Everywhere it's the same thing.... It is a struggle just to survive. The big buyers make all the money and they leave us the scraps. (quoted in Pugh 1990: 3)

Through these exchanges and dialogue farm leaders came to understand each other's realities and define the nature of solidarity. Lisa Chemerika, an NFU member, participated in an exchange with the Windward Islands Farmers' Association:

> It is amazing how much these experiences became part of our daily lives. I still keep in touch with some of the people I met on my first exchange, I still think about the people I met, I still think about the Caribbean and I wonder how they are surviving. You are so far away from home and it is all so foreign but it is amazing to go to a country where things are so different yet there are so many similarities because Canada and the Caribbean are export-based economies. . . . These were very political exchanges. We would spend hours and hours discussing the history of agriculture, the international economy, analyzing the current situation, the role of peasant organizations and how they are organized.... It forced us to really think about and understand better what was going on in our own countries. These exchanges were about getting to know one another and building relations of trust and respect.

This prior knowledge of, and experience and personal contact with, each other's work and realities contributed significantly to the success of the farm organizations in reaching the high level of agreement reflected in the Managua and Mons declarations. Armed with this kind of social capital, a sophisticated collective analysis based on daily realities, a collective will not to be "disappeared," and a commitment to build alternatives to neo-liberalism, many of the farm leaders who had participated in exchanges within and beyond their regions were inspired to give birth to the Vía Campesina.

The roots of the Vía Campesina, then, reflect a long history of agrarian movements actively engaged in the struggle for social change. Most of the organizations existed initially at the local and/or provincial levels and had subsequently converged into national organizations as agricultural and rural policies fell increasingly under national jurisdiction. In some cases, when farm policy was being defined at a regional level, farm organizations repositioned themselves by creating new umbrella organizations such as the CPE and ASOCODE to articulate cohesive positions and mobilize collective action. However, the CPE and ASOCODE also sought to work beyond the regional level.

In his presentation to the UNAG congress, Paul Nicholson, representing the CPE, retraced the steps which had brought the eight peasant and farm organizations together in Managua. He explained that following a very productive exchange with UNAG representatives involved in the Campesino a Campesino program who had spent some time in the Basque country, the General Assembly of the CPE had approached the UNAG and other key organizations in Europe and the Americas with the idea of gathering together at the UNAG congress in Managua to develop a joint statement to inform the general public about the destructive impact of neo-liberalism and to identify alternatives in the agriculture sector. Those alternatives included the formation of an international peasant movement. As Nicholson (1992: 1–2) explained at the UNAG congress:

> We have come in support and solidarity, but let's be clear, we have come to do more, we need more, the economic and social crisis of peasant society demands that we do more. Our strategy is to open ourselves to society, to the consumers, environmentalists... but principally to agrarian organizations who defend small and medium scale farmers. If we have similar problems, together we need to find solutions.
>
> We need to present our proposals in a united way to international fora. There is no doubt that now is the opportune historic moment. Let's not fool ourselves, this process demands exchanges of information, internal debates, an elaboration and process of work and rapprochement. We need a framework of distinct relations, of greater rapprochement....
>
> Our interests are debated in Brussels, Geneva and Washington and we also should be there. *Compañeros*, there will be difficult situations and as is logical we will not agree on everything. But, we will go forward on that which is common. Our enemy is not the European or North American peasant, the war is not among us peasants but between models of development. The challenge for us is to create this common space and publicize it to the world.

In forming the Vía Campesina these same farm organizations, which were experienced in working at the local, national, and/or regional levels, were pushing boundaries. As decision-making on food and agriculture was increasingly transferred to global institutions linked to the global marketplace, they were actively forging broader international links. By entering the international arena the Vía Campesina effectively created a much-needed and progressive alternative to the International Federation of Agricultural Producers.

More Than One Farmer's Voice
— Empowering an International Peasant Voice

When the Uruguay Round kicked off in the resort of Punta del Este in 1986 the international farm voice was dominated by the only major international farmers' organization in existence at the time, the International Federation of Agricultural Producers (IFAP). Founded in 1946, IFAP was established primarily to help prevent food shortages like the ones that had occurred during the Depression of the 1930s and World War II. According to its constitution, IFAP (n.d.) aims to "secure the fullest cooperation between organizations of agricultural primary producers in meeting the optimum nutritional and consumptive requirements of the peoples of the world and in improving the economic and social status of all who live by and on the land."

To reach these goals, one of IFAP's key strategies is participation. By promoting itself as the organization of "world's farmers," IFAP has succeeded in carving a space for itself in a significant number of international institutions. The organization has General Consultative Status with the Economic and Social Council of the United Nations and actively participates in consultations with a number of organizations such as the World Health Organization, International Fund for Agricultural Development, International Labour Organization, FAO, OECD, World Bank, GATT, and WTO (Karl 1996: 131).

With a membership totaling 110 national organizations from seventy-five countries (thirty of them in developing countries), IFAP works hard to promote the interests of its membership. It seeks unity among farmers by focusing on commonalities rather than differences. Reaching a unified position on trade, however, proved to be a difficult task. There was, for example, heated debate on this issue during the IFAP World Farmers Congress held in November 1997 in Buenos Aires. As Lee Swenson, president of the U.S.-based National Farmers Union (a prominent IFAP organization), reported, "It is evident that farmers throughout the world oppose trade expansion because of the threat existing trade agreements present to their livelihood." Swenson cautioned the IFAP leadership that it was "obvious" that IFAP was "greatly divided on the trade issue, and should not pretend to be otherwise during the next GATT Round" (quoted in McBride 1998: 1).

Divisions in the international farm community reflected what was happening on the ground at the national level. As the GATT Uruguay Round progressed, farm organizations around the world worked hard to influence the positions of their national governments, and divergences in positions and strategies on the complex questions of agricultural liberalization became increasingly pronounced. Those who opposed the trade agreements were often slated as being anti-trade and protectionists — though in reality, most of them were not against trade per se but were rejecting the terms, conditions, and processes being proposed in regional trade agreements and the GATT/WTO. They were seeking to establish a fair and socially responsible trade regime.

Indeed, in some countries farm organizations were at the forefront of national struggles against liberalization and globalization, while others were actively working with governments to promote those approaches. For example, in India, the demonstrations of the Karnataka State Farmers Association against the WTO were countered by the Shetkari Sangathana, which wholeheartedly accepted liberalization as an effective way of moving Indian farmers out of poverty (Brass 2000b: 108–112). In an interview with the *Economic Times* (2000), Sharad Joshi, leader of the Shetkari Sanghatana, argued, "The solution [for Indian farmers] is nothing short of pulling ourselves up by the bootstraps and altering our very style of agriculture." He suggested that government intervention in agriculture was a major barrier because "anything which is protected gets stifled." In Canada the NFU's more critical position on trade was completely rejected by many of the agricultural commodity groups and the Western Canadian Wheat Growers Association, while the Canadian Federation of Agriculture's reformist position aimed at making trade work better for farmers. In Europe the CPE's calls for food sovereignty were countered with the pro-liberalization stance of the Comité des Organisations Professionnelles Agricoles de l'Union Européenne (COPA) and the Comité Général de la Coopération Agricole de l'Union Européenne. Clearly, the farm community was divided on the issue of further liberalization in agriculture.

These national and regional divergences were subsequently catapulted into the international arena with the emergence of the Vía Campesina. Despite IFAP's claims to be *the* world farmers' voice, numerous peasant and farm organizations in the North and South did not and still do not belong to that organization — for a number of reasons. For one thing, the IFAP has for quite some time had the reputation of representing the interests of larger farmers primarily based in the industrialized countries (PFS 1993a: 6). IFAP membership has included mainstream farm organizations such as, among others, the American Farm Bureau Federation, commodity groups, farm businesses, and farm organizations linked to agro-industry.[1] Wayne Easter, president of the Canadian NFU from 1982 to 1992, says that at one point the NFU seriously contemplated membership in IFAP but ultimately opted not to join after concluding that the body simply did not represent the interests of smaller farmers.

The question of membership costs is also a factor. IFAP membership fees have been based on a formula that in some cases can run up to tens or even hundreds of thousands of dollars. For many financially strapped peasant organizations these membership fees were simply out of the question.

IFAP and Agribusiness

The Saskatchewan Wheat Pool, which became part of the IFAP through its membership in the Canadian Federation of Agriculture, is a prime example of a Canadian agricultural organization with corporate interests.

Originally a farmers' grain purchasing co-operative, the Saskatchewan Wheat Pool expanded dramatically in the 1990s by enhancing its grain-handling capacity "around the world" through the construction of overseas terminals and by diversifying its portfolio through a series of acquisitions in the agri-food processing industry, including meat-packing facilities and the Robin's Donuts chain of coffee shops. It also invested in "world-scale" hog production operations in its home base of Saskatchewan, and restructured itself to become publicly traded on the Toronto Stock Exchange (Ewins 2002: 10–11). The restructuring and expansion of the Saskatchewan Wheat Pool became the centre of heated debates among the farming members of the co-operative. For all intents and purposes the Saskatchewan Wheat Pool is no longer a farmers' co-operative run by farmers; instead, it functions more like a company ruled by a CEO and a strong management team.

In addition, some organizations did not join IFAP simply because they had never been approached and did not know of its existence.

The tension among some Vía Campesina organizations regarding IFAP has a long history. Many had had direct experience with IFAP organizations at the national level. Often, IFAP members were seen as those representing larger producers working in mainstream farm organizations. Rafael Alegría recounts that some IFAP members were known as "official" organizations — that is, organizations that had either been created by the government and/or received a large proportion of their funding from government sources. These organizations often advocated national and international agricultural policies that others judged to be detrimental to peasant agriculture.

These ideological differences and divisions led to conflict at the international level when attempts were made to bring IFAP into the process leading up to the constitutive meeting of the Vía Campesina held in Mons in May 1993. Doubts surfaced when some organizations realized that Kees Blokland, a staffperson with Paulo Freire Stichting (PFS) — the NGO that farm leaders had asked to help co-ordinate the follow-up to the Managua Declaration — and UNAG had actively sought IFAP's involvement. The UNAG and PFS had held discussions with IFAP Executive Committee members and the president of IFAP in attempts to convince that group to join the Vía Campesina project (*Intercambio* 1993a: 19). Nico Verhagen, a co-ordinator of the CPE (1990–99) and a technical support to the Vía Campesina, says this was something that the CPE, among others, could never support.

Blokland focused on the notion of *concertación*, which envisioned the Vía Campesina as a process open to as many organizations as possible, no matter their ideology.[2] As PFS (1993a) explained it, the process attempts "to bridge a worldwide gap between organizations, which do not initially consider themselves as natural allies, despite the fact that they all represent a rural population with a common interest as agricultural." The organizations involved carry out participatory research focusing on policy issues, "with an educational character for all those involved." The PFS added:

> This means that participating in this process not only entails an explicit definition of one's own strategy, but also that this strategy is submitted to other participants for assessment, evaluation and discussion. "Change" is the final aim. This "change" can reach as far as economic development, institutional environment, existing organizations and participants themselves. (PFS 1993a: 6)

The CPE was not the only organization that opposed the PFS's proposal for how peasants and farmers should work together. IFAP, too, had reservations since — among other reasons — *concertación* would ultimately compromise its own policies (PFS 1993a: 10–11). Although Blokland encountered difficulties in his attempts to build alliances between the conventional organizations of the IFAP and the organizations involved in the post-Managua process, the PFS (which clung to its view that the main goal of the meeting should be to establish an agricultural research agenda) remained convinced that *concertación* — a concept that had emerged in a particular context, at a particular point in history, and with particular social actors — could be globalized through the Vía Campesina (*Intercambio* 1993b: 4).

The tensions concerning the viability of *concertación* as an effective strategy to ensure the well-being of farming families came to a head at the constitutive meeting of the Vía Campesina in Mons. I was the NFU representative at this conference, and I remember that when IFAP's involvement was discussed it was clear that the majority who had gathered at the meeting did not see and could not imagine IFAP as the legitimate voice of peasant and small-scale farmers. These more critical peasant and farm organizations had no interest in strengthening links to an international organization that they believed had diametrically opposing interests to theirs; after all, in some countries the IFAP organizations had consistently blocked progressive farm policy and were even considered by some to be the enemy. As Verhagen puts it:

> I think that it was very clear we did not want *concertación* with organizations with interests represented by the IFAP. In Europe we had had the experience that dialogue was not possible, that these organizations sought with all their efforts to eliminate critical voices and that *concertación* as it was conceived by the PFS was not going to produce anything interesting. It would only be an instrument to silence, to "keep busy" the critical voices.

Instead, most of the organizations gathered in Mons effectively distanced themselves from IFAP by forging a new and progressive alliance.

Since the early 1990s IFAP has engaged in more concerted efforts to recruit members from developing countries; it made strong headway in 1991 when UNAG became responsible for IFAP in the Latin American region. Since the formation of the Vía Campesina, IFAP has also made structural changes to better integrate organizations from developing countries. At its 34th World Farmers' Congress in May 2000, IFAP took steps to facilitate the entry of organizations from the South by lowering membership fees. It also decided to restructure its Development Co-operation Committee to provide funds (channelled through Northern IFAP members) to help strengthen farmers' organizations in developing countries (IFAP 2000b). IFAP's conference report states:

> For a trial period of two years, all farmers' organizations from developing countries, which meet the criteria for membership laid down in the IFAP Constitution, but are currently not *strong* enough to join IFAP as full members, will be invited to join the IFAP Standing Committee of Agriculture in Developing Countries (SCADC) and the IFAP Development Co-operation Committee (DCC) for a flat fee annual contribution of US$200.... Membership of these committees would bring the organizations concerned into IFAP's Development program. It is hoped that, as a result of this, these organizations would become *strong* enough to join IFAP as full members, pay the formula subscription rate and then be able to take part in all IFAP activities including voting in elections and standing for office in IFAP. (emphasis added)

The newly elected president of IFAP, Jack Wilkinson, announced his desire to double membership by recruiting even more organizations from developing countries (Wilson 2002c: 12). Wilkinson stated that farm organizations from developing countries should "have the same kind of infrastructure, the same ability to work and trade on the international market, as we take for granted here." In the context of the WTO, Wilkinson argued that there was "the need for developing country farmers to have the information and analysis they need to push for a deal that will benefit them."

Although presumably well intentioned, these changes would only accentuate the differences between the Vía Campesina and the IFAP. Clearly, they reflect a traditional developmentalist mindset within the IFAP. That is, the IFAP structures themselves (the Standing Committee of Agriculture in Developing Countries and the Development Cooperation Committee, for example) suggest a view of clear divisions between the North and South. Perhaps most striking is the view that farmers' organizations in developing countries must be assisted so that they can "catch up" and become as "strong" (read financially secure) as their Northern counterparts. The approach also assumes that peasant organizations in developing countries do not yet have an analysis and that these groups, like the IFAP, want to engage with the WTO. Significantly, at the meeting of the IFAP Standing Committee on Agriculture in Developing Countries, which took place in the framework of IFAP's 34th congress, the session began by deleting from the agenda a discussion of developing country activities because no report existed (IFAP 2000c).

The very existence of the Vía Campesina is clear evidence that not all farmers speak with the same voice. Divisions among farm organizations at the national level became manifested at the international level. On the one hand, national organizations that saw a future in liberalization and globalization joined the IFAP. On the other hand, those that embraced an anti-corporate and global justice stance joined the Vía Campesina.

The Paternalistic Embrace of NGOs

The farming people organized in the IFAP and the Vía Campesina do not, of course, function in a vacuum. When the Vía Campesina surfaced, the international space was also filled by numerous national and international development NGOs as well as research institutions working on issues of agriculture and food security. Because many of these NGOs worked closely with rural organizations — and even though the NGOs had not been given the mandate — they often found themselves "representing" and speaking "on behalf" of and defending the interests of peasants and small-scale farmers in the international arena.

Even with the best of intentions, this type of interlocution can often lead to misrepresentation. Farming people often did not recognize their own voices when they were communicated back to them. Consequently, not only did the Vía Campesina work hard to distinguish itself from IFAP, it also sought to distance itself from the paternalistic embrace of well-intentioned NGOs. In doing so it raised the critical issues of representation, interlocution, accountability, and legitimacy.

Conflictual relations between professional NGOs and grassroots social movements working at the international level are common. Often the conflicts are characterized by different goals, different ways of working, and the unequal access to human, financial, and political resources that leads to skewed power relations. The same conflicts can arise between NGOs working on international issues of agriculture, trade, and food security issues and an agrarian social movement like the Vía Campesina. NGOs tend to be well staffed, with highly educated, experienced, multilingual, articulate, and mobile personnel; they understand technical language and concepts, are able to gain access to significant funding, and have developed excellent research capacities. While the Vía Campesina does succeed in obtaining funds to participate in key events and campaigns, core funding is virtually non-existent. With few technical support staff, the Vía Campesina depends primarily on volunteer farm leaders who tend to head national farm organizations that are already overstretched with work on local and national issues. These organizations are severely understaffed and suffer from a constant lack of funding.

Many Vía Campesina organizations had direct experience and were only too familiar with the inequities and power dynamics of the peasant movements–NGO relationships.[3] The differences were clearly evident when I was conducting research with peasant organizations in Bolivia and Honduras in the early 1990s (Desmarais 1994). When I visited NGOs doing work "with" rural organizations, I saw multi-room offices outfitted with computers, air-conditioning, comfortable chairs, and a secretarial staff. When I entered the one- or two-room offices of peasant organizations, I might only see an old typewriter and old wooden benches.

While some NGOs cultivated respectful relations with and won the collaboration of peasant organizations, others did not. Some NGOs took advantage of opportunities created by the new economic and political context of the 1980s and 1990s to better "represent" and "speak on behalf" of peasant organizations in policy development negotiations. Some, engaging in "participatory development," used their association with peasant organizations to gain access to precious funds available for work in the countryside and then channelled these funds to pursue their own goals rather than meeting the needs of the local organizations. Others used financial resources to co-opt peasant leaders; still others undermined peasant organizations by bypassing the decision-making processes and structures that ensured accountability within peasant organizations. Concerns about these NGO practices were repeatedly raised in numerous peasant gatherings that I attended at the local, national, and international levels throughout the 1990s.

The persistently negative experiences that they had with NGOs working in the countryside prompted some peasant leaders, like ASOCODE's Wilson Campos (1994: 214–21), a founding member of the Vía Campesina, to declare: "We don't need all those NGOs.... We farmers can speak up for ourselves. Already too many people have been taking advantage of us, without us getting any the wiser for it." Indeed, Campos explained that in forming a new rural social movement, ASOCODE, Central American peasants were articulating a clear message: they openly rejected the traditional, paternalistic funder/recipient model, and all of the relations that this entailed, in favour of a development model imagined by and administered by peasants themselves. In doing so, peasants in Central America successfully reclaimed the space that NGOs had occupied on their behalf since the 1960s.

The questionable practices that NGOs engaged in at the national and regional levels were replicated at the international level. Some NGOs clearly saw the need for and fully supported the consolidation of an independent farmer-led voice and presence in the international arena with the creation of the Vía Campesina. Others, however, were reluctant to share the space they had long dominated; the very formation of a movement that was working hard to carve out a space in the international arena that could be filled by peasant and farm voices was deeply threatening. For example, some well-intentioned NGOs spoke of the importance of working with farmers, but farm leaders would be invited to international events only if and when funds remained after the NGO staff had been taken care of. Others fully supported farmers' participation as long as they had full control over which farmers were selected. Still others, who saw themselves as social movements, assumed that farmers' interests were identical to their interests and often conditioned their financial support on the participation of NGOs in farmers' deliberations. The Vía Campesina, like ASOCODE, could not tolerate these practices and sought to rectify the situation by establishing some ground rules.

The "Difficult Birth" of the Vía Campesina

Various aspects of these dynamics were at play at the constitutive meeting of the Vía Campesina held at Mons. Indeed, these strained interactions not only preceded the creation of the Vía Campesina but also caused the new formation to have, as Nicholson puts it, a "very difficult birth." They would continue to plague the movement throughout its first year of existence and would help to shape future Vía Campesina–NGO relations.

Earlier, at the Managua meeting in 1992, for example, while farm leaders acknowledged the important human and financial contributions of the PFS and supported the NGO's role in helping to co-ordinate the next stage, some leaders questioned the future role and place of an NGO among agrarian organizations (EHNE 1992). This initial doubt escalated to tension and open conflict during the Mons conference as disagreements between the PFS staff and farm leaders centred on three key issues: the very purpose or raison d'être of the Vía Campesina, who should make up the membership, and the role of NGOs in the new organization. As the NFU representative I actively participated in reshaping the process and content of this conference and observed, first-hand, the tensions between peasant organizations and the PFS staff.

In supporting the follow-up to Managua, the PFS was to work directly with a co-ordinating committee (ECODEM), whose membership included Nicholson of the CPE, Jorge Hernández of ASOCODE, and Wayne Easter of the NFU in Canada (PFS 1993a: 24). Two short months after the Managua meeting, for further discussion the PFS sent out two documents outlining a basic framework for international co-operation among farmers. The PFS had worked hard at pulling together a detailed project proposal centred around the creation of the Vía Campesina as an international forum of farm organizations that would apply for funding for alternative and sustainable research policy development and rural projects. When inviting farm leaders to Mons to participate in the Vía Campesina, the PFS specified that this project would entail the "Constitution of the Research Programme of Farmers' Organizations." The preparatory documents to the Mons conference stated:

> The Research Programme is a participatory research effort seeking renewed coordination with study centres, taking farmers' priorities as starting-point. It is an organizational effort as well, strengthening the participants' organizations. It is a political effort oriented to gain more influence in the government policies to be formulated and in the channeling of funds towards projects originating within the farmers' movement itself. Finally, it is a platform for exchange and mutual assistance, aiming at restructuring of technical assistance from farmer to farmer. (PFS 1993a: 1)

Even though the PFS had consulted on a regular basis with ECODEM and had sent farm leaders an earlier draft of the project proposal for feedback, by the time they arrived at Mons, many — including some members of ECODEM — had serious reservations about the project being proposed by the PFS. As farm leaders informally exchanged impressions and ideas on the way into town from the airport or over dinner and wine. it became quite clear that others shared their individual doubts. Somehow, the farmers' forceful call, voiced in Managua, for an alternative development model built through collective analysis, joint action, and solidarity among peasant and farm organizations in the North and South had been translated into an international farmer-led research project.

Further doubts about the PFS surfaced the first day when the creation of the Vía Campesina was announced at a public event held on May 14 to celebrate the tenth anniversary of the PFS. To many participants this event seemed quite odd, because they had not yet engaged in any debate, or defined any plan, or, in fact, created or defined the Vía Campesina. Some of the peasant leaders felt as though they were being used, as if they were being put on display, to highlight a successful NGO project. Throughout the day farm leaders also discovered that the official launch of the Vía Campesina as a research project had been featured in a PFS publication one month earlier, and that the PFS had also already approached potential funders (*Intercambio* 1993b: 1–2).

Farm leaders — led primarily by ASOCODE, CPE, and the NFU — believed that they themselves should have complete control over the content and process of the conference and the Vía Campesina project itself. They proposed substantial changes to the agenda that had initially been drawn up by the PFS, broadening the discussion beyond the research proposal framework. Many of the organizations present in Mons had not participated in the Managua meeting, and it was seen as critical to offer them opportunities for exchange of information and analysis about the agricultural realities in their respective countries. This step would enable farm leaders to get to know one another, and only then would they more easily move to collective analysis and defining a way forward. The research project proposed by the PFS could potentially be one aspect of future work; but because it was not considered central, farm leaders wanted to shift discussion of it to the second day of the conference. More important was the need to revisit the Managua Declaration to ensure that all participants were in agreement with it and to use it to explore the possibility of creating an international movement.

PFS staff person Blokland rejected this change in the agenda. Although he considered himself as being at the service of farm organizations and worked for an organization that claimed to be "a service organization for agricultural organizations" (PFS 1993a: 7), he was clearly not satisfied to play a facilitative role. Years later, while reflecting on the meeting in Mons, Blokland (who in 2000–02 was vice-chair of the Development Cooperation Committee of IFAP) would say in an interview:

> They [CPE and ASOCODE] wanted to gather around an ideological project. There are those who see rural people as being divided into two camps: the big landowners and small farmers and farm work-ers.... I see a much more complex world and not just a division in two camps. The major conflict of farming people is against other sectors of society, that is, industry. The peasant movement would be much stronger if it could bring together the economic power of big farmers with the political power of peasant organizations.

By this, Blokland is referring specifically to his proposal for IFAP organizations to be invited to participate in the Vía Campesina project.

The farm leaders had a different way of conceiving an alternative development model. Most importantly, they sought to form a farmer-led, autonomous peasant and farm movement of progressive organizations that would strive to build the capacity to articulate joint positions and policies in opposition to the neo-liberal model advocated by many national governments and international institutions. Many of the farm leaders gathered in Mons did not see IFAP as an ally. Indeed, they saw the formation of the Vía Campesina as a much needed and radical alternative to the IFAP. As Jun Borras, of the KMP and one of the founding members of the Vía Campesina, recalls: "What? The Vía Campesina as a 'research project'? KMP's understanding at that time was this, and this is very vivid in my memory, the Mons meeting would aim to form an international peasant movement and that it would be a progressive alternative to IFAP."

The tension and conflict at Mons escalated to the point where the PFS representatives angrily walked out of the meeting. Farm leaders essentially took over the meeting, proceeded to discuss what they felt were the most critical issues, and collectively defined the purpose, structure, and ways of working of the newly formed international peasant and farm movement. In recognition of PFS's work in the past, and its efforts in bringing them together in Mons, the newly formed international peasant movement requested that the PFS work as the Technical Secretariat of the Vía Campesina. The Technical Secretariat was to play a facilitative role, take direction from, and support the Co-ordinating Commission (PFS 1993c).

Throughout the first year of the Vía Campesina's existence, tension between the Vía Campesina and the PFS surfaced again and again as Blokland — who became responsible for the Technical Secretariat — refused to accept the farmers' vision for the Vía Campesina, attempted to impose his own vision, and took on a more directive role. This approach, as Borras points out, was a clear violation of the agreement with the Vía Campesina and of the mandate that had been given to the PFS. Heightened concerns about the PFS's role were voiced at the meeting of the Co-ordinating Commission of the Vía Campesina (held in Lima, Peru) in the framework of the CLOC congress on February 21–25, 1994:

> In order to avoid the misconception that La Vía Campesina is the initiative of an NGO, we wish to clarify immediately that La Vía Campesina is the initiative of peasants and that the PFS only lends its services to the secretariat. We must avoid having the secretariat speak in the name of particular organizations in political and trade union discussions. The coordinating commission should be provided with brief information and consulted as to how to carry out the activity. (Vía Campesina 1994a: 9)

On April 29, 1994, nearly a year after the Vía Campesina emerged, two members of the Co-ordinating Commission, the CPE and the KMP, met with the board of the PFS to discuss some of the difficulties they were experiencing with the Technical Secretariat and to clarify the Vía Campesina's vision regarding the role of an NGO in supporting the Vía Campesina. By that time the CPE, as general co-ordinator of the Vía Campesina, had consulted various participating farm organizations and the Co-ordinating Commission had discussed the issue at length. The results of these consultations were communicated to the PFS board. The Co-ordinating Commission representatives stressed that the Vía Campesina was an autonomous and independent farmers' movement with a "political and trade union feature" and the PFS must restrict its activities and actions to supporting the Co-ordinating Commission rather than attempting to direct the Vía Campesina and be the public face of the organization (Vía Campesina 1994c: 3–5).

This encounter did little to end the ongoing tensions. Most revealingly, in a lengthy June 1994 letter written to the Vía Campesina members (including the NFU), Blokland criticized the CPE in its role of co-ordinator and clearly refused to accept the outcomes of the Mons meeting. He wrote:

> Last May 16th, the CPE finalized its period of general coordination of the Vía Campesina. A short while previously, it had begun to get involved in the founding of a new international peasant organization. Should their objectives be realized, they will establish an organization of global scope that works to oppose the policies of

the GATT, World Bank and the IMF, with a strong emphasis on protest. This decision on the part of the CPE had been expected, since
the organization lacked a world-wide framework of like-minded
organizations who could help them to strengthen their positions.
Within the scope of their work with La Vía Campesina they have
been able to identify those organizations with whom they can begin
to formulate this new project....

Unfortunately... the CPE seems to have confused its role as general coordinator of La Vía Campesina with that of being promotor
for a new international peasant grouping. They took advantage of
the discussions held in Lima and the visits from representatives of
the democratic KMP of the Philippines and of ASOCODE in order
to refine their ideas. We, in our position of secretariat of La Vía
Campesina, wish to clarify that the new international organization
— whose name and initials we don't yet know — like its members,
will continue to coordinate its efforts towards the generation of
agricultural and economic alternatives with other organizations
that participate in the Vía Campesina platform. That is, despite
some problems of conceptions and coordination, we have had no
indication that the CPE and/or others who are forming the new international farmers' organization wish to divorce themselves from
the Vía Campesina process. We issue this clarification in light of
the fact that some participants have understood that the new international organization was to be a substitute for La Vía Campesina,
leaving to one side those organizations that choose not to form part
of the new international grouping. This is not so. La Vía Campesina
will continue to exist as a platform with an open character that was
founded to generate alternatives; and, on the other hand, a new
international peasant organization will also exist. (Blokland 1994:
1–2)

In short, despite the Mons meeting's forceful rejection of the PFS's concept
of a linked farmer/NGO research project and the formation — after PFS staff
had angrily stormed out of the meeting — of an international farmer and
peasant movement entitled the Vía Campesina, the PFS was claiming that
the Vía Campesina was a "platform" that it had the power to define.

What the PFS failed to accept was that the majority of farm leaders who
had gathered in Mons had rejected the idea of creating a farmers' platform
to raise funds for alternative research and projects in favour of creating an
international, farmer-driven, autonomous peasant and farm movement. In
Mons farmers had taken ownership of the Vía Campesina, and then they
had spent the following year giving the movement shape, form, and content to fit their needs. The Vía Campesina leaders sought to "ground" the
organization at the local level and the movement, as a result, was gathering

momentum (ASOCODE 1994). The European organizations in the CPE had established closer ties with their counterparts in different regions as a result of joint actions in protests against the GATT in Geneva. The Vía Campesina organizations from North America, the Caribbean, and Central America had met in Tegucigalpa, the capital city of Honduras, and developed a plan of action for dividing co-ordination tasks among the English- and Spanish-speaking areas, bringing other like-minded organizations into the movement, and organizing exchanges among participating organizations. In November 1994, for example, the NFU hosted an ASOCODE delegation of representatives from Guatemalan, Honduran, and Nicaraguan peasant organizations, which involved visits to farms and discussions with the NFU's general membership, tours of co-operative production facilities, and exchanges with the NFU leadership. Links among Vía Campesina organizations in Central America, the Caribbean, and South America were extended and further strengthened with the creation of CLOC. In its first year the Vía Campesina issued two press releases: one opposing the GATT Marrakesh decisions and another in support of the Zapatistas in Chiapas (Vía Campesina 1994b, 1994c). Contrary to the criticisms raised in Blokland's letter, the CPE, as general coordinator, was carrying out the important job of co-ordinating this emerging international movement.

In suggesting that the CPE had completed its term as general co-ordinator, the PFS failed to mention that the Coordinating Commission, after consultation among the participating organizations, had requested that the CPE stay on in that role until 1995. For its part the CPE was feeling the pressures of its own limited capacity and argued that the position should be rotated to avoid centralization, but it reluctantly accepted the extension (Vía Campesina 1994e).

In assessing the continuing conflict, Nicholson of the CPE stated his belief that the root of the problem was structural:

> I am convinced that the frustrations that we have had were due to the wrong initial structure: the fact of asking an NGO to play the role of a farmers' organization leads to an inefficient and distrustful situation.... The birth of the Vía Campesina has not been easy and while we were on our way of defining our strategy the PFS has had an important role in this process. We also have to note that... it is clear that going on with such an unclear situation, as to OUR role and THEIR role, will lead us to a rupture which is harmful for the Vía Campesina and for the Paulo Freire Foundation. (Vía Campesina 1994c: 6)

A month after receiving Blokland's letter, the Vía Campesina, reiterating many points it had already raised with the PFS board, informed the president of the PFS that the Vía Campesina Co-ordinating Commission was taking over the role of Technical Secretariat (Vía Campesina 1994d). The

Co-ordinating Commission stressed that although the PFS's services in the capacity of Technical Secretariat were no longer required, it did hope that future collaboration would be possible. As it turned out, there was to be no future collaboration between the PFS and the Vía Campesina.[4]

Carving Out an International Peasant Space

In entering the international arena the Vía Campesina struggled for autonomy and challenged NGOs to define their relations with peasant organizations. Tensions between the increasingly vocal international peasant movement and NGOs would surface again and again.

The Vía Campesina made its first real appearance in the international arena at the Global Assembly on Food Security held in Quebec City in 1995 to celebrate the 50th anniversary of the FAO. As the only representative of a farm organization on the Steering Committee of the Global Assembly, the NFU worked hard to ensure that Vía Campesina representatives were invited as facilitators and panelists in group discussions and plenaries to present the perspective and experience of food producers. As Nettie Wiebe points out, this was no easy task because the NFU had to convince urban-based and urban-biased NGO organizers that peasant leaders were "capable and articulate" enough to provide an analysis of the impact of neo-liberalism in the countryside. But in the Quebec events peasant and farm voices came through loud and clear as one farm leader after another eagerly came to the microphone to explain how things really were in the countryside. Most began their interventions by proudly declaring their allegiance to the Vía Campesina. For the first time in an international arena dominated by NGOs, farm leaders worked in a concerted and collective fashion to speak about their own realities in their own voices and reflecting their own analysis.

In acknowledging the great interest expressed by the NGOs in working with the newly emerged peasant movement, the Vía Campesina sought to establish working ties by organizing an NGO forum concurrent with its Second International Conference in Tlaxcala, Mexico. The NGO Parallel Forum was designed to allow the non-governmental organizations a chance to hold their own discussions as well as participate (as observers) in various parts of the Vía Campesina conference. But the NGO Parallel Forum did not attract many NGOs, for a number of reasons. The Vía Campesina had carefully selected a limited number of NGOs to be invited, but did not raise funds specifically for the Forum, and some NGOs were simply not interested in participating. In addition, the Vía Campesina was so fully occupied organizing the content, logistics, and process of its own conference that it paid little attention to the NGO Parallel Forum. It also delayed making a decision about whether or not the Forum would actually take place. This whole issue was further complicated by unresolved disagreements in the organization of the main conference. It had been originally scheduled for the Philippines to be led by the two Filipino Vía Campesina organizations (the KMP and the Demokratikong Kilusang Magbubukid ng Pilipinas, dKMP), but conflict between the two groups had eventually necessitated relocating to Mexico.

While only ten NGO representatives participated, the NGO Parallel Forum did yield important results. In a presentation to the Vía Campesina Conference summarizing their deliberations, NGO representatives argued that NGOs should:

- Step aside
- Extend assistance to POs [people's organizations] only when requested
- Create more power and opportunities for POs. (quoted in Vía Campesina 1996b: 65)

Furthermore, the NGO representatives clearly understood the need to transform the existing relations between themselves and the peasant organizations. They could contribute to this by redefining their roles, forging links, and developing mechanisms to ensure that NGOs would better support the initiatives of peasant organizations. They stressed that this approach would only work if and when NGO-PO relations were based on the principles of "equal partnerships, mutual respect for each other's autonomy and independence, transparency and accountability" (Vía Campesina 1996b: 65).

The conclusions of the NGO Parallel Forum were heavily influenced by a presentation from Eduardo Tadem (1996), "Reflections on NGO-PO Relations." Tadem, a representative of ARENA (an Asian NGO working on rural issues), provided a historical overview, analysis, and suggestions for possible future directions of PO-NGO relations in the context of rural Philippines. His main argument was that in the Philippines, people's organizations had been around much longer than non-governmental organizations, and that NGOs had assumed a critical role in providing a "legal window to the outside world" for POs when most of them were forced underground during times of heightened repression. Since the 1970s the Philippines had experienced a considerable growth in NGOs, and their role was expanded to include advocacy, electoral politics, and delivery of services. Tension and conflict between NGOs and POs ensued when both attempted to work together on joint programs and campaigns. Tadem argued that NGOs were necessary when the political context did not allow POs to function, but when political conditions are such that POs' actions are no longer restricted, NGOs should be disbanded or take on new roles.

Some NGOs were not ready to accept that kind of subordinate role. They argued that it was a mistake for the Vía Campesina to have organized a separate NGO meeting and that NGOs should have been invited to participate in the Vía Campesina Conference proper. They stressed that, after all, NGOs and POs were involved in the same struggle — they were on equal footing, all stakeholders should sit at the same table right from the start, and it was unproductive to create divisions where none exist.[5] These comments reflected a complete lack of understanding (or denial) of the existing power dynamics; they also demonstrated a lack of respect for the process of dialogue and negotiation that farmers and peasants believed they needed among themselves as part of building an international movement. Perhaps more importantly, these observations revealed the reluctance of some NGOs to give up the space they had long dominated in the international arena. Not surprisingly, these same NGOs, after realizing that they could not direct the Vía Campesina, went on to organize major international events "for" peasant and farm organizations — events that, while often well-intentioned, could lead to a more submissive farm movement.

An example was the international peasant gatherings promoted by the French-based Fondation Charles Léopold Mayer pour le Progrès de l'Homme (FPH). The most recent, "Encuentro Campesino Mundial: Los Campesinos Del Mundo Frente a los Desafíos del Siglo XXI" (Global Peasant Gathering: Peasants of the World Facing the Challenges of the 21st Century), was held in Yaoundé, Cameroon, in May 2002. The invitational literature outlined the various challenges that peasants and indigenous movements face and noted that the gathering would address the need for: 1) organization, mobilization, and establishing alternatives, 2) collaboration and building alliances among different sectors, and 3) analysis of the current context to better develop strategies and proposals (Marzaroli n.d.). These are, of course, all challenges that peasant movements, especially the Vía Campesina, had already been working on for quite some time.

According to Rafael Alegría, the Vía Campesina declined the invitation to participate in helping to organize the Global Peasant Gathering for a number of reasons. First, his organization could not identify, to its own satisfaction, the long-term goal of the gathering. Second, the Vía Campesina had just organized its own global peasant encounter in the form of its Third International Conference. Lastly, it was working hard at strengthening already existing global and regional spaces for peasant dialogue and action.

Indeed, an event like the Global Peasant Gathering seemed to be isolated — quite separate from events already planned by the regional and international peasant organizations themselves — and unlikely to strengthen farm movements at a global level. While the conferences might offer wonderful opportunities for dialogue and exchanges of information, they offered little hope for on-the-ground follow-up because they did not appear to be connected to any established structure or plan of action. Such events, often initiated by NGOs, can be counterproductive: they duplicate efforts already well underway, and they use precious financial and human resources that could otherwise be used more effectively by existing movements.

Tension between the Vía Campesina and NGOs resurfaced at the November 1996 NGO Forum on Food Security, held parallel to the World Food Summit in Rome. The Vía Campesina refused to sign onto the

NGO Declaration, arguing that the statement did not adequately address the concerns and interests of peasant families. The Vía Campesina, after lengthy consultations with farm organizations at the national, regional, and international levels, had come to Rome with a new concept — that of food sovereignty — as a solution to world hunger and poverty. Although food sovereignty was included in the title of the NGO Declaration, the statement did not elaborate on the concept or explain how it could be implemented. In refusing to sign the NGO Declaration, the Vía Campesina expressed disappointment with the limited content of the statement and frustration with an exclusionary process (Vía Campesina 1996d). The Vía Campesina had brought over sixty delegates to the WFS events, and many of them did not speak English. With limited translation services during the NGO Forum on Food Security, many of the delegates found that they simply could not participate in any significant way.

The Vía Campesina's forceful rejection of the NGO statement at the WFS was, in many ways, a turning point for relations between the emerging peasant movement and NGOs. Through the Vía Campesina, farm leaders had carved out a space and were filling it with peasant and farm voices articulating their own agenda. The Vía Campesina was demanding respect for this newly created space, and it desperately needed time for farmers from around the world to meet, engage in collective analysis, and define common positions. Only then could the new organization move towards joint action with NGOs. In so doing the Vía Campesina would challenge NGOs to respect the different ways of working of grassroots social movements and NGOs. The Vía Campesina was sending a clear and direct message to the NGOs who had long dominated the international arena: NGOs could no longer "speak on behalf of" or as representatives of peasants and farmers. Just as importantly, the Vía Campesina challenged not only who would speak, and on whose behalf, but also what would be said and how to arrive at a collective position.

In June 1997, seven months after the WFS, some Vía Campesina leaders met with a number of mostly European-based NGOs to pursue issues raised in the NGO Parallel Forum and the outcomes of the WFS. The NGOs who participated in this meeting were Brot fur die Welt, Crocevia, Oxfam-Solidarité, DanChurch Aid, Comité Catholique Contre la Faim et Pour le Développement (CCFD), Transnational Institute, and Coopibo, a Flemish development NGO. This encounter was an important step because it allowed farm leaders and NGOs to further discuss some of the major bottlenecks in working together. They worked towards understanding each others' constraints and identifying issues and areas in which joint actions were possible. The meeting raised three major points: first, that NGOs needed to respect that the Vía Campesina was in a stage of internal strengthening that limited its capacity to respond to external requests; second, that there was a need to recognize the different mandates of farm organizations and NGOs working at the international level; and third, that the Vía Campesina did not want its relationships with NGOs to be founded exclusively on funding possibilities (CPE 1997). The meeting agreed on the need for a Code of Principles to be shared by the NGOs and the Vía Campesina and set the stage for future collaboration among organizations that had a common vision.[6]

The roots of the Vía Campesina stretch back to years of international exchanges among like-minded and progressive farm organizations. The movement coalesced in the North and South around common objectives: an explicit rejection of the neo-liberal model of rural development, an outright refusal to be excluded from agricultural policy development, and a firm determination to work together to empower a peasant voice and to establish an alternative model of agriculture. The Vía Campesina's rapid growth combined with its increasing presence and visibility strongly suggests that IFAP was not meeting the needs and interests of many peasant and farm organizations concerned with social justice as well as economic well-being. Indeed, the Vía Campesina surfaced as a progressive alternative to the IFAP. While both organizations embrace farming families, the Vía Campesina represents somewhat different constituencies; it takes different positions and engages in different strategies.

Since its inception the Vía Campesina has sought to establish the terms and conditions of collaboration and co-operation with NGOs and other institutions. On a number of occasions and at different stages it has engaged in continued attempts to work with NGOs, and has made concerted efforts to redefine relations between NGOs and farm organizations. In doing so it has openly challenged NGOs' assumptions, the "place" of NGOs in the international arena, and the ways in which they work with peasant organizations.

The Vía Campesina's experience with the PFS raises a number of critical issues, starting with how NGOs conceive of and practise the concept of participation. The PFS, like many "progressive" NGOs, professed a commitment to participatory development and placed high value on the need for a farmer-driven process. The PFS did consult with some farm organizations in the preliminary stages leading up to the formation of the Vía Campesina. However, when it became clear that farm leaders sought to go beyond the research policy framework that the PFS had worked so hard to formulate, the NGO resisted this move and failed to demonstrate the flexibility needed to facilitate the full participation of farm leaders. Participation demands more than consultation with a few; it involves continuing discussion and an acceptance of the very real possibility of significant and swift shifts in direction. The peasant and farm leaders who met in Mons wanted power to define their own alternative vision and needed mechanisms to make this vision a reality. As the PFS's actions demonstrated, the larger question of what the Vía Campesina was to be was not up for debate. Instead, the PFS drew boundaries. "Participation" was to be constrained to a focus on a pre-designed, manageable, and predictable program (that most certainly fit well into the NGO mindset) — that of policy research.

The PFS's refusal to accept and respect the decisions made by farm leaders in Mons highlight issues about the place and role of NGOs. Clearly, the PFS believed that its vision for what the Vía Campesina should be and do was superior to what farmers and peasants envisioned. This "we know what is best for you" approach has been all too common in a long history of rural development in which rural people's knowledge and peasants' experiences are denigrated and devalued, only to be replaced by science-based programs and the ideas of "experts" or others. When faced with the initiative presented by farm leaders, the PFS refused to give up ownership of the idea of the Vía Campesina and persisted in imposing its vision and views. The PFS refused to accept a subordinate place — whereby it would play a supportive rather than directive role — as requested by farm leaders. In doing so it seriously threatened to undermine the autonomy of peasant and farm organizations.

4. "The WTO... Will Meet Somewhere, Sometime. And We Will Be There"

> The imposition of the WTO and regional trade agreements is destroying our livelihoods, our cultures and the natural environment. We cannot, and we will not, tolerate the injustice and destruction these policies are causing. Our struggle is historic, dynamic and uncompromising.... This is a peasant struggle for all of humankind....
> —Bangalore Declaration, Vía Campesina, Oct. 3, 2000

La Vía Campesina maintains that the globalized industrial model of agriculture, together with increased liberalization of the food trade, is leading to the destruction of biodiversity and subsequent loss of cultural diversity, further degradation of the environment, increased disparity, and greater impoverishment in countrysides everywhere. It argues that neo-liberal policies are sustained by human rights abuses and increased violence in the countryside — geared specifically to intimidate peasants — while economic liberalization endangers national food security and threatens the livelihood and very survival of peasant families. As a result peasant and farm families in both North and South are "disappeared" and rural communities are decimated.

Still, as the Vía Campesina (1996a) so defiantly stated during its Second International Conference in Tlaxcala, "we will not be intimidated" or "disappeared." Armed with a strong collective identity as "people of the land" and an uncompromising belief in their right to continue making a living by growing food in the countryside, Vía Campesina members are fighting for the very right to exist. This is not just a struggle for survival; it is a struggle to protect not only their communities and cultures but also their right to produce food in culturally appropriate ways for domestic consumption — through what they call food sovereignty.

This determination led the Vía Campesina to adopt a strategy of public and radical opposition to one of the key instruments of globalization, the WTO. Vía Campesina opposition to a WTO-directed globalization has taken a unique shape that differs dramatically from the approaches of other civil society organizations involved in agriculture and food security at the international level.

Farmers' and the WTO: Diverging Positions

The International Federation of Agricultural Producers (IFAP), like the Vía Campesina, firmly believes in the need for international trade regulations to establish fair rules and markets for food and agriculture. Unlike the Vía Campesina, IFAP ultimately took a pro-liberalization stance. Indeed, IFAP accepts the inevitability of the liberalization and globalization of agriculture while seeking ways of ensuring that farmers have the necessary tools to adapt to changing production and marketing policies. IFAP does not question the basic assumptions of the free-trade model. Rather, it sees the WTO as a legitimate institution pursuing the legitimate goal of freer trade, which it states should "serve to ensure that economic growth and greater integration of the world economy fulfils its potential to enhance the livelihoods of family farmers throughout the world, contributes to the eradication of poverty, and promotes an economically, socially and environmentally sustainable path for agricultural development" (IFAP 1998a: 4).

As such, IFAP positions on trade and the WTO are essentially conform-ist and reformist in that the organization seeks to make the existing model, structure and policies work better for farmers. The issue then becomes a question of ensuring that farmers' voices are heard in WTO deliberations and of exploring how to ensure that WTO agreements recognize the need to slow down the pace of free trade until countries in the South catch up. From this follows the need for the transfer of technology and for capacity-building in the South (IFAP 1998a, 2000a).

To advocate its position IFAP actively participates in the WTO. According to Sally Rutherford, former executive director of the Canadian Federation of Agriculture, IFAP member organizations are often invited to participate on official national government delegations, and IFAP itself regularly meets with the WTO Secretariat and staff in Geneva (Rutherford 2002). Through this level of participation — which demands a substantial level of financial and human resources — IFAP believes that it is succeeding in influencing international deliberations and ensuring that farmers' interests are met. For example, IFAP argues, "During the Uruguay Round, IFAP's proposal concern-ing the conditions of bringing agriculture under GATT's rules and disciplines were taken up." On an economic level IFAP believes that "the contacts established with the WTO and the OECD... allow farmers to make progress" in meeting the challenges of producing sufficient food for an increasing world population while also dealing with increasingly volatile markets (IFAP: n.d.).

One of IFAP's key objectives is to create and help to strengthen farm organizations especially in the developing countries, to improve farmers' ca-pacity and participation in national agricultural and food policy development (IFAP n.d., 1998b). For example, in 1993, the same year that the Vía Campesina emerged, IFAP launched "The Worldwide Action for Strengthening Farmers," an initiative geared mainly to developing countries. Later IFAP restructured its Development Co-operation Committee in an attempt to channel more funds — sometimes via Northern farm organizations — to Southern farm organizations. IFAP also works closely with the World Bank on issues of rural

---

The U.S. Farm Lobby

In 1998 *Fortune* magazine ranked the American Farm Bureau Federation as the fourteenth most influential organization in Washington; in 1999 it ranked twenty-first. According to the Center for Responsive Politics the American Farm Bureau Federation spent $4.56 million on lobbying in Washington in 1998 alone. In addition, state farm bureaus spent another $250,000 (Monks, Ferris, and Campbell 2000: 50–51).

---

poverty and sustainable development. For example, the World Bank sponsored a number of farmers' workshops in developing regions and supported an IFAP Millennium Survey on Farmers' Organizations and Development to identify the needs and activities of farm organizations.

However, some of the industrialized-country farm organizations that belong to IFAP have no need for such support. The American Farm Bureau Federation, for example, is one of the most influential groups in Washington, spending millions of dollars lobbying U.S. politicians. Some of the European IFAP members are also members of COPA, an umbrella group of mainstream European farmers' organizations that have close links to and influence in the European Commission. These powerful players have clout within IFAP itself, and given COPA's close connections to agribusiness and large agricultural co-operatives, we can probably safely assume that it exerts influence on European government decision-making. Perhaps not surprisingly, then, the IFAP report on the Doha WTO Ministerial conference ignored the questionable processes leading up to, and the tactics used, in the Qatar gathering and essentially congratulated the WTO for succeeding in launching the so-called "Development Round" (IFAP 2001).[1]

The Vía Campesina's position on the WTO differs significantly. Although the Vía Campesina is by no means opposed to agricultural trade, it approaches trade from a human rights perspective rather than the exclusive market-driven approach advocated by the WTO and its proponents. Instead the Vía Campesina insists, "Food is first and foremost a source of nutrition and only secondarily an item of trade." Hence, agricultural production must be geared primarily to ensuring food security under the terms of food sovereignty: "Food is a basic human right. This right can only be realized in a system where food sovereignty is guaranteed" (Vía Campesina 1996c: 1–2). Furthermore, the Vía Campesina (2000f: 1) openly rejects WTO decisions that impose a "forced liberalization of trade in agricultural products across regions and around the world" — a practice that results in "disastrously low prices" for many of the crops produced. These policies have harsh results:

> As cheap food imports flood local markets, peasant and farm families can no longer produce food for their own families and communities

and are driven from the land. These unfair trade arrangements are destroying rural communities and cultures by imposing new eating patterns everywhere in the world. Local and traditional foods are being replaced by low priced, often poorer quality, imported food-stuffs. Food is a key part of culture, and the neo-liberal agenda is destroying the very basis of our lives and cultures. We do not accept the hunger and displacement. We demand food sovereignty, which means the right to produce our own food.

In advocating food sovereignty the Vía Campesina explicitly rejects what is perhaps the most significant principle of the WTO AOA, the "right to export" and the expanded power of the WTO in global governance over food, genetic resources, natural resources, and agricultural markets. This right to export is congruent with the WTO's view of food security, which is perhaps best defined as ensuring access to an "adequate supply of *imported* food" (Stevens et al. 2000: 3; emphasis added). Instead, the Vía Campesina argues that each country has the right and obligation to develop national agricultural and food policies that ensure the health and well-being of its populations, cultures, and environments.

The Vía Campesina (1999b: 1–2) argues that the WTO AOA and TRIPs were designed to protect agribusiness interests:

> Neo-liberal agricultural policies have led to the destruction of our family farm economies and to a profound crisis in our societies and threaten the very coherence of our societies: the right to produce our food for our own consumers, with great diversity in production and consumption according to cultural preferences. This touches our very identities as citizens of this world.
>
> The clearest example of the violation of our identity is the fact that TNCs are imposing genetically engineered food. In a recent move the US and the EU tried to bring the discussion on biosafety and GMOs — in essence, whether we have the right to protect ourselves against the importation of GMO products — in the WTO through a "Biotechnology working group." We consider this as a scandalous and provocative violation of our rights as citizens.
>
> Vía Campesina rejects the neo-liberal policies that push countries into cash crop export production at the expense of domestic food production. These policies contribute to low commodity prices, far lower than the real costs of production. Developing countries are forced to adopt these policies in order to pay their external debt. These countries must also open their borders to the importation of food which leads to even greater debt. The governments of the rich countries are giving massive subsidies without limit per farm in order to compensate price cuts and allow the TNCs

to buy cheaply. This way these public funds are a direct support for industry and not for farmers. This is a vicious circle which benefits only the TNCs.

There is no doubt that the WTO is an instrument that places greater control and profits in the hands of the TNCs. The WTO is a totally inappropriate institution for democratic decision-making and policy formulation on important issues such as food sovereignty, health and environmental legislation, management of genetic resources, water, forestry and land, and the organisation of agricultural markets.

At events surrounding the Seattle WTO Ministerial meeting the Vía Campesina (1999b: 3) reiterated the demands that it had voiced earlier at the Geneva WTO Ministerial conference:

- An immediate moratorium on further WTO negotiations.
- Immediate cancellation of the obligation to import five percent of internal consumption. Cancellation of all compulsory market access clauses.
- An evaluation of the impact of the Uruguay Round agreements and implementation of measures to correct the injustices.
- Take agriculture out of bilateral and regional trade agreements and the WTO.
- Create genuine international democratic mechanisms to regulate food trade while respecting food sovereignty in each country.
- Secure food sovereignty which means respecting each country's right to define their own agricultural policies in order to meet their internal needs. This includes the right to prohibit imports in order to protect domestic production and to implement Agrarian Reform providing peasants and small to medium-sized producers with access to land.
- Stop all forms of dumping to protect the production of staple domestic foods.
- Prohibit biopiracy and patents on life.

For the Vía Campesina, reforming the WTO is not a viable strategy, because the WTO's very purpose, practices, and policies are so fundamentally flawed. The Vía Campesina argues that the WTO's lack of transparency and accountability, accompanied by blatant undemocratic practices and links to agro-industry, makes it completely unsuitable as an international structure responsible for overseeing the food trade. Rather than restricting its efforts to "reforming" the WTO by negotiating what could be placed in the "green," "blue," or "amber" box, or making slight adjustments with the creation of a "development" or "food security" box, the Vía Campesina insists that agriculture and food should simply be taken out of the WTO: or, "Perhaps more appropriately, let's take the WTO out of agriculture."

Earlier, in 1996, the Vía Campesina appeared less able to deal with the potential power of a WTO that appeared to be still out of reach. At the time the Vía Campesina focused on opening spaces for deliberations on food security, and it challenged U.N. agencies such as the FAO to develop mechanisms to foster food sovereignty throughout the world. Consequently the Vía Campesina directed its efforts and resources to participating at the 1996 World Food Summit rather than attending the WTO Ministerial meeting in Singapore, which was held one month later. In 2001 the Vía Campesina continued to work primarily with alternative international agencies and focused on the WFS: Five Years Later, originally scheduled to take place in November, rather than on the WTO meeting in Doha. As Nico Verhagen, technical assistant to the Vía Campesina Operational Secretariat points out, the Vía Campesina's participation in the WTO would most certainly have contributed to legitimizing the institution's reach into agriculture and food. By working within the FAO — a relatively more farmer-friendly institution — the Vía Campesina could potentially help to shift (ever so slightly) the power dynamics between the FAO and other major agencies such as the IMF, World Bank (WB), and WTO. Nettie Wiebe explains this strategic decision:

> We are clear about the WTO: in principle this institution is pernicious for us. The FAO, in principle, is not a hostile venue for us. The U.N. is one of those last remaining multilateral institutions that might have some impact on its member agencies. There is within the Vía Campesina a struggle about how one should act vis-à-vis any U.N. operations: whether we should consign them all to having been taken over and contaminated by the WTO, or whether or not that is one of the places where there is some room to influence from one institution to another. In the end there was no conclusion that we have to abandon the FAO. It just turns out that the more it is influenced and dominated by U.S. foreign policy and WTO overlap, the less useful it becomes.

The Vía Campesina believes that new instruments and mechanisms must be established to develop and implement fair and socially responsible trade rules for agriculture and food; these would also have to be accompanied by a more democratically run, more transparent United Nations system (Vía Campesina 1999a). In this way trade regulations would have to comply with, rather than override, international agreements such as, among others, the International Covenant on Economic, Social and Cultural Rights (ICESCR), the Convention on Biodiversity and the Bio-safety Protocol.

The absolute right to food is a key to this ongoing debate. The Rome Declaration on World Food Security and the World Food Summit Plan of

---

The Human Right to Food

Article 25 of the Universal Declaration of Human Rights states, "Everyone has the right to a standard of living adequate for the well-being of himself and his family, including food clothing, housing." Article 11(1) of the International Covenant on Economic, Social and Cultural Rights (ICESCR) recognizes "the right of everyone to an adequate standard of living for himself and his family, including adequate food, clothing and housing, and to the continuous improvement of living conditions. The States Parties will take appropriate steps to ensure the realization of this right"

Article 11(2) of the ICESCR takes it a little further by declaring that governments recognize:

> the fundamental right of everyone to be free from hunger, [and] shall take, individually and through international cooperation, the measures, including specific programmes, which are needed: (a) to improve methods of production, conservation and distribution of food by making full use of technical and scientific knowledge, by disseminating knowledge of the principles of nutrition and by developing or reforming agrarian systems in such a way as to achieve the most efficient development and utilization of natural resources.

By September 2006 the ICESCR had been ratified by 154 countries. The right to food is also incorporated in the Convention on the Rights of the Child, the Convention on the Elimination of All Forms of Discrimination against Women (CEDAW), and the Optional Protocol to CEDAW.

Action adopted by heads of states in 1996 reaffirmed the fundamental right to food for all peoples and the obligation of each state to ensure the realization of this right. Article 25(1) of the Universal Declaration of Human Rights and Article 11 of ICESCR recognizes the human right to adequate food.

The ICESCR also acknowledges the right to self-determination: "The right of peoples to exercise sovereignty over their natural wealth and resources" as essential to ensuring the realization of human rights (Oloka-Onyango and Udagama 2000: 10). Furthermore, the ICESCR stresses, "In no case may a people be deprived of its own means of subsistence."

Yet Article XVI (4) of the Marrakesh Agreement to Establish the WTO clearly supercedes sovereignty in that all member states must alter their laws, regulations and administrative procedures to comply with WTO rules (Scholte, O'Brien, and Williams 1998: 3). The AoA also dramatically impinges on the ability of national governments to define their own national agricultural and food policies while at the same time forcing them to import 5 percent of national consumption of some products.

Ironically, then, international agreements give full responsibility to states to ensure the basic right to sustenance and oblige national governments to respect human rights — yet all states are bound by an international trade framework that undermines their ability to act. The Vía Campesina's calls for food sovereignty demand that trade *not* be the first priority over all else. Moreover, trade policies must respect, protect, and fulfill people's rights to sustainable production systems that yield safe and healthy food; the WTO must function within widely recognized limits of international human rights covenants. Since these principles would require a fundamental change in the conceptualization of the WTO — a change the WTO has given no indication it is willing to consider — the Vía Campesina demands that agriculture and food be taken out of the WTO's jurisdiction.

Initially the Vía Campesina position straddled the reformist and radical perspectives. Some Vía Campesina organizations, such as India's KRRS, clamoured for the abolition of the WTO. Others, like Canada's NFU and Mexico's UNORCA, argued that an international trade regulatory system was necessary to counter the skewed power relations and conditions enshrined in regional trade agreements like NAFTA. Still others, such as the Confédération Paysanne, believed that the Vía Campesina should work to reform the WTO to ensure that it complied with international human rights conventions. In the end, the Vía Campesina position was a compromise. Rather than calling for the complete disbanding of the WTO, the Vía Campesina demanded a reduction in the organization's powers by taking agriculture out of its jurisdiction, as well as the building of new structures within a transformed, more democratic, and transparent U.N. system.

WTO Spurs Worldwide Agrarian Activism

Certainly, one of the key sectors profoundly affected by the WTO and its new reach into agriculture consisted of the people who produce most of the world's food — small- and medium-scale farmers, which includes peasants, and especially women. Although the Vía Campesina, like IFAP, also engages with international institutions involved in defining agricultural and food policies, it approaches this engagement in numerous, and different, ways. In attempts to prevent or change policies and institutions that are hostile to peasants' and small farmers' interests, the Vía Campesina will engage in mobilization, mass demonstrations, and even direct action. Only in certain contexts that offer adequate space for negotiation will the Vía Campesina co-operate and collaborate to work for favourable policy changes. The Vía Campesina stresses that negotiation must always be accompanied by mobilization (Vía Campesina 2000c).

On December 3, 1993, just seven months after the Vía Campesina was created, its leaders joined over five thousand protesters to march on the GATT in the streets of Geneva. They called for an alternative trade agreement that put the needs of people ahead of profits. Addressing the rally, Nettie Wiebe declared:

It is unthinkable that decisions which will have important consequences for all of us be made hastily and in relative secrecy with so
little input from those whose livelihoods and lives are at stake. As
Canadian farmers we are particularly concerned that an international
trade agreement must not be used to destroy the food production
capacity and food self-reliance mechanisms within countries. Our
experience of ordering production domestically to achieve self-reliance and a fair price to farmers in egg, poultry and dairy production
without distorting international trade is successful. It could serve
as a model for others. A GATT agreement should not destroy such
systems. After all, the real reason to produce food is surely not to
increase trade and augment the profits of multinational traders, but
rather to feed people. (quoted in Pugh 1994)

The Vía Campesina captured the increasing frustration of farming
families in demanding the democratization of world trade talks and urging
"governments to negotiate a fair international trade order which pays fair
prices, does not destroy family farming and leaves each region with the possibility of securing its own food supply" (Vía Campesina 1993b).

At the second WTO Ministerial conference, held in May 1998, Vía
Campesina leaders returned to Geneva, this time joining a growing crowd of
over ten thousand demonstrators. After the first three years of implementation the WTO agreements had failed to bring any of their promised benefits
to the countryside. Indeed, Vía Campesina organizations had experienced
a deterioration in the social fabric of rural communities accompanied by a
decline in farm income as national governments altered and/or abandoned
programs and institutions to comply with the WTO regulations. The encroaching power of the multilateral institution and the acquiescence of
nation-states were clearly captured by President Clinton, who, in addressing the conference, declared, "Globalization is not a policy choice — it is a
fact."

The thousands of people marching in the streets of Geneva — many
of whom had contributed to the defeat of the Multilateral Agreement
on Investment — adamantly rejected this laissez-faire attitude towards
globalization and liberalization. While some of them, namely the People's
Global Action, clamoured for the abolition of the WTO, the Vía Campesina
demanded that agricultural negotiations be stopped, that agriculture and
food be taken out of the WTO, and that a comprehensive audit be carried
out to analyze the impact that the WTO AoA and WTO Agreement on Trade-
Related Aspects of Intellectual Property Rights (TRIPs) were having on food
security, food sovereignty, the environment, and the livelihoods of farming
families everywhere.

While demonstrating in the streets of Geneva, the Vía Campesina was
the only group to stress the need to reclaim agriculture in this way — re-

> ## People's Global Action
> The People's Global Action defines itself as an "instrument for co-ordina-
> tion" for social movements involved in resisting globalization and building
> local alternatives. The People's Global Action does not believe that lobbying is
> an effective tool for change; rather, it has embraced a confrontational approach
> consisting of non-violent direct action and civil disobedience. Since its inception
> in February 1997, the People's Global Action has organized Global Days of Action
> that involve anti-globalization demonstrations at G8 summits, WTO ministerial
> conferences, and meetings of the International Monetary Fund and the World
> Bank. In 1999 the People's Global Action organized an intercontinental caravan
> for solidarity and resistance that brought 450 representatives of organizations of
> farmers, fisherfolk, indigenous peoples, and anti-dam movements to Europe.
> Source: PGA's website <www.agp.org> (accessed July 13, 2006).

flecting the significantly different "place" and hence unique perspective
of the food producers embraced by the movement. For unlike many other
individuals and organizations — such as NGOs, government bureaucrats,
and government officials — the members represented people whose very
survival and livelihoods depended on farmer-led fundamental changes in the
production, marketing, and trade of food. According to the Vía Campesina
(1998a: 1), "International trade must serve society," and the current rules
and structure of global food trade were designed primarily "to shift control
over a basic human right [such as food] out of the hands of people and their
governments" to better serve the interests and bottom line of agro-industry.
The Vía Campesina (ibid.) went on to argue:

> The loss of national food sovereignty within the WTO system is
> dangerous and unacceptable. Vía Campesina strongly objects to
> the conduct of negotiations in agriculture under the terms of the
> World Trade Organization.... The agreements are defined by big
> industrialised countries... and multinational corporations with little
> participation of other countries and social movements. These enti-
> ties are acting without... responsibility or accountability, thereby
> degrading both people and natural resources.

By the time of the third Ministerial conference two years later, resistance
had escalated dramatically. Tens of thousands of protesters representing a
wide range of people from environmentalists, labour, indigenous groups, and
students to church groups and women's organizations took to the streets
in Seattle. Once again, farmers were at the forefront of resistance to the
corporatization and globalization of agriculture as Vía Campesina leaders
demonstrated in front of a downtown McDonald's restaurant and the offices
of Cargill in Seattle. They also joined labour leaders at the head of a fifty-
thousand-people-strong peaceful demonstration against the WTO. By this

time the Vía Campesina was convinced that the WTO was incapable of reform and sought to delegitimize it as an institution responsible for agricultural trade by reiterating demands that agriculture and food should be taken out of the WTO and that food sovereignty be respected (Vía Campesina 1999b).

Protest in the streets — the "Battle of Seattle" as the media coined it — together with increasing internal opposition by some developing countries contributed to the WTO's failure to launch the Millennium Round, which in turn prompted questions about the WTO's legitimacy. As *The Economist* (1999a: 17) stated:

> The fiasco... dealt a huge blow to the World Trade Organization and to prospects for freer trade. The WTO's credibility is lower than it has ever been.... The Seattle summit has also raised doubts about whether the WTO's unwieldy structure and arcane procedures can cope with 135 member-countries all demanding their say.

The setback was seen as a resounding victory for many social justice movements around the world. The WTO could no longer ignore the rising voices of dissent emanating from growing, well-organized, visible, and vocal civil society movements. Power had shifted, if only slightly, as globalization from above was now effectively being countered by a new international force: globalization from below. As *The Economist* (1999a: 18) reported:

> The debacle in Seattle was a setback for freer trade and a boost for critics of globalization.... The NGOs that descended on Seattle were a model of everything the trade negotiators were not. They were well organised. They built unusual coalitions (environmentalists and labour groups, for instance, bridged old gulfs to jeer the WTO together). They had a clear agenda — to derail the talks. And they were masterly users of the media.... In short, citizens' groups are increasingly powerful at the corporate, national and international level.

By the time of the fourth Ministerial conference, held in Doha, Qatar, proponents of liberalization were desperate to get the WTO back on its feet. The lengths to which the WTO was prepared to go is perhaps best reflected in the world leaders' agreement to postpone the World Food Summit: Five Years Later (originally scheduled to take place days prior to the Doha talks) due to security risks following the attacks of September 11 in the United States.[2] Yet they refused to delay the trade talks. Negotiations took place in a heavily militarized, fortress-like conference site. (This, of course, is a sad commentary on the priorities and morals of government leaders: focusing on increasing trade over solving hunger and poverty.)

Holding the WTO conference in Doha, Qatar, a monarchy where little public demonstration or civil disobedience would be tolerated, helped to

ensure the smooth running of events by severely restricting on-site opposition from civil society organizations. The WTO Secretariat and the Qatari
government, claiming a severe lack of lodging facilities in Doha, authorized
the entry of a limited number of NGOs into the country. A total of 400 NGO
and business representatives participated in the official meetings (Blustein
2001b); only sixty of these were "genuine" organizations in that they were
not controlled by government or business interests (Bello 2001a: 6). At the
Seattle Ministerial meeting 1,300 NGO and business representatives received
accreditation. Hence, in Doha the WTO did succeed in greatly limiting the
presence and actions of the opposition. By reshaping the nature of permitted civil society opinion in this way, the WTO then attempted to interpret
the world according to its own self-limiting perspective. Commenting on
the involvement of NGOs in Doha, the director general of the WTO, Mike
Moore, said, "I think we're getting more support from NGOs," as the majority
of the organizations gathered focused on lobbying (rather than protesting)
by working on or with national delegations (quoted in Pruzin 2002: 8).

Still, the opposition was not completely co-opted or silenced. The sixty
representatives of more action-oriented and critical NGOs and social movements — including one Vía Campesina representative — who did make it to
Doha engaged in daily protest, and they kept the rest of the world informed
with regular reports on the process of deliberations. Perhaps more importantly,
the WTO was powerless to stop the hundreds of thousands of people from taking to the streets around the world in their respective countries to resist the
launching of a new round of trade negotiations. Although these events were
not covered in many of the Northern media sources, civil society organizations participated in teach-ins, rallies, parades, and public actions in over sixty
cities in — among other countries — Australia, Austria, Bangladesh, Bulgaria,
Canada, the Czech Republic, Denmark, Finland, France, Germany, Honduras,
Hong Kong, India, Indonesia, Italy, Japan, Lebanon, Malaysia, the Netherlands,
New Zealand, Nigeria, Norway, Philippines, Russia, Slovakia, South Africa,
South Korea, Spain, Sweden, Switzerland, Thailand, Tunisia, and Turkey (Vía
Campesina 2001a). Once again, farm and peasant organizations belonging to
the Vía Campesina actively participated in many of these protest events.

Local and National Resistance to the WTO
Farmers' protests against the liberalization of agriculture are not limited to
the WTO Ministerial conferences. Agrarian resistance is most often expressed
at the more local or national level, and in some cases farmers' organizations
are at the forefront of national struggles against liberalization. In Taiwan,
for example, several thousands of farmers, faced with the impending opening
of their markets to U.S. pork and poultry, threw pig shit at U.S. government
offices in their country (*WTO News* 1998: 1). Violence broke out as thousands
of farmers in South Korea participated in anti-WTO protests (*Agence France
Press* 2001b).

Within the Vía Campesina, the transnational dimension of local and national resistance is perhaps best reflected in the struggle against the introduction and imposition of genetically modified, transgenic seeds — together with new international intellectual property rights contained in the TRIPs. For the Vía Campesina, this new technology represents a direct attack on peasant farmers: it means the effective expropriation of the essential means of production. Consequently, the struggle over seeds is intensifying. From the Confédération Paysanne's denaturation of Novartis GMO seeds in France (Bové 1998), the KRRS's destruction of Bt-cotton fields in India, the MST's blocking of Argentinean ships delivering genetically modified seed to Brazil (Osava 2000), to the Canadian NFU's work against the introduction of genetically modified wheat (NFU 2003), peasants and farmers are refusing to let transnationals take control over seeds.

For the Vía Campesina the struggle over the ownership and control of seeds is so critical that farm leaders are prepared to cross national borders to engage in direct action on foreign soil. For instance, in addition to local and national resistance, in January 2001 the Vía Campesina went one step further as farm and peasant organizations converged in Brazil to participate in the World Social Forum in Porto Alegre. Here, Vía Campesina leaders joined the MST and other Brazilian social movements in direct action; they uprooted three hectares of Monsanto genetically modified soya and occupied the stores and laboratories where seeds were being distributed. In doing so, the Vía Campesina broke new ground as peasant farmers engaged in their first transnational (or cross-border) direct action. Perhaps equally important, the Vía Campesina did not restrict its actions to a national government; instead, it targeted a multinational company.

Interestingly, the government of Brazil retaliated by attempting to expel the internationally well-known spokesperson of the Confédération Paysanne, José Bové, but surprisingly there were no arrests of MST leaders. This response was a far cry from the repressive actions formerly condoned by the government of Brazil against the MST and may have had something to do with Vía Campesina's collective actions following the killing of nineteen Brazilian peasants on April 17, 1996. The international pressure that the Vía Campesina and other organizations were able to exert on the Brazilian government, together with the strength and support that the MST has within its own borders, may well have played a significant part in the government's decision to restrict actions against the MST while focusing retaliation on a foreigner.

But perhaps the earliest and certainly the largest displays of farmer opposition to the liberalization of agriculture have taken place in India. Every year the KRRS, a regional co-ordinator of the Vía Campesina, organizes massive rallies on Gandhi's birthday, October 2. In 1991 more than 200,000 farmers gathered to protest the liberalization agenda contained in the Dunkel Draft Treaty of the Uruguay Round. Just one year later the crowd had grown considerably: over half a million Indian farmers gathered in Bangalore to launch the Seed Satyagraha.[3] The KRRS repeatedly called on the government of India to reject the Dunkel Draft Treaty and the TRIPs. Given the cultural significance of seeds in Indian agrarian communities, the TRIPs was of great concern because it effectively threatened to transfer the ownership and control of seeds away from farmers and into the hands of TNCs. In the interests of protecting the autonomy of small farmers the KRRS articulated a number of demands, including: 1) decisions regarding the Dunkel Draft Treaty should not be made in the absence of public debate, including consultations with farmers organizations and all state legislatures; 2) farmers have the right to produce, save, and sell seeds; 3) governments must oppose the patenting of intellectual property rights on living organisms; and 4) transnational seed companies must not be allowed entry into India (Assadi 1995: 194). By 1993 opposition to liberalization had gained momentum as the KRRS joined other key peasant organizations, such as the Bharatiya Kisan Union of Uttar Pradesh and Punjab, in a massive all-India rally held on March 3 that year in Delhi.

When the Central Government of India largely ignored the KRRS's demands, farmers were forced to engage in direct action. On December 29, 1992, after having served "Quit India" notices to a number of multinationals, KRRS members raided the offices of Cargill Seeds India and torched company documents. Some seven months later activists attacked another Cargill office in Bellary. Subsequently the direct actions of Indian farmers gained international recognition when they targeted other multinationals that were trying to establish themselves in India. In 1996 the KRRS ransacked the Kentucky Fried outlet in Bangalore and engaged in a public awareness campaign linking health and food safety concerns to the encroaching presence of TNCs in food production in India. Later the KRRS launched a campaign of civil disobedience called Operation "Cremation Monsanto" involving the burning of Bt cotton plants grown on test field sites under the guidance of Mahyco Monsanto in various parts of Karnataka (*The Times of India News Service* 1998; *The Hindu* 2001). On June 18, 2002, KRRS members entered a shop selling Bt cotton seeds in Davangere and burned the seeds (KRRS 2002). The campaign continued sporadically over the next four years.

The actions and strategies of the KRRS illustrate the acuity with which Indian farmers, most of them illiterate, so rapidly understood the immediate social, cultural, and economic ramifications of decisions being made half a world away in Geneva. As KRRS president M.D. Nanjundaswamy explained, the KRRS membership clearly understood that the WTO agreements represented an issue of national security: while greatly benefitting the agri-food transnationals and seed companies they would usurp peasant autonomy and destroy the livelihoods and displace millions of small Indian farmers — a human tragedy on an immense scale — in a country in which 70 percent of the population is rural.

The KRRS did not restrict its actions to influencing the national and state governments; it directly targeted the forces pushing globalization, the transnational corporations. According to T.N. Prakash, an agricultural economist who closely followed the situation, through their public actions the farmers successfully captured the public's attention, thus effectively placing the WTO, and India's role and position within it, in the midst of a public debate. Although the KRRS may not have seen any immediate results from the actions, it did succeed in educating the public (and government officials, for that matter) and mobilizing different sectors to action; in so doing, the organization, according to Prakash, may well have helped to shift public opinion to some degree. Indeed, former government officials — such as V.P. Singh (a former prime minister) and S.P. Shukla (a former ambassador to GATT and a secretary in India's commerce and finance ministries) — began to openly criticize the WTO as well as India's lack of leadership in challenging the multilateral institution (Frontline 2001; Shukla 2001). This remarkable outcome may help explain the more prominent and less reticent role that Indian negotiators took at the fourth Ministerial conference in Doha. Indeed, India's actions almost provoked the collapse of the talks.

Farmers' Different Strategies: Participation and Mobilization

The Vía Campesina's growing presence in the international arena has attracted the attention of an increasing number of NGOs and international institutions — the World Bank, FAO, Commission for Sustainable Development, and the Global Forum on Agricultural Research, among others — that seek to legitimize their policies and programs through the "participation" of this growing international peasant movement. For its part, the Vía Campesina's experience in the international arena has taught it important lessons about the limitations and very real dangers of this participation.

The Vía Campesina's experience with the Global Forum on Agricultural Research (GFAR) is particularly illuminating. GFAR, formed in 1996, seeks to establish a global system for development-oriented agricultural research by building partnerships and strategic alliances in efforts to reduce poverty, build food security, and better manage natural and genetic resources. In a May 2000 conference held in Dresden, Germany, GFAR brought together key stakeholders: representatives of government departments of agriculture, national and international agricultural research institutions, NGOs, Monsanto and Novartis, the Vía Campesina, and IFAP. The expressed goal of the conference was to reach a consensus on the future direction of agricultural research — not an easy task given that consensus-building is always a difficult process, and sometimes an impossible one, especially when participants have diametrically opposed interests. GFAR resolved this challenge by simply fabricating consent. In the final hour of the conference the organizers congratulated the participants for having reached agreement on the Dresden Declaration, which reiterated a faith in science, trade, biotechnology, and genetic engineering as solutions to poverty, food insecurity, loss of biodiversity, and environmental degradation. Most of the stakeholders present, including IFAP, agreed with the declaration — with the Vía Campesina and a number of NGOs being the exceptions. The Vía Campesina (2000a), sticking to its principles, not surprisingly asserted the crucial necessity of research being farmer-driven and designed to meet the needs and interests of small farmers and peasants rather than remaining in the hands of agribusiness

Immediately following the conference the Vía Campesina issued a press release highlighting its objections to the numerous ways in which peasants and small farmers had been excluded from participating in the debate: they were not invited to speak in the plenaries, there was no translation in the small-group sessions, critical themes were marginalized, and in a zealous attempt to reach consensus the Vía Campesina's very public opposition had been conveniently ignored and purposely omitted. But perhaps the ultimate in exclusion was the conference organizers' insistence that in future assemblies Vía Campesina representatives were welcome to participate as "farmers" but not as representatives of the Vía Campesina. The crux of the matter was that the GFAR structure allowed for only one seat for farmers' organizations on its Steering Committee. As the Vía Campesina (2000a) pointed out, "This condition denies and eliminates all necessary aspects of our vision, accountability and representation which are central to the Vía Campesina's organizational activities." The Vía Campesina demanded that GFAR create a space specifically for organized peasants and small farmers.

A year later GFAR proposed a co-operation agreement with the Vía Campesina. Among other things, GFAR expressed interest in helping the Vía Campesina improve its web page and suggested that the Global Forum could assist IFAP and the Vía Campesina in establishing common interests and positions (GFAR 2001: 3–4). The Vía Campesina saw this proposal as a clear sign that GFAR, once again, was ignoring its demand that space be created specifically for an organized peasant voice. Consequently, the Vía Campesina opted not to sign the co-operation agreement, opting instead for "non-active" participation — in other words, agreeing to maintain a limited presence and participation.

Conflating IFAP and the Vía Campesina into just one space, thus providing only one voice for organized peasants, small- and medium-scale farmers, and large producers, has been a common tactic on the part of international institutions that have invited the Vía Campesina's participation. While IFAP appears to be interested in building consensus among all farmers by maintaining that the organizations share common concerns and are increasingly speaking the same language, Vía Campesina leaders view these conditions as being of little value — indeed, disillusioning and even disempowering. As Nettie Wiebe sees it, in the very process of developing a joint IFAP/Vía Campesina position, often all of the issues are reduced to the lowest common denominator, thus effectively robbing the statement of its original meaning and intent. The resulting positions no longer reflect the needs and demands of Vía Campesina organizations.

Perhaps more disturbing, as Nico Verhagen, the Vía Campesina's technical assistant explains, the tactic is aimed at erasing the fundamental differences between the two international farm organizations. It not only contributes to diluting and silencing opposition but also attempts to weaken the alternatives advocated by the Vía Campesina. For example, at the GATT demonstrations in Geneva on December 3, 1999 the Confédération Paysanne, accompanied by Vía Campesina leaders, did meet with the director general of GATT, Peter Sutherland, but the delegation, according to Wiebe, had little opportunity to voice its concerns. Sutherland waved off any opposition by stating that in meeting with IFAP, which he said had demonstrated support for the GATT negotiations, he had already effectively consulted with farmers around the world.[4]

Although the Vía Campesina did initially share the farmers' space with IFAP in some contexts that were judged to be less significant, it eventually stopped doing this. Now, as a matter of principle, the Vía Campesina actively resists assimilation, and it pressures international agencies to acknowledge that it represents distinct constituencies who have a different way of seeing the world and who propose different solutions to meet their needs and interests. The Vía Campesina generally insists that it be allowed to speak on its own behalf in all spaces. As a result the Vía Campesina has carved out a space for itself among key international institutions, which now meet with IFAP and the Vía Campesina separately or provide spaces for each. Given IFAP's relatively more reformist/conformist stance towards agricultural trade in the WTO, the Vía Campesina refuses to collaborate with the International Federation of Agricultural Producers in these crucial negotiations.

For example, in preparation for the Geneva WTO Ministerial meeting in 1998 a Vía Campesina organization, the Union de Producteurs Suisses — now called Uni-Terre — worked with other national organizations such as the Union Suisse de Producteurs (a member of IFAP and COPA) in the hope of presenting a joint IFAP and Vía Campesina declaration to Renato Ruggiero, the director general of the WTO. Gérard Vuffray, a farm leader with Uni-Terre, explains that at the national level organizations quickly reached agreement, and with significant compromise the statement was approved at the European level; but the initiative collapsed at the international level. Following lengthy internal deliberations, which led to an increasingly critical position vis-à-vis the WTO, the Vía Campesina opted not to sign the declaration and not to meet with Ruggiero. This was a significant decision because it clearly demarcated the field between the farm organizations working inside and outside of the WTO: on the inside was IFAP, which was better equipped and better situated (geographically and ideologically) to "participate"; on the outside was the Vía Campesina, standing its ground firmly. The Vía

Campesina chose non-participation in an effort to delegitimize the WTO, influence public opinion, and mobilize collective action.

For the Vía Campesina participation is charged with political and economic consequences. The Vía Campesina is acutely aware of how participation can be used to co-opt a movement, thus effectively diluting or silencing opposition. Its own participation can help to legitimize the institution — including its processes and policies — that is attempting to draw it in. This becomes of particular concern when international institutions attempt to merge business interests, NGOs, and social movements into one "multi-stakeholder" site. As Paul Nicholson states:

> Multilateral institutions tend to slot us all into one space — a space that we must also share with agribusiness. This multi-stakeholder process is the bureaucratization of participation. It smells rotten and effectively serves to distance the base. It is not only a problem of methodology; it goes much deeper. It is a process that dilutes and lightens the content, makes it politically correct, and ultimately renders the result useless.

More importantly, this kind of "participation" can easily undermine popular movements. The Vía Campesina has an elaborate and carefully groomed system for being accountable to, and consulting with, its grassroots organizations. Clearly, this representational structure and various consultative processes heighten the organization's legitimacy as an authentic representative of peasants' and farmers' interests in the international arena. But it also makes decision-making a more convoluted and time-consuming endeavour, thus often trying the patience of NGOs and other institutions that are not encumbered by such structures and that seek more immediate responses to global events. The Vía Campesina would rather give up participation in certain international fora than compromise its commitments to building a peasant and farm movement built on relations of trust, respect, gender and ethnic equality, and accountability.

The Vía Campesina takes representation very seriously; it also jealously guards its autonomy in decision-making on issues of participation and representation. When the movement receives an invitation to attend a given event for instance, it makes every attempt to engage in democratic decision-making when choosing the best person to go on its behalf. In this process the Operational Secretariat or any of the regional co-ordinators to the ICC normally sends out a letter providing details about the invitation. Decisions about whether or not the Vía Campesina should participate and who the representative might be are usually made via e-mail within a two-week period. The final decision can rest on a number of factors. For example, the ICC may believe that one particular region has more expertise on the subject or needs more exposure and experience in the international arena. Other internal dynamics, such as the Vía Campesina's commitment to gender balance, or the ICC's desire to make a strategic choice to support a national struggle by sending a representative engaged in a similar struggle, can also enter into play. Even so, these internal dynamics can be undermined when the institution or NGO organizing the event handpicks a Vía Campesina representative, or when an invitation comes at the last minute, thus making it impossible for the organization to engage in democratic decision-making. To avoid that type of scenario, as much as possible — and to protect its collective structure and internal decision-making processes — the Vía Campesina (2000b: 2) defends its rights to define the terms and conditions of its participation:

> The Vía Campesina must have autonomy to determine the space it will occupy with the objective of securing a large enough space to effectively influence the event. It is not acceptable to participate on the invitee's terms in ways which subsume or erase our identity and use our credibility without giving us space to articulate our own interests and select our own representatives.

Given the importance of agriculture in trade negotiations, national governments and the WTO understandably recognize that it is in their best interests to be seen as consulting with the world's farmers while advancing global trade policies. But active participation at this level requires a substantial range of human and financial resources, something that grassroots organizations like the Vía Campesina simply do not have. Inside the WTO there is no space for the Vía Campesina to secure control and influence on the ultimate outcome of decision-making; Vía Campesina positions seriously question the neo-liberal orthodoxy, and dissension is rarely, if ever, allowed on national government delegations. As a result, while IFAP sits at the WTO and OECD tables representing the world's farmers, the Vía Campesina is out demonstrating in the streets in attempts to influence public opinion. Vía Campesina organizations also work to influence the positions of their national governments. Judging from the WTO's increasingly fragile legitimacy and declining credibility both in (certain) government circles and the general public, the Vía Campesina tactics would seem to be succeeding.

Building Strategic Alliances with Selected NGOs

Although Vía Campesina–NGO relations have been marked, from time to time, with conflict and tension, they are also a source of great power. The Vía Campesina, well aware of its limitations, became convinced that building alternatives to the neo-liberal agenda being promoted by the WTO, IMF, and WB would only occur with a cross-cultural, cross-sectoral convergence of grassroots social movements working together with the more professionalized (but critical) NGOs. As the Vía Campesina's internal guidelines on international relations and establishing strategic alliances (2000b: 1) argue:

The Vía Campesina has succeeded in establishing itself as an important global voice for peasant and small-scale farmers in less than a decade of work. It has done so by articulating a strong peasant agenda, mobilizing and working in solidarity across great geographic and cultural diversity. In order to build on those gains and become a more effective force, it is imperative to continue to build strategic working relations with others who support our agenda and to effect changes in the international institutions and agencies which are currently destroying peasant agriculture.

While the Vía Campesina's trump cards were legitimacy, accountability, on-the-ground experience, and mass-mobilization capacity, progressive NGOs could contribute much-needed expertise in research-lobbying, knowledge of global trends, and the ability to gain access to desperately needed funds for campaigns and mobilization. Consequently the Vía Campesina pursued close working relations with a carefully selected group of NGOs that not only shared a similar analysis and vision but also embraced the greater participation of social movements.

Still, the existing imbalances and asymmetrical power relations between NGOs and peasant organizations (see chapter 3) have made the creation and work of coalitions challenging. It took years of working together before the Vía Campesina succeeded in building relations of trust and respect with key NGOs. Also, the Vía Campesina needed to build and consolidate itself further as an international movement so that it could more confidently voice positions that accurately reflected the needs and interests of its constituency. Only then could it more easily move towards building strategic alliances with NGOs. Indeed, not until after the Seattle WTO Ministerial conference would the Vía Campesina begin to work in a concerted fashion in the international arena with NGOs on issues of trade and agriculture. Thereafter the Vía Campesina would not only help to legitimize NGO campaigns but also provide content and direction.

At the Geneva WTO Ministerial conference in May 1998, the Vía Campesina spent most of its time in internal deliberations to define a common position on the WTO. It also worked more closely with social movements linked to the People's Global Action than it did with NGOs. Following the Geneva meetings many of the groups that had successfully helped to defeat the Multilateral Agreement on Investment embarked on a year-long "No New Round: Turn Around Campaign" leading up to the Seattle WTO conference. This campaign eventually brought together 1,500 organizations from eighty-nine countries from around the world; they demanded a moratorium on further WTO negotiations, an assessment of the impact of decisions made so far, and a rejection of the introduction in the negotiations of new issues such as investment and competition. While many Vía Campesina organizations participated actively in this campaign at the national level, the Vía

Campesina was not fully on board at the international level.

In Seattle, however, the Vía Campesina adopted its "globalize the struggle, globalize the hope" strategy; it forged links with a number of key NGOs and consolidated alliances with other sectors in efforts to build a worldwide movement to develop alternatives to the neo-liberal model advocated by the WTO. The Vía Campesina focused on work with a number of strategically selected NGOs and social movements that shared common ideologies and similar visions for social change. Some three months later the Vía Campesina joined those who had worked on the No New Round campaign to elaborate a new strategy, "Our World Is Not for Sale: WTO — Shrink or Sink! The Turn Around Agenda." Nicholson explains that although the Vía Campesina did not sign this document, the movement was certainly connected to the process. By the time this statement was redrafted into "Our World Is Not for Sale: WTO Shrink or Sink," the Vía Campesina was ready to become a signatory.

The WTO, recognizing the need to open space and engage in discussion with civil society organizations, organized an NGO Symposium to be held in July 2001. Still, in the eyes of many social movements and NGOs, the WTO — even after having made commitments in Seattle to greater transparency and democracy — was not demonstrating any measurable reform. Focus on the Global South, a Bangkok-based independent research and policy institute with staff in Geneva, prepared monthly reports on WTO negotiations and interactions. The articles explained in detail the secretive, non-transparent, and exclusive process and practices of the WTO leading up to the fourth ministerial conference. Perhaps more disturbing, the powerful WTO actors and the WTO Secretariat itself were pushing for the launching of a comprehensive new round in Qatar — a move clearly indicating that the WTO was also ignoring the demands of the more than 1,500 organizations from eighty-nine countries that supported numerous developing countries' calls for a focus on implementation rather than defining a new round.

With no real possibility of reform in sight, many social movements and NGOs concluded that the WTO's symposium with civil society was simply a public relations exercise. Consequently, the Vía Campesina, working in coalition with other social movements and NGOs, held a press conference and launched the "Our World Is Not for Sale: WTO Shrink or Sink" strategy, centred on eleven demands aimed at reducing the power and scope of the WTO, resisting the launching of a new comprehensive round, and developing a sustainable, socially just, and democratically accountable trade system.

Given the restrictions posed by holding the WTO Ministerial conference in Doha, the Vía Campesina worked as part of a core group of the Our World Is Not for Sale coalition in developing a three-pronged strategy.[5] First, national and local events aimed at educating the general public and national officials would be organized to coincide with the Doha Ministerial meetings. Second, a major regional civil society organizations' forum on globalization

> ## Eleven Demands of Our World Is Not for Sale
>
> - No WTO expansion
> - Protect basic social rights and environmental sustainability
> - Protect basic social services and... the ability of governments and people to regulate in order to protect the environment, health, safety, and other public interests.
> - Stop corporate patent protectionism: seeds and medicine are human needs, not commodities.
> - No patents on life
> - Food is a basic human right:... protect genuine food sovereignty
> - No investment liberalization: The WTO Trade-Related Investment Measures (TRIMs) must be eliminated.
> - Fair trade:... special and differential rights for Third World countries
> - Prioritize Social Rights and the Environment.
> - Democratize decision-making
> - Dispute the [dispute settlement] mechanism
>
> For the full text of the Our World Is Not for Sale coalition, see the Council of Canadians website <http://www.canadians.org>.

and the WTO would take place in Beirut to bring together local and regional movements, strengthen their links to counterparts internationally and act as a civil society counterpoint to the official WTO conference. The final, and certainly the most creative, strategy was to organize an Activist Armada that would float from Al Aqaba, Jordan, to Doha carrying some two- to three-hundred activists, and a Fisherfolk Flotilla that would sail from Mumbai. The Vía Campesina consolidated ties with the World Forum of Fisher People and subsequently farmers and fishers agreed to collaborate in organizing anti-WTO actions. All of the organizations involved in the Our World Is Not for Sale coalition were committed to non-violent and peaceful protest; all those on board the boats would be required to sign a Peace Pledge, thus effectively distancing themselves from the fringe groups engaging in violent tactics.

The September 11 terrorist attacks in the United States forced the coalition to abandon the flotilla plan and thus substantially reduced the presence and actions of social movements and NGOs in Doha; but mobilization did not cease. Indeed, more people took to the streets in more places around the world than ever before. Resistance to the WTO had never been stronger, and positions and alternatives were now more clearly defined. For example, only days before the Doha Conference began, the Vía Campesina's lone calls (voiced as early as the Geneva Ministerial conference in 1998) for food sovereignty and the removal of agriculture from the WTO were now being supported by numerous social movements and NGOs from around the world with the launching, on November 6, 2001, of the "Priority to Peoples' Food Sovereignty — WTO out of Food and Agriculture" campaign.[6] The press release accompanying the statement explained:

> Peoples' food sovereignty is a call to governments to adopt policies that promote sustainable, family-farm based production rather than industry-led, high-input and export oriented production. This entails adequate prices for all farmers, supply-management, abolishment of all forms of export support, and the regulation of imports to protect domestic food production. All food products should comply with high environmental, social and health quality standards. This includes a ban on GMOs and food irradiation. Peoples' food sovereignty also includes equitable access to land, seeds, water and other productive resources as well as a prohibition on patenting of life. (Peoples' Food Sovereignty 2001a: 1)

The campaign stressed that to ensure food sovereignty governments must act immediately to remove food and agriculture from the WTO's jurisdiction and to begin working on an new multilateral framework to govern sustainable agricultural production and the food trade.

However, after the fiasco of the Seattle WTO conference, another collapse in trade negotiations was simply not acceptable for the proponents of liberalization. And despite internal and external resistance, the WTO fourth Ministerial conference in Doha concluded with a ten-page declaration. Upon returning home some government officials were clearly jubilant that Doha had not been a repeat of Seattle. For example, U.S. Trade Representative Robert Zoellick stated, "The members of the World Trade Organization have sent a powerful signal to the world.... We have removed the stain of Seattle." Canada's minister of international trade, Pierre Pettigrew, reiterated: "We have turned the page on the Seattle failure" (Morton 2001: 1–2). Others linked the opposition to terrorism and couched the successful launching of further liberalization in terms of "development." As President Bush said, the WTO promised to bring "prosperity and development for all." He went on to say that the meeting's declaration

> sends a powerful signal that the world's trading nations support peaceful and open exchange and reject the forces of fear and protectionism.... Today's decision offers fresh hope for the world's developing nations.... It reflects our common understanding that a new trade round can give developing countries greater access to world markets, and lift the lives of millions now living in poverty." (Office of the Press Secretary 2001: 1)

Similarly, EU Farm Commissioner Franz Fischler was jubilant with success as he declared:

Peoples' Food Sovereignty Proposals for an Alternative Framework

An alternative international framework involves:

- A reformed and strengthened United Nations committed to protecting the fundamental rights of all peoples and responsible for developing and negotiating rules for sustainable production and fair trade.
- An independent dispute settlement mechanism integrated within an international Court of Justice.
- A World Commission on Sustainable Agriculture and Food Sovereignty to assess the impact of trade liberalization on food sovereignty and food security, and be responsible for developing proposals for change. This commission could be directed by civil society organizations and movements, elected representatives and appropriate multilateral institutions.
- An international and legally binding treaty that defines the rights of peasants and small producers to the necessary assets, resources and legal protections required to exercise their right to produce. Such a treaty could be framed within the U.N. Human Rights framework and linked to already existing relevant U.N. Conventions.
- An International Convention to replace the current Agreement on Agriculture and relevant clauses in other WTO agreements. Within an international policy framework that incorporated rules on agricultural production and trade of food this Convention would implement the concept of food sovereignty and the basic human rights of all peoples to safe and healthy food, decent and full rural employment, labour rights and protection, and a healthy, rich and diverse natural environment.

Source: Adapted from Peoples' Food Sovereignty 2001b: 7. For the complete statement please see <www.peoplesfoodsovereignty.org> (accessed Jan. 23, 2007).

Today we have kicked off a party where everyone gets a prize. Agriculture was one, but not the only key point in the end game. I do not know whether we have written trade history today. But I do know that history will remember these days in Doha, when the free world backed multilateralism by opposing isolationism, when developing and developed countries opted for trade instead of terrorism. (European Union 2001: 1)

The Economist (2001: 65–66) insisted that the Doha deal was a "big win for poor countries" and that "contrary to much conventional wisdom, the WTO is the poor countries' friend."

The winnings at Doha were not as straightforward as all that; indeed, the process and outcomes remained controversial and pointed to only a fragile recovery of the WTO. Even the E.U. Trade Commissioner Pascal Lamy described the Doha process as "medieval" (quoted in Bello 2001b). As *The Economist* (2001: 65) itself explained, in Doha the WTO was "saved from the oblivion to which a failure might have condemned it." A deal was struck only as a result of drawn-out, "tortured" negotiations that were interspersed with "last minute panics" triggered by recalcitrant India. Analysts from developing countries were more critical of what happened, how it happened, and why. Shukla (2001: 8) stated:

> What has happened in Doha is the beginning of the final assault of global capital on the economic sovereignty of the nation-states, particularly of the Third World.... One of the main contradictions of the times is the WTO. It has a façade of democratic structure and rules of functioning. It is at the same time a non-transparent, non-participative, and undemocratic institution. Its very birth was occasioned by the processes and motivations characterised by those attributes. It talks of one vote for one member and decisions by prescribed majorities. It never flinches from forcing the will of the two powerful capitalist entities on the unwilling and screaming majority of Third World countries. It swears by consensus, but it reaches the consensus by suppressing or ignoring dissenting voices. It markets its predatory designs in the name of liberalisation and freer exchanges. The fundamental reason why things happened the way they happened in Doha is our failure to recognise the contradiction and seize the opportunity that the contradiction itself provides to turn it upside down.

Social movements and NGOs, including the Vía Campesina, were among the few actors to publicly challenge the WTO on the undemocratic and discriminatory process leading up to Doha and to shed light on the manipulative tactics and continued lack of transparency exhibited at the Ministerial meeting itself.[7] Contrary to promises made to reform the very practices that precipitated the debacle in Seattle, the WTO had continued much as before. Charlene Barshefsky, a former U.S. trade representative who played an important role in the Singapore, Geneva, and Seattle WTO Ministerial meetings, said the WTO process "was a rather exclusionary one. All meetings were held between 20 and 30 key countries.... And that meant 100 countries were never in the room" (quoted in Bello 2000: 5). Walden Bello noted that in the attempts to reach consensus in Seattle, Barshefsky had threatened delegates with exclusion, stating,

> [I] have made very clear and I reiterated to all ministers today that, if we are unable to achieve that goal, I fully reserve the right to also use a more exclusive process to achieve a final outcome. There is no question about either my right as the chair to do it or my intention as the chair to do it. (quoted in Bello 2000: 5)

According to social movement and NGO representatives present in Doha, the initial drafts presented by the chairman of the General Council and the director general did not contain the concerns of many developing countries, even though many of them had presented concrete proposals and positions; no brackets or covering letter accompanied the drafts, thus giving the impression of consensus. In addition to the Green Room practice — which involved inviting carefully selected governments to hold "informal meetings" — six "friends of the chair" were appointed as facilitators to aid in reaching a consensus on the declaration. There were no stated criteria or process of selection of these "green men," and all but one came from the pro-new-round camp. Finally, some developing country delegates claimed that arm-twisting tactics such as threats to financial aid were used to win their support. In assessing the process and outcome, the Vía Campesina joined numerous organizations from around the world in denouncing the outcome of Doha as "Everything but Development" and once again rejecting the legitimacy of the WTO:

> The outcome of Doha, especially the Ministerial Declaration and the work programme, does not have public legitimacy....
>
> We condemn the non-transparent, discriminatory and rule-less or arbitrary methods and processes presided over by the WTO Director General and the Secretariat and directed by the major developed countries. Such behaviour and processes are particularly disgraceful for an international organization that boasts that its core principles are transparency, non-discrimination and the rule of law. We therefore commit ourselves to raise public awareness worldwide on the disastrous implications of the Doha outcome, and the processes of shame that produced the outcome. (Joint Statement of NGOs and Social Movements 2002: 3)

As the work of the Our World Is Not For Sale coalition demonstrates, resistance is becoming more organized, inclusive, sophisticated, and pro-active. Immediately following Doha the coalition gathered in Brussels to analyze the post-September 11 context and develop worldwide strategies for continuing WTO resistance and mobilization. This time the gathering included the active participation of the Vía Campesina and the World Forum of Fisher People together with the labour movement and NGOs. Concerted efforts were made to overcome existing imbalances, bridge differences, and explore effective ways of working more closely together. Despite increased security measures and the clamping down on dissent following September 11, coalition participants agreed that resistance would continue. As Tony Clarke from the Polaris Institute said when summarizing the results of a discussion on future strategies vis-à-vis the WTO: "We own the streets. Direct action remains a key element of our movements. They will not take the streets away from us."

The terrain of struggle is expanding to include not only continued resistance at the international level but also more work at the local and national levels. Contrary to mainstream media reports, opposition to globalization and liberalization is not restricted to only a few hundred fringe anarchists whose sole mission appears to be the destruction of property and grabbing media headlines. Movements working in coalitions are publicly distancing themselves from those who advocate violence. Peaceful opposition to the WTO has risen dramatically, and there are no signs that it will subside in the near future. As declared in the last line of the statement "Porto Alegre II: Call of Social Movements" — signed by thousands of representatives of social movements and NGOs who had gathered together with the four thousand representatives of the Vía Campesina in Porto Alegre in February 2002 — the "WTO, IMF and WB will meet somewhere, sometime. And we will be there!"

Persistent Power Struggles

These developments do not mean that all social movements and NGOs agree on strategies vis-à-vis the WTO and agricultural trade. Indeed, differences of opinion came to the forefront, and divisions became more pronounced, at the NGO/CSO Forum on Food Sovereignty held in conjunction with the World Food Summit: Five Years Later in Rome in June 2002. Essentially, a major struggle occurred over the conceptual framework for future action. On the one hand were those who believed in a reformist approach, which includes increasing market access for Southern countries; improving the WTO Agreement on Agriculture with the introduction of a "development box" to allow developing countries the option of protecting their farm sectors and staple crops to help ensure food security; and the adoption of an international code of conduct, convention, and/or covenant on the right to food. This position essentially accepts the idea that increasing international agricultural trade is beneficial; that it is an important strategy in improving the well-being of farming families and will thus alleviate hunger and poverty; and that the WTO's jurisdiction (albeit under fairer trading rules and more democratic governance) over agriculture and food can be maintained. (For example, see Oxfam International 2002; Christian Aid 2001.) Advocates of this position see working inside the WTO as an important site of struggle.

The Vía Campesina, together with other critical social movements and NGOs, adopts the more radical approach of food sovereignty, which, as Nettie Wiebe (2002) puts it, "is really a rescoping of the problem."

> Food sovereignty challenges the whole globalization agenda on the basis that you could achieve food sovereignty in local and regional areas, both in markets and governance and in resource access. This is by far the most imaginative and creative approach; it has the most potential to actually change the story. Food sovereignty is a much

broader concept that creates an environment or a framework that
is more conducive to the realization of the right to food.

A food sovereignty approach involves delegitimizing the WTO by taking
agriculture out of the WTO — or the Vía Campesina's more recent and
stronger demand of "taking the WTO out of agriculture" — in favour of
building alternative, more democratic, and transparent structures. It also
involves the ratification of an International Convention on Food Sovereignty
to govern food production and international agricultural trade. The logic
of delegitimization entails a refusal to participate in the WTO itself and
working on the outside at strategic times to mobilize collective action and
ultimately shift public opinion.

The idea of food sovereignty was first introduced by the Vía Campesina
at the World Food Summit in the NGO Forum on Food Security in 1996.
Indeed, one of the main reasons that the Vía Campesina refused to sign on
to the NGO Declaration was because it did not offer a real alternative; the
declaration was constrained within existing frameworks. According to Wiebe,
in refusing to accept the NGO Declaration, the Vía Campesina effectively
carved out a space for itself by putting the concept of food sovereignty on
the map. Interest in the concept spread quickly, and the idea was increasingly found in documents addressing different aspects of food security.
For example, European NGOs formed a Belgian-based Food Sovereignty
Platform specifically for advocacy around the issue of food sovereignty;
the concept was at the heart of discussions at the World Social Forum held
in Porto Alegre, Brazil, in January 2001; an international forum on food
sovereignty was organized in Havana in August 2001; and the Green Party
of the European Parliament held a three-day conference on the concept in
December 2001.

By the time of the WFS: Five Years Later, food sovereignty had become
the rallying cry for an increasing number of peasant organizations and social
movements around the world in search of alternatives to the WTO. This is
evidenced by — among other things — the development of the Our World Is
Not for Sale: Priority to People's Food Sovereignty — WTO out of Food and
Agriculture campaign and the results of the Strategy Workshop on Taking
WTO Out of Agriculture organized in July 24–26, 2001, in Penang, Malaysia.
Consequently, the Vía Campesina worked hard, along with other members of
the International Planning Committee responsible for organizing the NGO
Forum, to ensure that food sovereignty would frame deliberations at the
NGO/CSO Forum on Food Sovereignty in Rome in 2002. As the very name
of the forum suggested, and Forum outcomes entitled "Food Sovereignty:
An Action Agenda" indicate, the discussion had clearly moved beyond food
security to food sovereignty.

The concept of food sovereignty has now entered more official circles.
For example, Jacques Diouf, the director general of the FAO, communicated

the FAO's commitment to collaborate fully with civil society organizations and social movements on the food sovereignty action plan (FAO Director-General 2003). Reports to the Commission on Human Rights, submitted by the United Nations Special Rapporteur on the Right to Food, advocates food sovereignty as a way of ensuring people's rights to food and food security (Ziegler 2003: 21, 2004).

Yet how can we explain the resistance on the part of many NGOs to explicitly adopt a food sovereignty approach at the NGO/CSO Forum on Food Sovereignty? Wiebe suggests a number of possible reasons for this resistance. First, since the concept is relatively new, many NGOs simply did not completely understand its full breadth and scope. Prior to and since the WFS in 1996, many NGOs had adopted a (more restrictive) right to food discourse and worked long and hard on developing legally binding instruments to ensure the realization of the right to food at an international level. Considerable ground had been gained in this area, and the right to food was perceived by many as a realistic and realizable goal.

The Vía Campesina, on the other hand, had initiated international discussions on food sovereignty during its Second International Conference in Tlaxcala in April 1996. Subsequently it had spent six years elaborating the concept through consultations and debates at the local, national, regional, and international levels. Peasant and farm organizations clearly understood that nothing less than radical transformation was needed to stop the ongoing displacement, marginalization, repression, and persistent impoverishment of rural peoples. Reforming or "fixing" existing structures would do little to stop the increasing levels of hunger, depopulation, and environmental devastation in rural areas. By introducing food sovereignty, the Vía Campesina was clearly challenging everyone concerned to think outside of the boxes — technological fixes, liberalization, deregulation, and privatization — that often characterize policy deliberations about food and agriculture. In assessing the NGO/CSO dynamics, Wiebe says that by the WFS: Five Years Later in June 2002:

> We [the Vía Campesina] simply assumed because the NGO forum was called food sovereignty that this would be the central focus of discussion. The Vía Campesina just kept putting different elements of food sovereignty on the agenda. And, this is where the Vía Campesina was deemed to be strident and obnoxious in that we kept intervening in the workshops and presenting positions as if everyone knows that we are talking about food sovereignty, about taking agriculture out of the WTO.... For the Vía Campesina it was a major opening.

But, as she also pointed out, some NGOs were highly dissatisfied with the Vía Campesina's approach:

Suddenly they [NGOs] found that the language has shifted around them so that now the right to food was subsumed within a bigger, more comprehensive agenda of food sovereignty. Something that seemed realistic [the right to food] was suddenly subsumed under what seemed to many something quite unrealistic.

[Consequently,] some NGOs felt discomfited, displaced, really unhappy about the whole process. And, some felt threatened, frankly threatened. They felt uncertain, they felt like they had somehow been re-ordered into a category where they did not feel authentic and they really resented it....

The idea that the peasants who come off the land, who don't know what from what, will then demand all kinds of things which we all know institutionally are not even realistic.... It seems to me that there are some places where we should just look it in the eye and see that here are people who have finally, in one little venue arrived in a place in a big enough force and made up their minds that they are not going to take that. They are going to put something else on the table.

And, it was particularly awkward. In the official summit people can consign it immediately to the marginal. But in the NGO summit because there has been all this language of empowering people and people speaking for themselves, and giving voice to the marginalized and capacity building it was harder... to just consign it to the margin.

For some NGOs, it is extremely difficult (if not ideologically impossible) to give up the space they had long dominated. It was equally difficult for them to alter their carefully crafted strategies vis-à-vis the WTO, *even though* the major representative movement of peasants and small farmers had made its demands clear. According to Gustavo Capdevila (2002), two weeks after the NGO/CSO Forum on Food Sovereignty a number of NGOs "speak[ing] out on behalf of poor farmers" presented a petition to the WTO that sought the strengthening of the Agreement on Agriculture through the introduction of a development box.[8] It seems that at the final moment, once again, NGOs were convinced that they knew what was best for farming peoples.

This inside-outside struggle on future action again brought out the different aspects of the traditional practices characteristic of relations between NGOs and peasant organizations. For example, in commenting on the belligerent resistance of farmers' representatives to discuss the reformist approach in Rome, one NGO representative (who will remain anonymous) went so far as to suggest that these farmers simply were probably not real representatives, that they clearly didn't know what was best for their own good, and that they needed to be educated:

Given that they [those opposed] were not ready to discuss the views being put forward by Friends of the DB [Development Box], this silenced many voices who would have perhaps wished to contribute. That the DB calls for support for farmers, food security and rural development and yet this was being rejected by these groups calls into question whether they are really farmers talking for themselves or whether they are "representatives" of farmers who are sometimes out of touch with the situation on the ground and who do not always have the farmers' interests at heart. Farmers all over the world are calling for support for agriculture and the DB would be one such tool that would make it possible for governments to support farmers in developing countries....

I think that debate on the DB is still possible. But there is need for more sensitization of the DB, especially among FARMERS who are the ones that feel the pinch and are the main beneficiaries of the DB. *We may talk on their behalf*, we may even politicize issues (as this was partly the case in Rome) but for them, it's not politics. It's survival. (emphasis added)

The language and intent here are striking: Farmer and peasant representatives simply do not understand what is best for farmers. These "representatives" are, therefore, not legitimate. NGOs will continue to speak for farmers until more "sensitized" and legitimate farm representatives are identified — people who presumably understand that the "development box" and inclusion are what is best for them.

External forces spurred agrarian organizations in the North and South to build an international peasant and farm movement. The Vía Campesina's positions and strategies differed from other social actors involved in deliberations on agriculture, food, and trade at the international level, which helped the Vía Campesina to consolidate itself as a strong and united peasant voice. While IFAP and many NGOs believe that reforming the WTO is possible, for the Vía Campesina there is little option but radical transformation. This is a struggle in which Vía Campesina organizations have long been engaged and one to which they remain committed. Developing alternatives to globalization and the WTO is the very raison d'être of the Vía Campesina.

5. A Fine Balance: Local Realities and Global Actions

> But here is the key issue. *Que bien* (how wonderful) Seattle. How wonderful India in their struggle against Cargill and other transnationals. But what about the process of construction? How much have we advanced on that front? Yes, we are gaining experience, yes, there are confrontations, and yes, there are possibilities of building a global movement. But this doesn't depend on a global process. The consolidation of alternatives rests completely on what is happening at the local level, it depends on the development of organizations in their regions, in their countries. This gives viability to a global process. —Pedro Magaña Guerrero, former national peasant leader, UNORCA

Global forces seep down to the local level in a myriad of diverse ways. Local struggles, therefore, take different and sometimes unexpected shapes.

When I originally started thinking about how to do a book on farmers' struggles, my plan was to focus research on three different but key issues in three different locations: the efforts of peasant organizations to put in place a new law of rural development in Mexico, the struggle over genetically modified seeds in India, and efforts to maintain supply management and orderly marketing in Canada. As it turned out — even though I had consulted at considerable length with Vía Campesina leaders — when I went to Mexico to begin this work, farm leaders there stressed that looking at only one aspect of their work would seriously misrepresent what their organization was all about. It seemed that I needed a much broader research agenda. The Mexicans argued that if I truly wanted to understand how their organization worked at the national level, I should travel to various parts of their country and examine the issues, strategies, and alternatives being developed at the local level in response to the globalization of agriculture.

This shift in focus reinforced the idea that globalization takes diverse forms and depends on a specific context. You cannot study the global aspects of social movements in isolation from the local. As Ann Florini (2000: 218) puts it, "Global movements don't float free in a global ether." What I needed to understand in looking at the larger role of La Vía Campesina was this dialectical relationship between the local, the national, and the global.

The Significance of Local and National Organization

La Vía Campesina depends on strong local and national peasant organizations. Yet some of these organizations suffer from numerous problems — lack
of resources, weak leadership, regional and personal jealousies, ideological
splits, a declining or inactive membership base, and co-optation from governments and NGOs — that have afflicted rural organizations everywhere.
In many ways, the strength of national farm organizations depends largely
on how quickly they can deal with these kinds of problems and reposition
themselves in a rapidly changing environment.

The MST, the Vía Campesina Regional Co-ordinator for South America,
believes that completing the task of building and maintaining strong politicized national organizations in the context of the globalization of agriculture
is perhaps one of its most precious accomplishments. As João Stédile, leader
of Brazil's MST, says:

> By the simple fact of existing for 18 years, a farmers' movement
> [the MST] that contests the ruling class in this country can consider
> itself something of a triumph.... But maybe the greatest success is
> the dignity the Sem Terra farmers have won for themselves. They
> can walk with their heads held high, with a sense of self-respect.
> They know what they're fighting for. (quoted in *New Left Review*
> 2002: 91)

The MST has become one of the most influential and powerful social movements in Brazil partly due to its success in empowering local communities
through consciousness-raising, collective direct action such as land occupations, and establishing local economies. Meanwhile, it also concentrates on
winning over public opinion in urban areas and on developing a wide and
diverse network of allies at an international level.

Similarly, the Confédération Paysanne — a member of the Coordination
Paysanne Européenne (CPE), the Regional Co-ordinator of the Vía Campesina
for Europe — is gaining ground in France as it works more closely with
urban-based groups on issues of food safety, GMOs and campaigns against
malbouffe in favour of sustainable farming. José Bové and François Defour,
two of its leaders, define sustainable farming as "farming that respects the
farmer and meets the needs of society" by re-establishing direct links between
producers and consumers (Bové and Dufour 2001: 202). As Dufour (ibid.:
26–27) explains:

> Town-dwellers understand that an attack on the countryside and
> the quality of its produce is an attack on the relationship between
> the farmer, his land and the consumer....
>
> Agricultural identity is part of this: you don't have to be a
> farmer or live in the country to feel rooted in the land. Such roots

---

The Confédération Paysanne and McDonald's

In August 1999 farmers gathered at a rally in Millau, a small town in southwest France in the Larzac region, an area known for its Roquefort cheese. They were there to protest the U.S. government's retaliation against the European Union's refusal to comply with a WTO directive that allowed the importation of hormone-fed beef into Europe. In response to the E.U.'s stance the U.S. government had slapped a 100 percent customs surcharge on imports of Roquefort cheese to the United States. As a consequence of that surcharge exports had fallen dramatically, and farmers' incomes had plummeted. Both the French and European governments claimed that their hands were tied; farmers would not be compensated. The issue left farmers with no other recourse but to take direct action.

That day in Millau, members of a local sheep and milk producer organization and the Confédération Paysanne led a non-violent and symbolic action: the organizational dismantling of a McDonald's outlet still under construction. The group piled door frames and partitions onto tractor trailers and then, accompanied by children, women, farmers, and townspeople, began a procession that made its way to the office of the local government.

For farmers organized in the Confédération Paysanne, McDonald's was the perfect target: it represents the epitome of industrialized agriculture, economic imperialism, the power of transnationals, and *malbouffe.*

---

connect all parts of the country in a unifying whole, and this can't be undermined by Europe or globalization. The McDonald's issue came just at the right time to stir up such feelings. Even the most liberal economic milieux had to admit that the downgrading of agriculture and its appropriation by factories was [sic] destroying those roots. People don't want to be uprooted. This is essentially what public opinion boiled down to....

The Confédération Paysanne also garnered more support in the countryside, as evidenced by the results of elections to the Chambers of Agriculture; the organization's share of the vote rose from 21 percent in 1995 to 28 percent in 2000. The increasing national popularity of the Confédération Paysanne is undoubtedly also due to its charismatic spokesperson, José Bové, who first gained notoriety when he and his colleagues from the organization engaged in direct action by dismantling a McDonald's outlet in Millau, France.

No one could have predicted the impact that this single action would have, not only in France but also around the world, as the imprisonment of four farmers, including Bové, made headlines worldwide. Bové has since become something of a national hero, an international farm activist cum media star, and has often been a spokesperson for the Vía Campesina. His interviews with the likes of Mike Moore (former WTO director general) and

Hugo Chavez (president of Venezuela) are significant news events, as is his participation in human rights missions, social movement gatherings, and anti-globalization protests in, among other countries, Colombia, Mexico, Brazil, and Palestine.

But it would be a mistake to focus on Bové as an individual — the movement, after all, is not about one man. Rather, this high profile speaks more to the acuity with which the Confédération Paysanne successfully played the media to further the struggle to protect the interests of peasants and small farmers and build alternatives to corporate agriculture. Moreover, the Confédération Paysanne was extremely adept at capturing the interest of the growing global social justice movements and using its links to the Vía Campesina (through the CPE), other social movements, and NGOs around the world to publicize and garner support for its actions. Over 100,000 people (double the number of protesters at the "Battle of Seattle"), including leaders of the Vía Campesina, converged in Millau to witness the trial of the leaders of the Confédération Paysanne, who faced criminal charges for their action at McDonald's. As Bové and Dufour (2001) explain, the trial was symbolic; in reality it was globalization, the WTO, and *malbouffe* that were all on trial. The Confédération Paysanne uses non-violent direct actions to focus the public's attention, educate citizens on an issue, and foster public debate with the ultimate goal of shifting public opinion and mobilizing action. If the media insisted on personalizing issues and events — which it always does — the charismatic Bové could easily play this role, but without ever losing sight of the collective force he helped to build.

Globalization, however, systematically undermines farm organizations that advocate in favour of small-scale agriculture. Canada's Stuart Thiesson maintains that this tendency makes the maintenance of strong, coherent, national peasant and farm organizations a continuous struggle. As supportive agricultural policies give way to neo-liberal approaches, rural infrastructure and farmer-friendly marketing structures collapse and support programs are dismantled — leading to greater impoverishment and the subsequent depopulation of rural areas. Thiesson explains that those who do remain on the land are forced to seek off-farm work, thus greatly limiting the amount of time available to participate in farm organizations. Moreover, the demise of small-scale farms has been accompanied by the consolidation of larger farms, which in turn makes it increasingly difficult for an organization struggling to protect small-scale agriculture to recruit members. As a result many farm organizations have experienced a persistent decline in membership and reduced activity. The NFU's membership, for example, has fallen dramatically since the mid-1970s.

Perhaps more importantly, in many ways the nature of peasant and farmers' struggles has changed considerably. For instance, the NFU and its predecessor, the Saskatchewan Farmers Union, had fought long and hard with provincial and national governments to successfully build alternatives such as orderly marketing boards and supply management systems that worked in farmers' interests. With the NAFTA and WTO frameworks, these alternatives have consistently come under threat (Qualman 2002: 5).[1] Consequently the NFU is forced into a defensive position in which it spends precious resources primarily to protect existing programs. In a conversation with Nettie Wiebe, Winnie Miller, in her nineties and a long-time farm leader in Saskatchewan, explained that the shift from being a builder of alternatives to becoming a protector had undermined people's personal energy and the organization's morale. She was able to compare the struggles of earlier years to those of the 1990s:

> Times were much harder in that we were poorer, but times were much easier because we were working to build something, and there was all of that energy to build. And now… you have to try to protect what we built and it's almost a losing battle. How can people be enthusiastic and excited and forward-looking when the best they can achieve is to stay where they are, to protect what they have?

Thiesson agrees that the shift can lead to disempowerment:

> I suppose if you keep on losing battles all of the time, it makes it appear as though you are not effective. And that makes it difficult for you to go out and make claims of how relevant you are in terms of protecting the interests of farmers. So that's not an easy sell when you can say, well, come on and join us because we have lost all of these battles.

Furthermore, in the new global trade environment the Canadian Government, like most governments around the world, now faces considerable limitations in the types of programs and structures that it can establish in the agriculture sector. As globalization undermines the power of the state to define national policies, most farmers' organizations — which had developed considerable capacity in lobbying government officials — must also now find new ways of working.

Bringing the Global Back Home

To be effective the Vía Campesina must ensure that its international work is firmly rooted in local realities. Otherwise, it has little or no relevance for the peasant and farm organizations on whose behalf it speaks in the international arena. Perhaps just as importantly, the Vía Campesina's international efforts must also be brought back to the local level. In doing so, local organizations are strengthened. According to Víctor Suárez of ANEC,

> Through the Vía Campesina one feels part of an international or global effort for the defence of common concerns. You get the

sense that your organization and your work are shared with others in many countries. This is very important, this sense of being part of an international struggle around common objectives. It gives you strength, it gives you more confidence, it gives you more influence. Also, the perspective that you gain by having access to information about the international and global conjuncture from the logic of small producers everywhere — this generates a very important perspective of socialization during a process of globalization. If you have elements of the global situation you have tools for negotiation in your local struggles and in public policies in your own country — this is very valuable.

This drive for cohesion is more or less what happened, for example, when the NFU, after participating in numerous visits to different countries, eventually consolidated its international work by creating institutional linkages with the youth of WINFA in the Caribbean and the women of the UNAG in Nicaragua (see chapter 3). From 1993 to 1996 the NFU assisted ASOCODE in co-ordinating the Vía Campesina region encompassing Central America, North America, and the Caribbean by taking over the tasks of co-ordination and communication with organizations in English-speaking countries. Between 1996 and 2000 the NFU played a key leadership role in the Vía Campesina as a regional co-ordinator, member of the ICC, and co-ordinator of the Vía Campesina Women's Commission. It was also the Vía Campesina representative in the Sustainable Agriculture/Food Systems Caucus in the United Nations Commission on Sustainable Development. At the Third International Conference of the Vía Campesina in Bangalore the NFU was re-elected as one of the regional co-ordinators for the North American Region.

In repositioning itself in the context of increased globalization the NFU adopted a two-pronged strategy: it sought to strengthen its ties at the international level through the Vía Campesina; but, just as importantly, it determined that international work must be brought back home in concrete ways. Wiebe describes how this occurred:

It became clear to us that far from being a provincial or even a national matter, this was an international struggle we were engaged in and that was for us the impetus of moving towards the Vía Campesina. We had to find counterparts elsewhere in the world that also shared our clear objectives of protecting the countryside and the possibility of small-scale agriculture and farm communities and understanding what that was really worth. The challenge for the NFU now is to engage itself at that level in such a way that farmers at the local level see that as an avenue of possible re-empowerment. Through our connections in the Vía Campesina farmers genuinely and literally can feel that they have representative voices at the WTO in Seattle, for example, or at international forums like the World Food Summit. But it is also important that people who gather together in their local groups have spaces and places where they can have real conversations about what is affecting them. The power of local organization and community-based organization is that it does allow people to take some of that international and national information and experiences, and collectively make sense of it on the ground.

To ensure that the global would resonate at the local level, the NFU created the International Program Committee (IPC) in 1995.[2] As coordinator of the Oxfam Global Agriculture Project I facilitated the work of the IPC and witnessed, first-hand, how the NFU changed as it gained more international experience. Through the IPC, the National Farmers Union expanded its international and development education program beyond the national office and Saskatchewan, where most of the activities had previously been concentrated. It also democratized the program as regional representatives from across Canada became responsible for decision-making and implementation; NFU locals and districts were linked up to the IPC through IPC regional chairs. The IPC held two meetings a year to design and evaluate a program that would focus on the NFU's participation in the international arena and help to organize Vía Campesina delegation visits to Canada to meet with NFU members at the local level. The IPC was directly accountable to and advised the NFU National Board of Directors on all international actions. It developed criteria for the selection of NFU representatives to international meetings and organized events in which these representatives could bring their international experiences back to their rural communities. The NFU international program also involved conferences and workshops, and the regular distribution of updates to the membership — outlining, for instance, major international debates on agricultural trade and food security. The updates also kept the membership apprised of the positions and actions of the Vía Campesina. Through the IPC the UNAG-NFU Women's Linkage was expanded beyond Saskatchewan to include NFU women in Prince Edward Island. Delegations from Vía Campesina organizations from Central America, the Caribbean, or the Philippines met first with national NFU officials and then travelled to several provinces to meet with members at the local level.

Most importantly, through the IPC the NFU gained complete decision-making control over all aspects of its international work. This was a significant change from ten years earlier, when the goals, objectives, and itineraries of international visitors (including peasant leaders) coming to Canada were determined primarily by NGOs that had international rural development programs. Although NGO-directed tours often included meetings with NFU representatives, and these events certainly exposed the NFU leadership to other situations and realities, the meetings remained somewhat isolated and ad hoc events. Moreover, the activities were designed more to meet the NGOs' goals for fundraising and/or legitimizing their efforts than to fit into the NFU's agenda for social change in rural Canada. For the NFU, international work was an integral part of its long-term vision for social change; but international work only made sense if it was grounded in local realities and if the international debates were brought back to the local level in concrete ways. Consequently, the NFU sought to establish an international program on its own terms and in ways that met its needs more appropriately. (Interestingly, Mexico's UNORCA went through a similar process. Pedro Magaña explains that UNORCA's initial exposure to international issues and farm organizations from other countries was also mediated by NGOs; but that during debates around NAFTA, UNORCA sought to break the cycle of working only through NGOs and effectively established direct lines of communication with peasant organizations elsewhere.)

By expanding its work to various regions across Canada through the IPC, the NFU increased its level of activity considerably. In just a sixteen-month period (1996–97), for example, NFU actions included:

- a four-member delegation that participated in a working tour to Mexico hosted by UNORCA, leading to a joint NFU-UNORCA project submission to establish alternative trade ties with Mexican farmers organized in the two bodies;
- a representative from the Belizean Agricultural Producers Organization addressed an NFU convention, and three NFU members then travelled to Belize to participate in an exchange organized by Belizean Agricultural Producers Organization;
- two NFU representatives went to the Philippines to meet with members of the dKMP and to plan for the People's Summit and other Asia-Pacific Economic Co-operation Forum activities scheduled to take place in Vancouver in November 1997; and
- the NFU hosted a two-person delegation from the Cuban Asociacion Nacional de Agricultores Pequeños, who met with NFU representatives in three Canadian provinces (NFU International Program Committee 1997).

The NFU's efforts were recognized as being innovative, participatory and relevant to local and international struggles. In 1995 the women of the NFU in Saskatchewan won a Global Citizen Award from the Saskatchewan Council for International Cooperation and three years later the Canadian Council for International Co-operation awarded the NFU the International Co-operation Award for its work with the Vía Campesina and grassroots farmers.

The more the NFU worked with Vía Campesina organizations, the more radical its stances in Canada became. Wiebe says that although in Canada the NFU is often seen as "pushing the margins," in the international arena she is "constantly reminded of how conservative" the Canadian organization is. In that arena, she says, "I am constantly learning."

> Vía Campesina organizations are far more radical in their analysis than the NFU.... It took these peasant movements to say unequivocally that the WTO is a malicious agenda against small farmers everywhere, and that we want agriculture right out of the WTO. It took the Vía Campesina to say this in order to strengthen the NFU position here at home in terms of our critique of the WTO. I don't think we would have ever dared in our context to take such a position on our own. We would have been laughed right out of the room; it would have been such a marginal unlikely position here in Canada.

After the Vía Campesina, "backed by millions and millions of farming families," demanded that agriculture be taken out of the WTO, according to Wiebe, "It gave the position a lot more credibility and it gave us the confidence to be able to do that more radical analysis and make the same demand at home."

The Vía Campesina also had a radicalizing effect on the NFU's position on genetically modified foods. The NFU had fought, and lost, a long fifteen-year battle against the introduction of plant breeders' rights in Canada, which left the organization with little energy to reactivate the debate. However, the NFU was forced to further define its position as the struggle over intellectual property rights and GMOs intensified at the international level as a result of the TRIPs agreement. As regional co-ordinator of the Vía Campesina, the NFU found it increasingly difficult to justify supporting the Vía Campesina's international demands for a complete moratorium on the production, marketing, and distribution of GMOs (and derived products thereof) unless the NFU itself had a solid position on the matter. Wiebe says it was the work of some Vía Campesina organizations, such as the KRRS in India and the Confédération Paysanne in France — which were engaging in direct actions against transnationals to resist the entry of transgenic seeds — that gave the NFU the impetus to be more critical of Monsanto in Canada and to articulate a firmer position on the use of genetic modification in agriculture.

Defining an NFU policy on genetically modified technology was not easy. On the one hand, some NFU members were completely opposed to its use in agriculture and food. On the other hand, as NFU vice-president Terry Boehm says, some NFU members had completely bought into the technology and as a result had altered their production systems. NFU women, in recognition of the organization's involvement in the Vía Campesina, had commissioned a policy discussion paper on agriculture and biotechnology in 1996 (Roppel 1996), but it was not until November 2000 that the NFU (NFU 2000b: 2) finally articulated a policy on genetically modified food, demanding, among other things, "a moratorium on the production, importation, distribution and sale of GM food until questions regarding consumer acceptance, human health, environmental implications, technology ownership, and farmer profitability are answered to the satisfaction of the majority of Canadians." As the Vía Campesina had previously argued, the policy declared, "'Terminator,' 'Traitor,' and similar Genetic Use Restriction technologies, along with the WTO's Trade-Related Aspects of Intellectual Property Rights (TRIPs) agreement, restrict farmers' right to save, trade and reuse seed. Thus, they are unacceptable."

UNORCA — Managing Diversity

The UNORCA leaders I talked to in Mexico described many of the same concerns that were raised by the NFU around the difficulties of organizing in the neo-liberal era. In light of the counter-reforms encompassed in market-assisted land reform programs, peasant organizations in many developing countries find themselves in a defensive mode in their struggles to defend the often deeply flawed agrarian reforms that were introduced in the 1970s and 1980s. Luis Meneses, a UNORCA executive co-ordinator states:

> The rural scene has changed substantially yet we want to organize like we used to in the past.... Changes are occurring so rapidly and are so extensive that farmers' organizations lack the capacity to control or influence the extent and speed of change. This is what lies behind the crisis in the peasant movement in Mexico. We are all in a defensive position, responding to the *embate* (violence, beatings, or blows) of the free market and the *embate* of the TNCs.

Neo-liberal globalization has led to rapid and dramatic change in the Mexican countryside, thus forcing UNORCA to rethink how it organizes.[3] For example, the *ejido*, once UNORCA's main organizational unit at the community level, is being dismantled in some states. Throughout the 1980s UNORCA focused on controlling various aspects of production and marketing by forming associations and co-operatives. With economic liberalization these small units simply cannot compete, and many have gone bankrupt.

The rapid change in policies was not met by equally rapid shifts in strategies on the part of farm organizations. Some organizations lost their focus, while others continued trying to find a way forward. Alberto Gómez of UNORCA says the group has found it increasingly difficult to organize in the countryside as a result of the social disintegration of the family:

> Not only is the *ejido* being dismantled in many areas by the restructuring of agriculture and the economy in general. It is also leading to disintegration of the most intimate of the social fabric, the family.

This is a important process of disintegration that is leaving us with a demobilized countryside, a paralyzed countryside, a dispersed countryside.

Given this situation, according to Gómez, UNORCA is concentrating its efforts on strengthening the organization. It now directs more resources to the formation of new leaders and leadership capacity-building at the local and regional levels so that community-based organizations are better equipped to work on locally based development alternatives. Suárez of ANEC points out that some people have criticized UNORCA for not participating in major national mobilizations and campaigns, for not being in the media — essentially for no longer being as visible and active as it was in the past. But Gómez argues that the viability, the very raison d'être, of UNORCA depends exclusively on the extent to which it is connected to the local and regional organizations and represents their interests at the national level. Rogélio Alquisiras Borgos, one of the co-ordinators of the Society for Social Solidarity of the Titekite Sanzekan Timeme in Guerrero, put it like this:

> The UNORCA serves us in many ways: it keeps us informed, it provides training, we learn of other experiences from around the country, and it gives us representation at a national level. The regional organizations, well, they are the *carne de su carne y sangre de su sangre* [flesh of our flesh and the blood of our blood]. The UNORCA would have no meaning if there were no regional organizations. The experiences and projects all take place at the local level. The concrete expression of alternative regional development occurs here at the local and regional levels.

In addition to institutional strengthening and leadership capacity-building, UNORCA and its affiliates have adopted numerous diverse and multi-pronged strategies in efforts to keep people on the land and improve the well-being of rural communities. The strategies differ from region to region and from organization to organization. For example, as Ernesto de Guevara Ladrón of the national office explains, in Chiapas UNORCA organizations are working primarily on issues of agrarian reform, indigenous self-government, management of natural resources, and human rights. In Michoacán, the local UNORCA organization has created a commercial business organization that pools fruit for export to the United States. In the process the organization has acquired an entrepreneurial vision, knowledge, and experience, and the local community now exhibits greater economic stability through increased employment. In Quintana Roo the Organizacíon de Ejidos de Productores Forestales de la Zona Maya is involved in agro-forestry projects involving the concept of the *milpa mejorada*. Women's groups there create and market arts and crafts, and the organization is now exploring the viability of ecotourism. In Guerrero UNORCA organizations produce arts and crafts and organic coffee for the fair trade-market. Magaña explains that at the national level UNORCA is now working with other peasant organizations, as a member of a national platform of farm organizations where it attempts to *"unorquizar"* (in true postmodern fashion, making a verb of their organization) the right-wing farm organizations to press for more equitable rural programs.

UNORCA fully recognizes that although globalization has undermined the power of the Mexican government, the state remains a key point of reference. As Servando Olivarria Saavedra, regional co-ordinator of UNORCA in Sinaloa, says:

> We can't put aside the work that needs to be done at the national level. We need to continue our internal struggle here in Mexico because there are many issues in the Law of Rural Development and other public policies that are uniquely and exclusively the re-sponsibility of our national government. Yes, some issues are now dictated by international organizations, but we need to constantly pressure our government so that those international institutions start from the point of view of the national. To stop working at the national level... I don't think so. We need to be at the international level, like we were at the WTO meeting in Seattle, but we cannot let go of the national. We have to be everywhere!

Finally, in 1997, as democratic space opened in Mexico, UNORCA leaders entered the electoral process by running for different parties to gain seats at the local, state and federal levels. From January to April 2000, five national UNORCA leaders were elected to the national and state congresses. In the state of Sonora alone, UNORCA leaders won four municipal presidencies, one federal position, and three state legislators (Molina 2000: 8). This strategy, as Magaña explains, was aimed at defining a new relationship between the state and peasant organizations to ensure that rural issues and the rural constituencies and their interests were put on the political agenda. In this way peasant organizations might gain more access to and control over the distribution of resources available for rural communities.

UNORCA members are conscious that they are new to the game of elec-toral politics, and they recognize the need to look carefully at the impact of this political strategy on the organization as a social movement. Another concern is the extent to which the strategy has helped UNORCA to influence implementation of progressive rural policies. Luis Meneses, one of the five national UNORCA leaders who won a seat in the Mexican Congress, told me that because of disenchantment with their experience within existing par-ties some UNORCA leaders were considering forming an alternative political party. Magaña, who also won a federal seat, asks:

> What have we learned from this? What has been the relationship between the peasant organization and the government where we

have succeeded in gaining local power? All of our principles, like autonomy, for example, what happens now that a UNORCA leader is the president of the municipality? Suddenly we have a key leader of the UNORCA in the municipal administration, but this leaves a huge hole in the leadership of the local organization because we have not been able to fill those spaces. What kind of relations — of critique, recognition, support — from the government to the organization and vice versa do you end up with? How do you support the actions of the government from the peasant organization, and how does the government support the peasant organizations?

Thus UNORCA continues to struggle with the multitude of tasks that its work demands. Its members feel the need to fight on many different fronts. Certainly, these tasks might be easier, more manageable, if the organization were to centralize decision-making and improve its national strategies, to dilute diversity in the name of efficiency. But if it did so it would ultimately and fatally weaken itself; it would no longer, then, truly represent the diverse interests of its members.

UNORCA brings together an estimated 2,700 organizations — these are unions of *ejidos*, production co-operatives or associations, and rural associations — with a total membership of over 400,000 affiliates (Molina 2000: 3). The fifteen years of experience that it has gained in building and maintaining unity among such diversity remains an invaluable gift to the Vía Campesina.

The Power of Domestic Conflicts

Other organizations have not been so successful at managing diversity at the national level. Conflicts and divisions occurring at the national level have come into play in the life of the Vía Campesina when organizations have attempted to use the international arena to gain leverage in a domestic dispute. The earliest of these was the split within the Kilusang Magbubukid ng Pilipinas in late 1993.[4] The split, first of all, raised issues about representation from the Philippines in the Vía Campesina, especially given the 1993 election, at the Mons conference, of the KMP as the regional co-ordinator for Asia. Some four months later a number of KMP leaders, who were among the founding members of the Vía Campesina, went on to form the Demokratikong Kilusang Magbubukid ng Philipinas. The remaining leaders of the KMP subsequently approached the Vía Campesina to challenge the dKMP's legitimacy as representatives of the Filipino peasant movement (KMP 1994). After hearing from both sides, the Vía Campesina leadership resolved that the dKMP should continue to participate in the ICC until elections could be held at the next international conference. Furthermore, the ICC clarified:

Great care has to be taken not to let national issues and conflicts to be drawn into the Vía Campesina. Neither can the Vía Campesina "intervene" in national domestic issues. The Vía Campesina wants to open the space for many organizations to join the Vía Campesina. The divisions between the peasant movement in the Philippines can only be resolved by the Filipinos. However, the Vía Campesina... must discuss the Filipino issues as far as how they relate to the work of the Vía Campesina. (Vía Campesina 1995: 3)

In the meantime, though, the dKMP and the KMP were unable to reconcile their differences — indeed, they were unable to work together — and the conflict greatly hampered the Vía Campesina's preparatory work leading up to the Second International Conference and NGO Parallel Forum, leading to a postponement and relocation from the Philippines to Mexico. The persistent conflict also meant that neither organization was elected as regional co-ordinator. Instead, the region designated this responsibility to the Assembly of the Rural Poor in Thailand.

Another concern for the Vía Campesina was an internal crisis within the KRRS in India. As regional co-ordinator for South Asia, the KRRS was scheduled to host the Third International Conference of the Vía Campesina in October 2000. Throughout the year preceding the conference Vía Campesina leaders received several communications from former KRRS members who had been expelled from the organization. These letters appeared to be geared specifically to discrediting the KRRS president, M.D. Nanjundaswamy, in the international arena. Based on its experience with the Filipino case, the Vía Campesina largely ignored the issue, deciding that it was clearly internal to the KRRS and not Vía Campesina business.

In the end, however, the internal KRRS conflict did spill into the Vía Campesina. The International Forum on Globalization, whose vice-chair at the time was Vandana Shiva, aligned itself with the dissenting KRRS faction to organize the International Seed Tribunal and a major farmers' rally just days prior to, and in the same location as, the Vía Campesina's international conference. The International Seed Tribunal was organized to run concurrently with and in opposition to the Seed 2000 Forum, a major international event seeking to promote the further introduction of biotechnology in agriculture. It seemed quite odd that a progressive NGO deeply concerned about the plight of the world's farmers had not sought the full collaboration of the Vía Campesina in planning a gathering focused on the protection and enhancement of genetic resources and the threats posed by transnationals. Interestingly but not surprisingly, while the International Forum on Globalization had invited farm leaders such as the Confédération Paysanne, National Family Farm Coalition, and the NFU to participate as representatives of their national organizations, the press coverage surrounding the event clearly referred to them as representatives of the Vía Campesina (*The New*

Indian Express 2000: 4), thus giving the impression that the Vía Campesina as an organization supported both the meeting and the dissident groups.

The internal conflict within the KRRS, combined with the increasingly visible differences among the two renowned Indian activists, led to tension within the Vía Campesina. Nanjundaswamy advised Vía Campesina organizations to boycott the International Seed Tribunal, and those who did choose to attend the Tribunal were later informed that they would receive no logistical assistance to get to the site of the Vía Campesina Conference. However, some Vía Campesina organizations, such as the NFFC, had already worked with and established good relations with the International Forum on Globalization. Dena Hoff, the NFFC representative to the Vía Campesina, says the NFFC believed that the Seed Tribunal should hear about the negative experiences of U.S. farmers with Monsanto as a way of encouraging further resistance to the introduction of genetically modified seeds into India. Moreover, NFFC members did not want to be forced into taking sides on an issue that they knew little about, and that at a distance appeared to be a personality conflict between two internationally known Indian activists. After seeking clarification (and not receiving any adequate responses) from the International Forum on Globalization, the NFU's Nettie Wiebe ultimately chose not to attend the International Seed Tribunal. Given a situation in which it appeared that peasant organizations were being used to score points, Wiebe expressed, in a letter to Nanjundaswamy, the frustrations felt by many others:

> I cannot support any initiative which appears to catapult the internal India disputes into the international arena with the potential of damaging the effectiveness of such international networks of progressive activists as we have to date been able to build. I sincerely hope that the issues can be resolved within your organizations in India without external intervention or aggravation. (Wiebe 2000: 1)

National Level Tensions and Responsibilities

Gatekeepers and bottlenecks also exist at the national level. Pedro Magaña explains that if the Vía Campesina wants to grow it has to develop relationships directly with the state-level organizations rather than working only at the national level:

> There is also a tendency within organizations to concentrate power and opportunities, which ultimately makes some individuals more indispensable than others. You really have to socialize the international relationship so that it will ultimately help to strengthen the national organization. As more people gain international experiences, this helps broaden internal discussions as they bring back other visions and other points of view.

La Vía Campesina acknowledges the great need to "socialize" the movement beyond those who have the opportunity to participate in its conferences, delegations, or actions, or those who represent the Vía Campesina in international events. While some Vía Campesina organizations have put great effort into socializing the Vía Campesina from the national to the local, others have not. For the Vía Campesina to mean anything at the local level ultimately depends on the existence of democratic decision-making structures and participatory mechanisms of its national organizations. Clearly, if the aim of the Vía Campesina is to help strengthen its member organizations, the movement as a whole cannot bypass the national to go directly to the local. That work is the responsibility of national organizations themselves.

Sometimes it is easier to work with organizations far away than with those nearby, in your own territory. The case of Mexico provides an example of the difficulties that the Vía Campesina faces at the national level. As a result of the Second International Conference held in Tlaxcala, five Mexican organizations joined the Vía Campesina.[5] Throughout their history these organizations have worked together with varying degrees of intensity on different issues. But in the late 1990s one of them, UNORCA, turned inward to focus more intensely on internal strengthening at the expense of maintaining strong ties to the others. This organizational strategy, of course, altered UNORCA's ability to co-ordinate Vía Campesina work among Mexican organizations; leading to far less communication, consultation, and collaboration. As Suárez, of ANEC, remarks:

> Certainly the problem is that at the national level the Vía Campesina organizations do not engage in joint work. We don't have the perspective of working together even though theoretically we do share similar orientations and agenda. We have never worked together — not for a Mexican project.... There is no communication, no relation and no co-ordination of the organizations that belong to the Vía Campesina in Mexico. If the link is supposed to be the UNORCA that calls us to tell us that there will be a meeting of the Vía Campesina and that there will be a discussion of a certain position... never. When the Canadian [a CUSO sponsored staff position based in the UNORCA office] was in Mexico there was a link but this was really an external connection that carried out this function on behalf of the regional co-ordinator, the NFU, or the Operational Secretariat... but the link was not internal to Mexico and it was not established by Mexican organizations.

Part of the problem came from a lack of resources: the NFU, as North American regional co-ordinator, simply did not have sufficient resources to do an effective job of co-ordination within the region as a whole and also within Mexico. Consequently the NFU worked successfully with UNORCA to secure a staff position with the expectation that the Mexican organization could then handle communication and co-ordination within the country. In doing so it did not take into account the very real possibility of national-level tensions and conflicts among the Mexican organizations. The NFU, as an outsider, had no way of understanding or handling tensions that were the result of historical experiences, jockeying for position in national agrarian struggles, differences in political strategies, outside intervention, or personality conflicts. Some of these factors were certainly at the heart of the rising tension between ANEC and UNORCA during this period.

According to Pedro Magaña, another factor leading to the lack of co-ordination at the national level in Mexico was that UNORCA was unaware of any clearly defined expectations, obligations, and responsibilities in its role as "informal" Mexican co-ordinator. All of this changed considerably once UNORCA was formally elected at the Third International Conference as one of the regional co-ordinators. Since then co-ordination and communication among the Mexican organizations seems to have improved.

The Mexican experience points to a number of major issues for the functioning of an international movement. First, if one of the basic aims of the Vía Campesina is to articulate a united international movement, how are we to understand a lack of solidarity, co-operation, and collaboration at either the local or national levels? Suárez argues:

> This puts into question the very principles of the Vía Campesina. In reality the issue really rests with the Mexican organizations. The best-case scenario is that we will someday create a kind of Vía Campesina within Mexico — that is, a process of national convergence and national action that expresses Mexican characteristics, that generates strategies of exchange and solidarity, constructs moments and spaces for co-ordination of action on the same issues that the Vía Campesina is addressing — all the while respecting each organization's identity, autonomy, spaces, and leadership.

Although the Vía Campesina certainly cannot force national organizations to work together, what if any is the Vía Campesina role — when tensions and conflicts do flare up at the national level? In the past the Vía Campesina has consistently shied away from "meddling" at the national level. Yet national conflicts, tensions, and differences can and do have an impact on the Vía Campesina at an international level — as in the case with the conflict between the dKMP and the KMP. The lack of co-ordination and communication also certainly limited the Vía Campesina in Mexico, at least temporarily.

Ultimately the Mexican organizations did end up working on a joint project. When faced with further liberalization in the countryside as per the agriculture chapters of NAFTA, all five Mexican Vía Campesina organizations coalesced in a strong coalition called El Campo no Aguanta Más, which led over two months of mobilization and subsequent negotiation with the

Mexican government. Although numerous factors led to the formation of this coalition, the organizations' international experiences, gained through their participation in La Vía Campesina and CLOC, were a contributing factor. Another major contributing factor was UNORCA's years of experience in managing the different interests of its own membership, which helped it to be a key leader within the El Campo no Aguanta Más.

Local Realities and Global Actions

The transformational potential of the Vía Campesina rests on the way in which it directs its actions at all levels — local, national, regional, and international. But as its organizations engage in collective action within their national boundaries, they do so with the knowledge that they are connected to the actions of organizations of men and women half a world away. As Wiebe explained:

> The difficulty for us, as farming people, is that we are rooted in the places where we live and grow our food. The other side, the corporate world, is globally mobile. This is a big difficulty for us. But our way of approaching it is not to become globally mobile ourselves, which is impossible. We can't move our gardens around the world. Nor do we want to. The way in which we've approached this is to recognize there are people like us everywhere in the world who are farming people, who are rooted, culturally rooted, in their places. And what we need to do is build bridges of solidarity with each other which respect that unique place each of us has in our own community, in our own country. These bridges will unite us on those issues or in those places where we have to meet at a global level. (quoted in Arcellana 1996: 10)

Building these bridges has required the recognition of key issues around which all members of the Vía Campesina, no matter where they were located, can organize.

Following numerous discussions within and among its eight regions, the Vía Campesina began to focus its work on eight key themes that resonate at the local, national, and global levels: food sovereignty, agrarian reform, genetic resources and biodiversity, human rights, gender and rural development, developing a sustainable peasant agricultural model, migration (urban/rural and international), and farm workers' rights (Vía Campesina 1998b, 2001b). The movement recognizes that each of these issues might not be a preeminent concern in all locales or for all Vía Campesina members. What is important is that all regions of the Vía Campesina acknowledge the validity and importance of these issues for peasants around the world and dedicate themselves to supporting struggles around these themes.

Historically, peasant and farm organizations have been most successful in bringing about change when they have made community-oriented issues a national concern. Perhaps the most important of these issues has been agrarian reform. Indeed, for most existing peasant and farm organizations it is the issue of access to land and security of tenure that has fuelled peasant activism — at the community and national levels — and led the cry for social justice in the countryside. This focus remains, but in view of the dramatic globalization of the agricultural economy, peasant organizations have also recognized the need to make community issues, such as agrarian reform and access to resources (seeds, credit, technology, markets, and water, for instance) not only national but also international concerns.

As one way of making this happen, on October 12, 1999, the Vía Campesina, together with an international human rights organization, the Food and Information Action Network (FIAN), launched the Global Campaign for Agrarian Reform. Under the campaign banner "Food, Land and Freedom," peasants joined human rights activists in twelve countries from Asia, the Americas, and Europe in mobilizations, land occupations, and other public events to demand the right to land and security of land tenure as a prerequisite to the human right to food as stipulated in Article 11 of ICESCR (Vía Campesina 1999a). The Global Campaign for Agrarian Reform involves work on a number of different fronts: support to organizations involved in national struggles for agrarian reform; exchanges between peasant organizations to examine the particular nature of struggle over land in various countries; lobbying governments and international institutions; and establishing an emergency network to facilitate international intervention in cases of human rights abuses in conflicts over land.

To provide background information for the annual meetings of the U.N. Commission on Human Rights,[6] the Vía Campesina began publishing an annual report highlighting various cases of violations of peasants' rights. For instance, *Violations of Peasants' Human Rights: A Report on Cases and Patterns of Violence 2006* discusses how representatives from Bangladesh, Indonesia, and Thailand were treated while they were detained and interrogated by the Hong Kong police during the sixth Ministerial meeting of the WTO held in Hong Kong in December 2005. The annual reports provide much-needed documentation of human rights abuses that peasant communities experience in their struggle for land, natural resources, and protection of biodiversity. They also support the Vía Campesina's efforts to secure an international charter or declaration on peasant rights.

April 17th — International Day of Peasant Struggle

The Vía Campesina's work, and growth — by necessity harvested from seeds rooted in the specifics of community and location — necessarily entail something of an intricate balancing act: with respect for the autonomy of each organization posited against the need for international co-ordination and collective action.

A key impetus for work in the sphere of transnational co-ordination came on the eve of the movement's Second International Conference, held in Tlaxcala in 1996. In Brazil, on April 17 — the day before the conference was to open — police had opened fire on a large group of demonstrators in the small city of Eldorado do Carajas in the northern state of Para, killing nineteen peasants (members of the MST). The Vía Campesina representatives from over sixty-nine farm organizations from thirty-seven different countries who had gathered for the conference in Mexico were quick to respond. They marched on the Brazilian Embassy in Mexico City denouncing the murders and demanding that the Government of Brazil conduct a full investigation to ensure that the perpetrators be brought to trial. Vía Campesina leaders later met with the Brazilian ambassador, who agreed to a future meeting with the president of Brazil. Several months later the Vía Campesina sent a delegation to meet with the government officials and the president of Brazil to discuss the status of the investigation.

In commemoration of the nineteen slain Brazilian peasants, the Vía Campesina declared April 17th an International Day of Peasant Struggle (in Spanish, "el Día Internacional de Lucha Campesina") against all forms of oppression of rural peoples — an event geared to highlight human rights abuses in the countryside and to focus the world's attention on the demands of farming families around the globe. Over the following years the number of organizations that participated in various events that day increased substantially. On April 17, 2000, for instance, hundreds of thousands of European, Central American, Mexican, Brazilian, Thai, and Indian peasants and farmers participated in some form of public action within their national borders.

Yet, in some ways, over the early years the April 17th actions remained a limited collective endeavour: each region was encouraged to mobilize, each was free to choose the focus of collective action, and the Vía Campesina Operational Secretariat would then simply report on these different actions. After the Tlaxcala conference the Vía Campesina consistently stated its desire to work in coalition with other movements to build a global movement aimed at transforming the neo-liberal agenda, but the organization showed few signs of moving forward in this area. It remained, in many ways, in a self-limiting phase, focusing on creating and defining a space for itself — a distinct, unique space that could be filled with peasant voices — and building from within. It was a time of institution-building and strengthening. The Vía Campesina could reach out to work with other sectors only after it became a more confident and mature movement.

A turning point in transnational focus and participation came in 2001, beginning with the World Social Forum in Porto Alegre, Brazil (January 26–29, 2001), where the Vía Campesina worked as part of the Social Forum organizing committee and also held workshops on three themes: the struggle against GMOs in favour of farmer seeds, the WTO and food sovereignty, and the articulation of farmers' struggles. By the end of the World Social Forum

The Massacre at Eldorado do Carajas

On April 17, 1996, according to information provided by the MST, Brazilian military police opened fire on a group of 1,500 people who were on a march to Belem, the capital of Para, to demand a legal resolution to a land occupation that over 4,000 people had carried out on the Fazenda Macaxeira (in the territory of Curionopolis) — some 650 kilometres from their planned destination. Under the pretext of ensuring that the marchers would not disrupt traffic, the Governor of Para sent in a battalion of 2,000 well-armed soldiers. When the demonstrators refused to get off the road the police opened fire, killing nineteen peasants and wounding thirty more.

The Brazilian government showed little interest in bringing the perpetrators of this brutal and repressive act to trial. The MST, through its presence and actions at the national level together with its strong international connections, persistently demanded that justice be administered. This pressure meant that the Brazilian authorities could not simply brush the issue aside. Legal procedures did begin in early 1997, but questionable methods and decisions by the authorities meant that no one was brought to trial. The MST took the case to the U.N. Commission on Human Rights for review, and in February 2000 the Commission notified the Chief Justice of Brazil that various aspects of the legal procedures were unacceptable. The U.N. Commission on Human Rights also encouraged the Organization of American States to examine the case.

In 2002 a sentence was finally handed down to one of the three police officers involved. However, none of the local authorities who were responsible, including the Governor of Para, the Secretary of Public Security, and the Chief of the military police were brought to justice.

over 184 organizations had committed themselves to supporting the Vía Campesina's international day of struggle. The Vía Campesina had broadened participation in the April 17th activities beyond its own Campesina organizations.

At that point the Vía Campesina began a concerted effort to focus the April 17th actions on the key issue of food sovereignty. The idea was to mount a unified campaign against low-priced food imports (dumping) and the introduction and imposition of genetically modified or transgenic seeds. The ICC prepared a succinct list of Vía Campesina demands and encouraged all participating organizations to approach their national governments and to urge those governments to develop food and agricultural policies based on the principle of food sovereignty. In February 2001 the Vía Campesina installed a website <viacam17april@yahoogroups.com> to promote April 17th as a day of worldwide mobilization and to facilitate discussion on strategies and actions. The e-group not only provided a forum for Vía Campesina organizations to share information about April 17th initiatives, but also clearly demonstrated the kind of broad support that the movement was garnering.

It is no accident that this broadening of support occurred in Brazil. Certainly, the MST's influence and leadership made a distinct contribution, because one of that organization's most successful strategies is to work cross-sectorally for social change in Brazil. As João Pedro Stédile stated in his address to the fourth congress of the MST in August 2000, social change can only be accomplished not by a vanguard group or party, but through the unity of forces and the hard work of organizing at the local level. Stédile argued:

> It is a long road that will be built by uniting forces among all people, not by one group of intellectuals insisting that it is the work of millions. It is not the MST, nor a single political party, rather it is the people organized into a large popular force that will effect change.... The work entails returning to work at the base, prioritizing political formation of our militants, implementing the pedagogy of example in daily practice and consolidating popular consultation with the aim of transforming existing forces to introduce political, social and economic change. (quoted in *ALAI-Amlatina* 2000: 1–2)

For Vía Campesina the combination of a more focused campaign around April 17th and the willingness to reach out to its allies led to more public activities after 2001. In some cases Vía Campesina organizations worked together among different regions. For example, the National Family Farm Coalition (in the United States) and the CPE issued a joint press release condemning the European Common Agricultural Policy (CAP) and the American Freedom to Farm Bill as anti-farmer, while urging their governments to adopt the concept of food sovereignty. The NFU-Canada worked together with CLOC in organizing a Farmers' Forum in Quebec City to voice peasant and farm leaders' promotion of food sovereignty and rejection of the Free Trade Agreement of the Americas (FTAA). However, in most cases Vía Campesina organizations mobilized at the local and national levels with peasants engaging in various forms of collective action — ranging from demonstrations, media work, workshops, and conferences to meetings with policy-makers to discuss alternative proposals of agricultural development — in a wide range of countries. In France alone the Confédération Paysanne and allies organized over fifty demonstrations — including going into supermarkets and putting stickers on foods known to contain GMOs.

On April 17th, 2002, farmers around the world — joined by an increasing number of urban-based non-governmental organizations, environmentalists, and human rights activists — once again made the news. In great numbers they took to the streets, engaged in land occupations, filled auditoriums and local halls, and organized public meetings and press conferences. They held briefings with governmental officials and did teach-ins. Vía Campesina organizations (and allies) in over thirty countries engaged in collective actions in their continuing struggle against the imposition of genetically modified technology. In the Netherlands, Vía Campesina leaders from Indonesia and Bangladesh joined Dutch farmers and activists from the international network Resistance is Fertile to "alter" a genetically modified seed test site and convert it into a sustainable biodiversity site. In Austria, as the government held public discussions on biotechnology and food, farmers there presented hundreds of potted forget-me-nots to members of parliament to remind politicians of the 1.2 million people who had signed the Austrian referendum against gene technology some five years earlier. The NFU and the National Family Farm Coalition announced that they were exploring joint actions to ban the introduction of Monsanto's genetically modified wheat (NFFC and NFU 2002). In 2002 throughout the Americas farmers and activists, spurred by the news of the genetically modified seed contamination of corn in Mexico, engaged in a week-long continental campaign against GMOs.[7] In some countries, such as Guatemala and Brazil, the struggle over seeds is fought alongside the struggle for land. In Guatemala, by nightfall on April 17, 2002, indigenous peasant organizations had occupied fourteen *fincas* (large private landholdings) covering over 5,076 hectares. The land occupations involved over 1,250 peasant families. In Brazil, land occupations and demonstrations in support of continuing land occupations took place in nine states.

The April 17, 2002, actions also protested the continuing repression of farm leaders. A Vía Campesina press release of April 17 that year listed the names of peasant leaders (and their organizations) who had been imprisoned in the Philippines, Colombia, Brazil, Bangladesh, Indonesia, France, and Bolivia for their struggle over productive resources. It also demanded that the perpetrators of massacres of peasant families that had occurred in Brazil and Colombia be brought to trial. Two months later the Vía Campesina's calls for justice were brought to the fore again. On June 8, 2002, just prior to the opening of the World Food Summit: Five Years Later, thousands of people from a variety of civil society organizations marched in the streets of Rome under the banner of "Land and Dignity!... Food Sovereignty for All!" to denounce the human rights abuses and repression suffered by peasants, farmers, indigenous peoples, and workers.

Rooted Locally — Working Globally

When the Vía Campesina was first formed it concentrated much of its resources on strengthening itself internally. It defined participatory and inclusive structures for communication, consultation, and co-ordination. Exchanges among participating organizations, regional meetings, international conferences, and organizing Vía Campesina delegations to international events were all critical to fostering an understanding of each other's realities and establishing common ground. Only then was the Vía Campesina confidently able to identify, analyze, and articulate positions on the common issues facing farming families everywhere.

Once the Vía Campesina had consolidated itself internally it began to reach out strategically to establish alliances with other progressive social movements, NGOs, and research institutions that shared a similar vision. It played a key role in bringing peasants' and farmers' perspectives to transnational networks such as the Our World Is Not for Sale coalition, the Alliance on Agricultural Research, groups working on patents and genetic resources, and the NGO International Planning Committee of the FAO World Food Summit: Five Years Later (Vía Campesina 2003a). It helped to create new networks like the Agri-Trade Group to focus attention more specifically on trade and agriculture. It also jointly launched international campaigns such as the Global Campaign for Agrarian Reform with the FIAN, and the International Seed Campaign with Friends of the Earth International. The Vía Campesina thus became more intimately linked to, and increased its role in, global social justice movements.

As a result of having firmly planted itself in the international arena, the movement has come under enormous pressure to be everywhere. The Vía Campesina has attracted the attention of global institutions and international NGOs that seek further legitimization by gaining its participation. The mere act of having coffee in an Italian café with a representative of a well-funded NGO has been interpreted as a partnership (Vía Campesina 2002h). On a weekly basis the Vía Campesina receives invitations to participate in events, join working groups and international networks, and meet with NGO representatives who are addressing issues related to agriculture and food.

The Vía Campesina's ability to respond adequately to these demands essentially rests on questions of the extent and capacity of the human resources available and international co-ordination. Given that most Vía Campesina representatives are recognized national peasant leaders in their own countries, all of whom already have overbooked agendas, their ability to fly off to international meetings is greatly limited. Even if and when Vía Campesina regional co-ordinators or working group members do agree to represent the organization at some international event, they sometimes have to cancel their participation at the last minute due to pressing work at home. This, of course, does nothing to boost the movement's reputation for reliability and effective organization. Although unfulfilled commitments are not as much of a problem as they were when the Vía Campesina was first formed, this problem does highlight the need to build a better understanding of the dynamics of a locally rooted international movement.

While strengthening its work at the international level the Vía Campesina may have sacrificed much-needed spaces for internal debate and organizational strengthening. Suárez comments:

> Understandably, the Vía Campesina has oriented itself towards campaigns and mobilizations as a key way of working. There is the WTO campaign, the agrarian reform campaign, this and that campaign. But there is no reflection about the internal functioning, and

discussion about the ways of working that we want at the national, regional, and international levels. I am not talking here about a rigid institution or a totally regimented organization. We are clear about the fact that the Vía Campesina is a movement. These are questions of strategies for internal construction.

These questions arise when Vía Campesina members are called to participate in international events. Vía Campesina delegates are in great demand as speakers and organizers of workshops and mobilizations; but often the organization itself does not have enough time for extensive internal debates about the issues, never mind discussion of internal organizational mechanisms (Vía Campesina 2003a).

As the Vía Campesina became a more prominent player on the international stage, there were signs that it had regressed internally. Alberto Gómez expresses the belief that a lack of close attention to the internal strengthening of the Vía Campesina resulted in less communication and fewer spaces for internal debate. Pedro Magaña argues that even the Vía Campesina meetings do not necessarily facilitate an in-depth exchange of the wide breadth of experiences, information, and ideas of its membership:

> The Vía Campesina could provide better opportunities for learning and leadership-building. For example, I would like to know what the NFU's experience with electoral politics is. I could provide the Vía Campesina with a report on our legislative work — our work on developing a new law of rural development in Mexico. These are also contributions to the Vía Campesina process. It is also the result of a collective analysis, of discussion of policies, of having the possibility — without having gone to Harvard or wherever — of knowing and understanding how government policies are affecting people in different countries. Our experience in developing this law was also a product of our experience within the Vía Campesina. But, in the Vía Campesina there was no real discussion or serious attention paid to the experiences we had had in Mexico. In the International Co-ordination Commission the regional reports seem to be more of a formality than anything else. They are not structured in a way to really facilitate real exchange.

Moreover, as M.D. Nanjundaswamy pointed out, not all information is disseminated, and given as well a lack of consistent consultation, the result is less democratic decision-making. In a constantly changing context this is dangerous ground. By concentrating information and decision-making in fewer hands the Vía Campesina risks not reflecting the needs and interests of its membership. It recognizes that this tendency is also a recipe for creating distance from the membership and potentially fostering conflict within the movement.

The Vía Campesina's expressed need and commitment to information-sharing and broad-based consultation assume a certain level of capacity for international co-ordination in the Operational Secretariat. But even there the leaders and personnel experience difficulty in separating the local from the global. In the former Operational Secretariat in Honduras, for example, both the Vía Campesina representative and the personnel are intimately involved in local farm politics and time-consuming party politics. For Doris Gutierrez de Hernandez, technical assistant to the Vía Campesina, the international movement "cannot and must not only exist out there in cyberspace. The Vía Campesina exists because of its local and national organizations so our work must also be grounded here locally."[8] But time spent on local organizing means less time dedicated to international co-ordination.

Although the Vía Campesina has a global structure, it is acutely aware of the importance of the regions and the base. When the Vía Campesina approaches the WTO, the U.N. Commission for Sustainable Development, or the FAO it does so while remaining deeply rooted in local issues and realities, and active in local struggles. Indeed, the international work of farm organizations is possible only if and when the organizations are strong and consolidated at the local and national levels. The base, articulated through the national and the regions, is the heart and driving force of the movement; local issues and local activism drive its global interventions. Just as importantly, the experience that local and national organizations gain in the Vía Campesina helps to strengthen their work at the domestic level. In some cases that experience also contributes to the adoption of more radical positions.

What is required, then, is truly a fine balance: to be representative and accountable the Vía Campesina must be rooted in local realities; yet as a transnational movement it must also engage in broad-based consultation, communication, and co-ordination on a regular basis. This is the only way in which it can continue to understand and place the specificity of local situations and local interests at the centre of international debates. The ability of the Vía Campesina to remain firmly grounded on the local while being thrust into the global sphere is perhaps one of the most significant contributions to our understanding of the nature, extent, and complexity of agrarian activism.

6. Co-operation, Collaboration, and Community

In successfully bringing together, as La Vía Campesina does, organizations of peasants, farmers, farm workers, and indigenous agrarian communities from a wide diversity of locations and cultures, the path has not always been smooth. Back-country roads are often not paved.

To build collaboration and co-operation among its membership the Vía Campesina uses various strategies and mechanisms that intersect at the local, national, and international levels. The movement's strategic work on questions of gender inequality and regional differences is a key part of this balancing act, part of its objective of building community.

La Vía Campesina and Gender

Rural women play a critical role in agricultural production and in maintaining the economic and social fabric of rural communities. Yet rural women still have limited access to economic and political power. In many cases women continue to be excluded from decision-making positions or involvement in policy development on issues that influence the well-being of farming communities.

In the beginning, all was not equal when it came to gender. The eight representatives who signed the Managua Declaration and all of the regional co-ordinators elected at the First International Conference in Mons were men. Indeed, the Managua Declaration of 1992 makes no mention of women or gender, and the Mons Declaration of the following year mentions women farmers only once. Still, the Mons Conference saw an increased involvement on the part of women farm leaders, who made up 20 percent of the participants. Interestingly, that conference also identified a specific need to integrate indigenous peasant organizations into the organization — a goal linked, in the discussions, with an understanding of the challenges faced by indigenous peasant women. On a number of occasions outspoken indigenous peasant leaders from the Andean region — most notably, Camila Choqueticlla of the Confederación Nacional de Mujeres Campesinas de Bolivia and Paulino Guarachi of the Confederación Sindical Unica de Trabajadores Campesinos de Bolivia — strongly articulated the specific situation and problems of indigenous peasants, including peasant women, that grew out of the implementation of neo-liberal policies in the country-side. The worldwide struggle of indigenous communities for ownership and control over productive resources is critically important — raising questions as to how the Vía Campesina deals with the social relations of ethnicity and contributes to this struggle. Although indigenous concerns were raised in Mons, Consuelo Cabrera Rosales, a Mayan peasant woman leader from Guatemala, suggests that the Vía Campesina still has a long way to go. She argues that if La Vía Campesina had integrated an indigenous as well as a peasant identity, its whole approach to land, the earth, and territory, and its vision for the practice of agriculture, would be considerably different from what it is now.

The Vía Campesina has taken concrete steps to address gender concerns. The Framework for Action (PFS 1993c) agreed to in Mons did specify advocacy for women's and men's rights in their struggle for land, recognized the critical role that women and youth play in rural organizations, and emphasized "the need to guarantee their full participation." However, the first International Conference failed to identify mechanisms that would ensure the meaningful participation and representation of women. As a result of that omission, three years later, by the time of the Second International Conference, women's representation had not improved: it remained at 20 percent of all delegates. The women who gathered in Tlaxcala had struggled for years in their own communities and organizations to integrate gender issues in debates around agricultural policy. For most, this was an ongoing struggle waged at the local, national, and regional levels. In Tlaxcala women delegates demanded no less at the international level, and the Vía Campesina was driven to take direct actions in this area.

Following a long and heated debate, both among women themselves and subsequently among the delegated body, the conference stipulated concrete steps towards gender equality. Essentially, the debate centred on what mechanism could best ensure women's increased participation and representation. Some participants argued for an affirmative action strategy whereby women would automatically have two seats on the ICC. Others asserted that women's effective participation at that level had to be based primarily on their leadership abilities and positions within their own countries and regions. Significantly, too, this was a debate that occurred amidst the internal power struggle between the Filipino groups within the East and Southeast Asian region (see chapter 5). An affirmative action strategy would have enabled one of these organizations to gain a place in the ICC. For some delegates, this was a clear case of women being used to pursue someone else's agenda. Ultimately, the Tlaxcala conference — informed by the conclusions of a meeting convened by the women and proposals from a conference working group on Rural Development, Living and Working Conditions, and Women — agreed to the formation of a special committee to work with women in the Vía Campesina (1996b: 41). Specifically, as the Vía Campesina stated, the mandate of this committee was to:

- Examine the specific needs, interests and concerns of women of

the Vía Campesina,
- Develop strategies, mechanisms and a plan of action to ensure women's equal participation and representation at all levels of Vía Campesina, and
- Establish lines of coordination and communication among women of the Vía Campesina. (Vía Campesina Women's Working Group 1996: 1)

Furthermore, the conference designated the only female member of the newly elected ICC — Nettie Wiebe — as head of this special committee, a position she held until 2000.

For most of the women, the formation of a special committee to deal specifically with women was not seen as a goal in and of itself. Many of these women peasant and farm leaders had had direct experience with and were acutely aware of the numerous limitations of women's auxiliaries and/or women's secretariats in mixed organizations. Rarely did these structures guarantee equal status; often they were subordinate to, and played a secondary role within, male-dominated organizations. Still, the women considered this step as an important means, a process, that could integrate women — and their concerns, needs, and interests — into the movement, facilitate collective analysis and collective action among women (as women), and potentially challenge male domination in rural organizations and within the Vía Campesina itself. Hence, the formation of a special committee gave women an important space in which they could organize themselves, with the ultimate goal of eventually reaching gender equality within the Vía Campesina.

The Women's Commission Meets in San Salvador

Vía Campesina women were quick to take advantage of the space they had won. Some four months after the Tlaxcala conference women's representatives from Europe, North America, and Central America gathered in San Salvador, the capital city of El Salvador, for the first meeting of the Vía Campesina Women's Working Group, which quickly became known as the Vía Campesina Women's Commission. Representatives from Eastern Europe, the two Asian regions, and South America were unable to attend. For some of them it was a case of insufficient funding, illness, or an inability to secure a visa in time. As well, two of the regions had not yet nominated their women's representatives.

This first women's gathering, hosted by the Women's Commission of ASOCODE, was expanded to a regional consultation and included several women peasant leaders from each of the seven Central American countries. The meeting, covering considerable ground, set the tone for future collaboration among women of the Vía Campesina.

As women spoke from their own experiences of working within peasant and farm organizations, a sense of camaraderie, sharing of insights, and respect for one another permeated the discussions of potential models and plans for work within the Vía Campesina. For many participants this was their first exposure to the movement — most of them had not attended the Tlaxcala conference — which meant that they necessarily spent a good deal of time learning more about the Vía Campesina itself — how it was formed, who was involved, and its goals and ideological foundations. They reviewed the conclusions of the conference working group on Rural Development, Living and Working Conditions, and Women, discussed the overall results of the conference, and expanded the original mandate of the newly formed Women's Commission to include building leadership capacity among women farm leaders. Moreover, women enthusiastically contributed to further defining the Vía Campesina's position on food sovereignty, which was to be presented at the World Food Summit in Rome in November of that year. They studied the draft position in detail and stressed a number of additional issues. For example, the women asserted that at the heart of food sovereignty was the notion that farming peoples "have the right to produce our own food in our own territory" (Vía Campesina Women's Working Group 1996: 6). The draft position recognized the need for sustainable farming practices to ensure environmental sustainability, and to this the women added the human health dimension. For women, as those primarily responsible for the well-being of their families, food sovereignty must also include a move to organic production or certainly a drastic reduction in the use of health-endangering chemical inputs and an immediate stop to the export of banned agro-chemicals. Finally, given the impact of agricultural policies on women's daily lives and their unequal access to productive resources (relative to men), women insisted that food sovereignty could only be achieved through women's greater participation in policy development in the countryside. All of these concerns were eventually integrated into the final draft, effectively integrating a gender analysis into the Vía Campesina position.

The Women's Commission agreed to work with three NGOs — ISIS International-Manila, and two U.S.-based organizations, the People-Centered Development Forum and the Women, Food and Agriculture Network — to organize a three-day Rural Women's Workshop on Food Security just prior to the WFS. The members of the Women's Commission believed that it was important that peasant women themselves be involved on the organizing committee of the event, rather than leaving the planning only to NGOs. The Women's Commission contributed much to this workshop: eighteen peasant women leaders from the eight regions of the Vía Campesina participated, and Vía Campesina organizations wrote four of the regional papers presented, providing much-needed information and analysis of what was happening in the countryside in each of these regions. The Women's Commission argued that the Rural Women's Workshop, together with their request to the ICC that each region should send one man and one woman, would help to ensure gender parity in the Vía Campesina delegation to Rome.

Finally, the first meeting of the Women's Commission also developed an action plan which included a number of goals: to get a functional Women's Commission up and running, with representatives from each of the eight regions of the Vía Campesina; to establish open lines of communication and co-ordination among the members of the Women's Commission; to communicate regularly with the ICC, to keep that body abreast of the specific concerns, needs, interests, and contributions of women; and to disseminate the results of the San Salvador meeting to all regions. Based on the success of the regional consultation approach, participants agreed that this type of gathering would be more useful than if they restricted meetings to the eight representatives on the Women's Commission.

This first meeting of the Women's Commission had been planned to coincide with two other significant events held in San Salvador: a gender workshop for ASOCODE and a meeting of the ICC. As a result the discussion of gender issues went beyond that particular group. Women's voices infused the ICC deliberations, and men participated in the gender workshop. Perhaps more importantly, the Women's Commission meeting grounded the Vía Campesina in local realities. As its final report stated:

> It was quite clear to everyone present that by putting the Gender workshop on the agenda [of the Women's Commission meeting], we were succeeding in making a local issue, the work of ASOCODE in this case, an international issue. This is precisely what the Vía Campesina is all about. The work of the Vía Campesina is not something that happens outside of or apart from the work of each of its participating organizations. Whatever issues the Vía Campesina works on should come right from the base, right from the local level. (Vía Campesina Women's Working Group 1996: 6)

This statement brought the Vía Campesina home, right into local rural communities, into women's households and their personal lives. In evaluating the Women's Commission meeting one peasant woman leader noted, "I've learned a lot more about the Vía Campesina now and feel that I am part of something much bigger than just my organization." Another woman said the regional consultation had succeeded in bringing women into the movement, making them feel like they were really part of a growing and powerful force. Yet another said, "I feel more confident; I can meet more challenges now."

All in all the three events in San Salvador proved to be excellent opportunities for building leadership capacity, with women both learning much about each other's realities and broadening the Vía Campesina position on food sovereignty by inserting their insights, experiences, expertise, and demands. Women left San Salvador convinced that there was a place for them in this newly created international peasant and farm movement, and many of them believed that they had taken concrete steps towards "making the Vía Campesina a movement for both men and women" (Vía Campesina Women's Working Group 1996: 6). They also recognized, though, that they faced a long process that would require their full engagement in a constant and uphill struggle for gender equality. Based on their daily lives and organizational experiences, the women were acutely aware of their unequal access to economic, political, and social power relative to men in the countryside. After years of struggle for women's equality, rural women's involvement in forums and structures responsible for policy development in the rural sector remained highly restricted. In most (if not all) countries, peasant and farm organizations were still male-dominated. The women involved in the Vía Campesina refused to accept these subordinate roles and positions. While acknowledging the long and bumpy road ahead, they enthusiastically embraced the challenge and vowed to take a leading role in shaping the Vía Campesina as a movement committed to gender equality.

Women on the Frontiers of Food Sovereignty

Since its formation the Vía Campesina Women's Commission has accomplished a great deal. The first task was simply bringing together women from diverse cultures and different contexts. However, from 1996 to 2000 the Women's Commission concentrated its work in the Americas, primarily in the three Vía Campesina regions in Latin America and Mexico. The Women's Commission, with funding from Promoting Women in Development at the Centre for Development and Population Activities (CEDPA), held a series of three regional workshops and exchanges among women in Central America, South America, and the Caribbean. The primary goal of this project, entitled "Peasant Women on the Frontiers of Food Sovereignty," was to increase women's participation and representation at all levels and in all activities of the Vía Campesina (Vía Campesina Women's Working Group 1997: 1). The workshops and exchanges were designed specifically to enhance women's involvement in policy development and actions on issues of food sovereignty and strengthen their capacity to organize at the international level (ibid.: 4). While the Vía Campesina Women's Commission was responsible for overall co-ordination, the regional workshops and exchanges were organized by the women leaders of three regionally based organizations, CLOC in South America, ASOCODE in Central America, and WINFA in the Caribbean.

The project was a huge success.[1] By exchanging ideas, information, and experiences women learned about the agricultural realities in different countries, broadened their understanding of the issues facing farming communities at the local, national, and international levels, and engaged in a collective analysis of the forces affecting the daily lives of people living in rural communities. The discussions ranged from human rights, struggles for genuine agrarian reform, biodiversity and genetic resources, management of natural resources, and the impact of agricultural trade, to different aspects of food sovereignty. Women also shared experiences about alternative pro-duction and marketing strategies, explored ideas about organizing in the countryside, and discussed strategies to address gender inequalities in their local and national organizations, at the regional level, and within the Vía Campesina. These face-to-face encounters among women were crucial in facilitating a greater understanding and building unity among the women of the Vía Campesina in the Americas. One assessment of the work done by the Women's Commission concluded:

> The common ground developed through the project ended a perva-sive sense of isolation and powerlessness among participants, who viewed their leadership training and exchange experiences as key to enabling them to participate in decision making and advocate on their own behalf. Participants gained an increased understanding of the root causes and validity of the issues they confront. Many also developed greater self-confidence and improved their ability to take on leadership responsibilities in their own communities and organizations. Most importantly, women learned that they did indeed have voice, experience, and expertise, and the ability to share this with others. (ICRW and CEDPA 1999: 4)

The women of the Vía Campesina believe that they must work together — on equal terms — with their male counterparts to build an alternative agricultural model. Hence, as they gained more experience and confidence in working beyond national borders women eagerly joined, in increasing numbers, the Vía Campesina's delegations to international events such as — among others — the World Food Summit and NGO Forum on Food Security in Rome (1996), the WTO Ministerial meeting in Seattle (1999), the Conference of the Global Forum on Agricultural Research in Dresden (2000), and the World Food Summit: Five Years Later and the NGO/CSO Forum on Food Sovereignty in Rome (2002). Organizing women's meet-ings immediately prior to these larger events and/or before Vía Campesina gatherings was another important strategy aimed at ensuring their greater participation and increased representation within the Vía Campesina. It was the strategy first used by Vía Campesina women when they co-organized the Rural Women's Workshop on Food Security just prior to the World Food Summit in 1996, and three years later the Women's Commission convened a meeting prior to the WTO events in Seattle. As a result women constituted 34.5 percent and 37.5 percent of the Vía Campesina delegates to Rome and Seattle, respectively.

This same strategy was used by Latin American women when they convened the First Latin American Assembly of Rural Women just prior to the general congress of CLOC held in Brasilia in November 1997. A total of 125 women participated in the Women's Assembly, and women subsequently made up 37 percent of the delegates at the CLOC congress.[2] Although the

---

**Excerpts from the Resolutions of the First
Latin American Assembly of Rural Women**

The organizations of CLOC/Vía Campesina should fully integrate women in all the spaces where decisions are made through — among other measures — technical and political training.

CLOC and the Vía Campesina should guarantee the equality of women's participation — at a level of 50 percent — in those spaces of coordination and all events.

CLOC/Vía Campesina should assume the development of a data-base about the realities of rural workers of the Americas and the Caribbean specifying the situation of women.

CLOC/Vía Campesina should organize an international event of rural women, directed to make their realities more visible and project their proposals to the world.

Strengthen the training school of CLOC — including the participation of 50 percent of women in its activities — and develop courses, workshops and seminars in the formation of leaders.

CLOC should develop a campaign in every country to value the forms of communication of women at the base, with the objective of recovering their self-esteem and to claim their right to communication...

Strengthen the Boletin Campesino [the Vía Campesina's newsletter] and other means of communication to address the themes and actions of rural women.

CLOC should create and strengthen spaces of organized and systemic denunciation of all forms of violence against peasant women and girls.

CLOC/Vía Campesina should develop campaigns against privatization of health services and education, and to fight against forced sterilization of peasant women, indigenous persons and blacks.

CLOC, at all levels, should revise its plans to ensure that it includes a cross-sectional focus on gender and direct these resolutions in concrete ways to daily action at all levels.

CLOC women did not reach their goal of gender parity, the extent and level of participation of women were unprecedented in what had until then been largely a male-dominated space. As a direct result of the First Latin American Assembly of Rural Women, women leaders arrived well prepared to contribute actively in discussions of policy development and advocacy plans throughout the CLOC congress. They readily joined working groups on agrarian reform, sustainable agriculture, indigenous and Afro-American peoples, environment and natural resources, human rights, culture and education, rural workers, and organizational matters. The significant presence of women was clearly visible as they joined men at the head table to give summary reports of the working group sessions and readily went to the microphones to express opinions on various topics.

The women's assembly had a significant impact on the results of the

CLOC congress in that they reflected a gender, as well as a class and ethnicity, analysis (Leon 1997). Perhaps more importantly, all of the resolutions and proposals of the First Latin American Assembly of Rural Women were approved by the whole CLOC congress, and many of these were in fact measures to help reach gender parity and gender equality, not only in CLOC but also in the Vía Campesina.

Clearly, Latin American women made significant progress as they became more visible and their voices became more vocal in the region and beyond. By the third congress of CLOC, celebrated in Mexico in August 2001, women surpassed their goal, representing 56 percent of congress delegates.[3] They were also making important contributions and influencing the gender dynamics of the Vía Campesina. In the process of organizing the First Latin American Assembly of Rural Women in Brasilia and the women's workshops in Central America and the Caribbean, the Vía Campesina Women's Commission and the Women's Commission of CLOC began working closely together to the point where divisions between the two entities became somewhat blurred. Indeed, the leaders involved began referring to themselves as the Women's Commission of CLOC/Vía Campesina as they vowed to work together to ensure follow-up on resolutions, commitments, and plans agreed to at the CLOC congress, the Latin American Assembly of Rural Women, and women's gatherings held throughout Latin America, and to work to co-ordinate the work of the Vía Campesina women in the Americas.

The Asian Peasant Women's Workshop

Although the majority of the interregional work done by the Women's Commission did take place in the Americas, the Asian women in the East and Southeast region also strengthened their communication and co-ordination links through the Asian Peasant Women's Workshop held in Bangkok, Thailand, in August 1999.[4] This workshop — organized in preparation for the Third International Conference of the Vía Campesina — was the first of its kind in the region and brought together peasant women from Thailand, Vietnam, Laos, Malaysia, Indonesia, Philippines, Korea, and Japan. Through reports of the situation in their respective countries, women identified a number of common issues: 1) "modernization" and liberalization of agriculture were exacerbating the plight of small farmers; 2) conflicts between governments, private sector, and local communities over productive resources such as water, land, forests, and coastal resources were leading to increased violence and repression of ethnic minorities who resisted encroachment; 3) "development" projects concentrated on large infrastructural projects were resulting in the forced displacement of peasant families; globalization was leading to the adoption of Western values, with the subsequent loss of local cultures; 4) there was a rise in domestic violence; and 5) rural women experienced increased discrimination as they were forced into low-paid and abusive work conditions in urban settings.

(The situation differed somewhat in Laos, and especially in Vietnam, where more pro-agriculture policies had contributed to a relative strengthening of peasant women's unions).

The workshop declaration (Asian Peasant Women's Workshop 1999: 12) demonstrates how women were acutely aware of the specific ways in which globalization and liberalization were hurting women because of their particular roles in the struggle for the survival and well-being of their families and communities:

> After years of struggle, Asian women still suffer and are marginalized in all levels of society. Economic policies have caused massive migration of women, displacement of women and discrimination in employment of women. Even if they are able to get jobs, women are paid less for the same type of job, become victims of contractualization and always "the last hired, the first fired." Gender inequality rooted in patriarchy still exists in Asian societies. Society regards women as second class, and their participation in decision making is still limited. Less education opportunities available to women has blocked their access to information, knowledge and skills. Violence against women remains a serious problem and has never been curbed. Indigenous people, as the minority in society, have been the recipients of development aggression threatening not only their traditions but their livelihood as well.
>
> Women peasants in Asia suffer layers of oppression. The control of the means of production such as land and the monopoly of natural resources by the landowners and capitalists have further worsened the poverty of peasants. Women who know how to manage natural resources are excluded. Women's limited access to knowledge of farming technology, training and capacity building has forced the deterioration of their livelihood. Social services such as health care, education, and subsidy for women are not the priority of governments. Many women are forced into menial jobs and prostitution as a result of worsening poverty.
>
> These conditions of women are the direct result of liberalization of agriculture in Asian countries....

This declaration greatly resembled the conclusions of the First Latin American Assembly of Rural Women. The participants at the Asian Peasant Women's Workshop, like those involved in the women's regional consultation in San Salvador, also learned about the Vía Campesina's efforts to put in place an alternative model of development — a model based on, among other things, gender equality. Recognizing their crucial role in local and national struggles, they vowed, like the women of CLOC, to play an important part in this international movement.

On the last day of the workshop sixty of the participants, armed with multilingual banners, demonstrated in front of the IMF office to protest against the institution's structural adjustment programs. Most of the participants then travelled seven hundred kilometres to visit with and lend moral support to the Pak Moon demonstrators — a community of over four thousand families who were facing forced relocation as a result of a major infrastructure project involving the building of six dams — who had been occupying the Pak Moon Dam site since March 23, 1998.

The International Women's Assembly

The Vía Campesina Women's Commission, with the approval and support of the ICC, went on to organize the First International Women's Assembly immediately preceding the organization's Third International Conference in Bangalore in early October 2000. This strategy, once again, effectively led to a considerable increase (albeit with great regional variation) in the number of women attending the conference as compared to the Second International Vía Campesina Conference (see Figure 6.1).

As one of its most important accomplishments, the First International Women's Assembly brought together women peasant leaders from seven of the organization's eight regions and facilitated their engagement in discus-

Figure 6.1 Comparison of Women's Participation
in the Tlaxcala and Bangalore Conferences

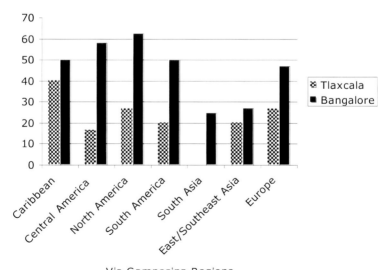

Via Campesina Regions

Source: Lists of delegates attending the Tlaxcala and Bangalore conferences

sions and decision-making on future policy directions. For some women, this was the first time they had crossed national borders, and through the Women's Assembly they were exposed to a whole new world. Not only did women deepen their understanding of the situation that women faced in their own regions, but they also learned about the struggles of counterparts from different continents. As one Indian participant said in her evaluation of the Women's Assembly: "I felt a closeness, almost like I had been to everybody's country without getting on a plane. I no longer feel alone." In addition to discussing the various draft Vía Campesina positions — on food sovereignty and trade, gender, agrarian reform, human rights and solidarity, alternative agriculture, and biodiversity and genetic resources — women analyzed the achievements they had experienced and the barriers and challenges they shared at the social, political, economic, and organizational levels. The Women's Assembly agreed that to realize the meaningful participation of women the Vía Campesina must, at a minimum:

- guarantee 50 percent participation of women in all decision-making levels and activities of the Vía Campesina
- maintain and strengthen the Women's Commission
- ensure that all Vía Campesina documents, training events, and discourse go beyond sexist contents and *machista* language. (Vía Campesina 2000i)

While the Third International Conference fell short of reaching the goal established by the Women's Commission and the ICC — that 50 percent of the delegates be women — it did take important steps in that direction. During the Third International Conference delegates unanimously agreed to a structural change to ensure gender parity. Previously, from 1996 to 2000, Nettie Wiebe was the only woman on the ICC. In Bangalore the Vía Campesina decided to expand the ICC from eight to fourteen regional co-ordinators — which was later expanded to sixteen with the addition of Africa as the eighth region.[5] Each region would have two regional co-ordinators (one man and one woman) elected by the region and responsible and accountable to the region. Furthermore, the women regional co-ordinators would meet prior to the ICC meetings and thus continue to function as the Women's Commission, but their work was now broadened to encompass the general work of the Vía Campesina. Whether this new structure would function well would depend on both regional co-ordinators assuming equal responsibilities for communication and co-ordination within their region — thus avoiding the situation in which women regional co-ordinators are relegated to taking care only of women's issues and organizing women within the region.

The Third International Conference also approved a "Vía Campesina Gender Position Paper," which clearly put women and gender issues at the

The Aracruz Action: Women Reversing Desertification

In a swift, well-coordinated action, women from the Vía Campesina organizations in Brazil, with support from some of their international counterparts, entered a large eucalyptus plantation owned by Aracruz in Barra do Ribeiro, Rio Grande do Sul and destroyed millions of seedlings as well as the on-site lab. By dawn, the forty buses carrying the women were heading into Porto Alegre, where the participants joined a massive march celebrating International Women's Day. Mud was washed from hands and shoes, little purple bandanas were stuffed into pockets or bags and the actors joined thousands of women and men on a march towards the Catholic University where the United Nations Food and Agriculture Organization was holding a conference on Agrarian Reform.

When we reached the conference site, pressure to gain entrance provoked an intense flurry of negotiations which resulted in permission for fifty women to clear security and enter the official conference venue. Two leaders from the Movimento dos Mulheres la Camponesa (MMC) read the peasant women's demands to the assembled delegates, calling for genuine integrated agrarian reform, an end to violence against women, gender equality, justice and solidarity:

> We are against green deserts, huge plantations of eucalyptus, araucaria and pinus that cover thousands of hectares in Brazil and Latin America. Where the green desert thrives, biodiversity is destroyed, soils are deteriorated, rivers are dried up and huge pollution of the paper factories threatens human health and water.... If the green desert keeps on growing, soon there will be no water and land to produce food. [quoted in Vía Campesina 2006a]

... The timing of the action worked to increase the public impact and information while decreasing the immediate danger to the participants. The FAO conference on Agrarian Reform in Porto Alegre ensured that the action gained widespread international attention, as the international press was already there. The presence of international dignitaries and delegates to the conference also limited the possibility of an immediate violent police response to the action. Neither the state nor the national government could risk images of police beating unarmed peasant women being broadcast globally from Porto Alegre.

March 8th is International Women's Day when women around the world remember their many struggles for justice, equality and dignity and celebrate the strength, joy and beauty of their aspirations and achievements. The women of Vía Campesina–Brazil added a significant page to that proud history in their courageous action to protect land, ecology and people's rights.

Source: Excerpts from Wiebe, "Women Reversing Desertification, forthcoming.

The Seedlings Broke the Silence

There was sepulchral silence

over the eighteen thousand hectares stolen
from the tupi-guarani peoples
over ten thousand quilombola families
evicted from their territories
over millions of litres of herbicides
poured in the plantations

There was a promiscuous silence

over the chlorine used
for whitening paper
producing carcinogenic toxins which affect
plants, animals and people.
over the disappearance
of more than four hundred bird species
and forty mammals
in the north of Espírito Santo

There was an insurmountable silence

about the nature of a plant
that consumes thirty litres of water per day
and does not give flowers or seeds
about a plantation that produced billions
and more billions of dollars
for just a half a dozen gentlemen

There was a thick silence

over thousands of hectares accumulated
in Espírito Santo, Minas, Bahia
and Rio Grande do Sul

There was an accomplice silence

over the destruction of the Atlantic Forest and the pampas
due to the homogenous cultivation of a single tree:
eucalyptus

There was a bought silence

over the voluptuousness for profit
yes, there was a global silence
over Swedish capital
over Norwegian companies
over large national stalls

    Finally,

there was an immense green desert
in concert with silence

II
Suddenly,
thousands of women got together
and destroyed seedlings
the oppression and the lie

The seedlings shouted
all of a sudden
and no less than suddenly
the smile of bourgeoisies became amazement
became a grimace, disorientation

III
The order raised incredulous
crying out progress and science
imprecating in vulgar terms
obscenity and bad language

Newspapers, radios, magazines,
the internet and TV,
and advertisers
well spoken businessmen
crawling advisers
clever technicians
reluctant governments
the yelling right
and all the centre extremists
in chorus, echo,
assemblies and declarations
to defend capital:
"They cannot break the silence!"
And cried for beheading!

Suddenly
no less than suddenly
thousands of women
destroyed the silence

On that day
the so called Aracruz land
the women from Vía Campesina
were our gesture
were our voice.

Source: Manifesto of men and women in solidarity with the peasant women
from Vía Campesina <www.viacampesina.org/>.

heart of the movement.[6] The position aimed at providing a gendered lens to help guide future Vía Campesina deliberations. The document stated:

> The global neo-liberal economic agenda is designed to enhance corporate profit and concentrate power without regard for the destruction of nature, culture, community or the well-being of people. The impact of these changes [is] most acute in rural areas where the brutal exploitation of the environment and the people of the land is an immediate daily experience for millions. Women experience the impact of these changes in different ways than their male counterparts because of their history, roles and relationships. Hence, it is fitting and necessary to articulate a gender analysis in order to shape inclusive, just and viable long-term solutions.
>
> The predominant current economic goal of increasing the production of saleable items assigns more value to industrial production than reproduction, manufacturing than nurturing, profits than people. This devalues the reproductive, regenerative forces both of the natural world and in human society. As the bearers of children all women are suffering from this fundamental shift in values. As those who grow food and take care of the land, peasant and rural women are doubly discounted and disadvantaged by the policies and social changes based on these neo-liberal values. These negative changes, coupled with a history of subjugation and voicelessness, often undermine the self-esteem and leadership confidence of rural and peasant women.
>
> However, women of the land are key to the building of healthy, sustainable rural communities, caring for the land and achieving genuine, long-term food security. Rural women produce much of the food that feeds families and local communities. They are historically and currently responsible for protecting and enhancing the bio-diversity which is vital to human survival. They are the beating heart of rural cultures. Genuine rural development, which includes cultural, social, economic and environmental rejuvenation, depends on rural women consciously and courageously taking a leading role. (Vía Campesina 2000c: 1)

The "Gender Position Paper" then elaborated on three main principles and commitments: equality and human rights, economic justice, and social development, each clearly specifying the particular role, position, needs, and interests of women. The gender position action plan stressed that the Vía Campesina must not restrict itself to integrating a gender perspective, but must also include a class and ethnicity perspective. Furthermore, it called for organizing gender workshops for both men and women, ensuring gender parity on all Vía Campesina delegations, working groups and exchanges, integrating a gender perspective in all Vía Campesina positions, and fostering better co-ordination and communication among all Vía Campesina organizations. (See Appendix C for the full text of the "Vía Campesina Gender Position Paper").

After its inception in 1996, then, the Women's Commission accomplished a good deal. By the Third International Conference, just four short years after the Women's Commission was created, women had gained considerable space in the Vía Campesina. They were now much more visible and active participants in decision-making and in various organizational activities. Paul Nicholson says that placing gender front and centre on the agenda forced the regions and their organizations to consider exactly how they would address the gender question and what actions were necessary to deal effectively with it. The Vía Campesina leadership began to make greater effort — with varying degrees of success and failure — to select women and men to represent the movement in international meetings. Certainly, a cursory reading of Vía Campesina documents demonstrates a shift from earlier days when women and gender were barely mentioned. The more recent positions and actions of the Vía Campesina do reflect, to varying degrees, more of a gender analysis.

Peasant women's recent direct action against Aracruz Celulosa, Brazil's largest paper-producing company, highlights the increasing visibility and significant contributions of women within the Vía Campesina. On March 8, 2006, over two thousand peasant women (accompanied by some men) participated in a well-planned and strategic move to stop the monoculture planting of eucalyptus. Their goal was to protect biodiversity, stop environmental degradation, secure access to land, and build food sovereignty.

Following the Aracruz action the police charged thirty-seven people, most of them women. A couple of weeks later, on March 21, 2006, the police raided the offices of the Movimento dos Mulheres la Camponesa (MMC), taking with them computers and files (Vía Campesina 2006b, 2006c). The Vía Campesina immediately began an international campaign, which gained momentum on April 17, 2006, the International Day of Peasant Struggle. The organizers circulated a list of those indicted by the police, along with a poem, "The Seedlings Broke the Silence," written by the MST. They asked supporters to send the poem to the governor of Rio Grande do Sul to demand an end to the repression and violence against Brazilian peasants.

The Struggle for Gender Equality Continues

Still, much work was left to be done — as typified by events that remained male-dominated. For example, when the Vía Campesina working groups on biodiversity and genetic resources and alternative agriculture held their first meetings in Spain in April 2002, and subsequently met with a number of NGOs to explore the possibility of establishing a farmer-led international alliance for research and development, only three of the twelve Vía Campesina representatives were women (Toner 2002). Only four of the thirty-eight Vía

Campesina delegates to the World Summit for Sustainable Development events held in Johannesburg in 2002 were women (Vía Campesina 2002g). While the ICC now has gender parity, not all of the female representatives are able to attend all of the meetings all of the time.

There are many reasons why women do not participate at this level. Perhaps most important is the persistence of ideologies and cultural practices that perpetuate unequal and inequitable gender relations. For instance, the gender division of labour means that rural women have considerably less access to a most precious resource, time, to be involved in leadership positions in farm organizations. Because women remain primarily responsible for the care of children and elders, they find it far more difficult than men do to leave their households for, say, a ten-day international farm meeting. Women's triple workday — involving reproductive, productive, and community work — also means that they are less likely to have time to participate in training/learning sessions aimed at leadership capacity-building. Women also have unequal access to productive, political, and economic resources, all of which greatly influence their capacity to be effective leaders. Women still face persistent social attitudes and norms that foster male dominance in the public sphere. As the First International Women's Assembly of the Vía Campesina pointed out, while women had made some advances in carving out more spaces as women's organizations and/or in mixed organizations, the specific condition and subordinate position of women relative to men in most (if not all) societies remain a key barrier to gender equality (Vía Campesina 2000i).

The work within the Women's Commission was also far from being completely easy. The Vía Campesina women acknowledge — among other things — the existence of destructive power struggles among women themselves (Vía Campesina 2000h). Also, women were not always conscious of their own cultural biases and lack of understanding, which led to cultural insensitivity. Understanding different gender dynamics in some of the Asian countries was particularly challenging for some representatives. Some women's representatives from Asia were not permitted to travel to meetings — even the Vía Campesina women's meetings — without their husbands being present. Consequently, in the Vía Campesina's Continental Rural Women's Workshop, organized in preparation for the First Women's Assembly and the Third International Conference, one Latin American, with little opportunity to understand gender dynamics in Asia, publicly claimed that the Latin American regions were far more advanced on the gender front than were those in Asia. (She was eventually replaced by her organization.)

The Women's Assembly did offer the opportunity to experience rich cultural exchanges and to deepen understandings and analysis of gender relations from diverse settings. Still, the gathering was not as successful as it might have been. The Latin American delegations had already met, and they came to Bangalore with fleshed-out proposals and wanted to see the

Women's Assembly move more quickly to articulate specific demands and define strategies. This was not necessarily a negative thing because it demonstrated the strength, commitment, and exuberance of the Latin American organizations in the Vía Campesina. But the more vocal and results-oriented Latin American delegations did tend to dominate the Women's Assembly as they grew increasingly impatient and frustrated with the pace of the meeting. This condition effectively silenced some participants and gave less room for Asian women to fully participate in their own culturally acceptable ways, demonstrating the need for an appreciation of ethnic and cultural variations among rural organizations in different parts of the world.

Most of these problems could have been avoided if the Women's Commission had held face-to-face planning meetings months prior to the events in Bangalore. The women who had organized the Latin American Assembly of Rural Women in Brasilia had stressed the importance of organizing one or two preparatory sessions. In their experience this advance work greatly contributed to the success of the women's assembly in Latin America because it facilitated greater understanding across cultures, allowed leaders to know each other, and helped consolidate a cohesive team (Desmarais and Wiebe 1998: 5). Had funding been available for the Women's Commission to plan ahead, as the ICC did on two occasions preceding the International Conference, the Bangalore Women's Assembly might have been a more unifying event.

The Vía Campesina Women's Commission suffered other major limitations and weaknesses, most of them institutionally driven. While all other ICC members were responsible for work only within their region, the NFU — as regional co-ordinator and co-ordinator of the Women's Commission at the global level — had twice the workload. Although the NFU's capacity to carry out these leadership responsibilities was facilitated by the technical assistance provided by the Oxfam Global Agriculture Project, it still was a onerous task for an organization with limited human and financial resources.

Then too, unlike the regional co-ordinators of the ICC, the representatives to the Women's Commission were not elected in Tlaxcala. Indeed, no formal process had been defined for the appointment, selection, or election of the representatives to the Women's Commission. In areas where women and/or men were already organized regionally, a democratic process did occur. For example, the CPE, ASOCODE, and WINFA did elect or appoint their women's representatives. But in the areas that had just started to work as a region it was often left to the regional co-ordinator, who presumably consulted his organization to make a selection. One full year after the decision to form the special committee was made in Tlaxcala, only four of the regions had women's representatives. In one of these regions the women's representative was purged from her organization by the ICC regional co-ordinator as a result of an internal struggle. The move occurred just over one year after her appointment, and her replacement was not selected for quite some time. For an extended period there was no women's representative for that specific region, a situation characteristic of two other regions.

The somewhat informal selection process also meant that the appointed representative would come to one meeting, only to be replaced by someone else at the next. At virtually every single meeting of the Women's Commission new players were sitting at the table. In addition to the lack of accountability and legitimacy this fostered, there was also a significant lack of continuity. Consequently, less work was done in the Women's Commission because a considerable amount of time was spent in orienting newcomers. Inconsistency also greatly hampered the Women's Commission's ability to build a strong, cohesive group. This feature differs dramatically from the experience of the ICC, whose members accumulated years of working together as a group, got to know each other as individuals and leaders, and consequently consolidated relations of camaraderie, trust, and respect.

That the Women's Commission was not "institutionalized" in practice led to a lack of clarity and eventually to conflict and tension between the Women's Commission and CLOC women leaders. Most of the organizations that belong to CLOC also participate in the Vía Campesina. Both movements embrace similar views and objectives but the Vía Campesina works at the global level while CLOC functions within Latin America. In Latin America CLOC has regional structures that are both different from and overlap with those of the Vía Campesina. This sometimes causes problems. For example, in their closely knit work together in the "Peasant Women on the Frontiers of Food Sovereignty" project — which effectively led to the formation of the Women's Commission of the Vía Campesina/CLOC — problems emerged when, in the context of limited funds, attempts were made to override the Vía Campesina structure with that of CLOC. For instance, when Vía Campesina funds were insufficient to cover the costs of this expanded commission, the Vía Campesina Women's Commission sought to ensure the participation of their own representatives in planning and co-ordination meetings, while the CLOC women worked towards the same goal. Moreover, some women of CLOC argued that their organization should be recognized as the regional entity responsible for the Vía Campesina in Latin America, and that by creating the Vía Campesina Women's Commission an external structure was being imposed.

Interestingly, the different structures of CLOC and Vía Campesina were not seen as a problem among the men of both movements, and no proposal for a structural change was ever put on the agenda of the Vía Campesina conference. One peasant woman (who wished to remain anonymous) says that tension around regional boundaries and organizational structures among some women also might have had more to do with internal power struggles and gender dynamics within CLOC itself, because at the time CLOC was going through a brief period of decreased activity and organization.

Clearly, the Vía Campesina has given women farm leaders opportunities to engage in advocacy and collective action on a range of issues at the international level. Through meetings, workshops, conferences, and exchanges women successfully established common ground. Through the Women's Commission the Vía Campesina increased women's participation and representation as women, in increasing numbers. Women joined their male counterparts in policy development and collective action. Still, the initial failure to institutionalize the Women's Commission greatly hindered the Vía Campesina's advancement to gender equality. The Vía Campesina's eventual structural change introduced gender parity on the ICC, yet it remained to be seen whether this mechanism would lead to the practice of gender equality. Even today women's unequal access to and control over productive, political, and social resources remains as a significant barrier to their equal participation and representation in the Vía Campesina. In many ways the Vía Campesina's success in reaching gender equality rests primarily on the persistent and concerted efforts of organizations at the local and national levels working to address the barriers to gender equality.

Regional Articulations — Strongest or Weakest Links?

The ability of the Vía Campesina to be an effective force for social change in the international arena depends on strong local and national peasant organizations that work together at the regional level. The development of effective and cohesive regions demands constant communication, co-ordination, open discussion, consultation, and strategic planning. It means following through on commitments and, perhaps most importantly, respecting decision-making structures and processes. This kind of structure is based on a number of assumptions: for instance, that national organizations within a region will work well together, and that regions will be able to find resources to build, maintain, and strengthen their own work. These conditions are among the most important challenges to the Vía Campesina.

When an organization seeks to join the Vía Campesina, the members in the region where that prospective member is located assess the application and approve it or not. The region then informs the ICC of the new member's entry. The ICC provisionally recognizes the new member, official recognition comes only at the international conferences that occur every four years. If necessary the ICC can intervene and overrule the region's decision — an action that must also be confirmed or rejected at an international conference — but rarely does so because of the tensions that might arise from the roadblock. What this entry process does is place greater decision-making at the national and regional levels. It respects how current members, especially at the national level, are surely more familiar with the history and politics of the applicant organization and thus better able to judge whether the organization truly embodies the ideals and principles of the Vía Campesina.

The membership mechanism helps to exclude the entry of organizations whose interests might be to divert, subvert, or undermine the Vía Campesina. But the entry process can also be used to restrict organizations whose participation could form a significant contribution to the movement. For example, for a number of years one of the Vía Campesina's stated priorities was to expand its presence in Asia; but a number of South Asian peasant organizations interested in joining found their way blocked at the regional level. K.S. Puttaniah, president of one faction of the KRRS, stressed that internal divisions and leadership styles were a problem in this regard, while M.D. Nanjundaswamy said that political differences and insufficient resources for regional co-ordination and communication were key reasons for the low membership numbers in South Asia.

In other regions some national organizations that are already members of the Vía Campesina have wanted to actively participate but encountered resistance from other member organizations within their regions. For example, on two separate occasions Costa Rica's Unión Nacional de Pequeños y Medianos Productores Agropecuarios (UPANACIONAL), a founding Vía Campesina member with years of international experience, notified the ICC that it was receiving very little information about the Vía Campesina in general, and that it was rarely invited to join the movement's delegations from Central America.[7] At the heart of the problem, no doubt, was an internal crisis in the late 1990s within ASOCODE, the Vía Campesina regional co-ordinator for Central America, which resulted in UPANACIONAL leaving the regional organization. UPANACIONAL remained a member of the Vía Campesina but for all intents and purposes was being effectively excluded from its activities. Although the Operational Secretariat did respond to UPANACIONAL's concerns, the Vía Campesina ICC failed to address this issue, which might help to explain why the UPANACIONAL did not participate in the Third International Conference.

The various regions also have considerable differences in capacity, which is at least partly due to history. While several regions already had organizations that worked at a regional level before the creation of the Vía Campesina, others had not. For example, the CPE as of 1986 had established a structure and mechanisms for communication, co-ordination, and co-operation among participating organizations throughout Western Europe. Similarly, ASOCODE established itself as a regional structure in 1991 and thus had two years of regional experience in Central America before joining Vía Campesina. Meanwhile, in North America, farm organizations had just barely begun to get to know each other in joint efforts to resist NAFTA. There had been little interaction between the Spanish-, English- and French-speaking areas of the Caribbean. Both Asian regions had virtually no history of regional interaction.

The Vía Campesina has not yet fully dealt with these regional differences. Nico Verhagen, technical assistant to the Vía Campesina, explains that while the Vía Campesina has allocated some funds for regional meetings, directed resources specifically to the Asian regions, and supported fundraising efforts of several organizations, in general these have been limited efforts. Regional capacity-building remains a key challenge. The Vía Campesina Three Year Plan (1999–2001) stressed the need to strengthen all regions by establishing eight regional secretariats to ensure greater co-ordination and communication within each region (Vía Campesina 1998b). Yet until 2003, very few Vía Campesina resources were actually allocated to this effort. Instead, regional strengthening depended almost exclusively on each region's ability to come up with its own funds for this purpose.

In some cases, this proved successful. For a period of three years a full-time person was stationed in the UNORCA office, and the NFU was provided with a staff person as technical support. But in the South Asian region little was accomplished because the regional co-ordinator, the KRRS, depends entirely on funds raised from its membership and volunteer leaders. The KRRS also had no experience in securing funds from outside sources such as non-governmental organizations. As Nico Verhagen points out, the problem may not simply be an issue of lack of experience. In some cases farm organizations in India are not allowed (or may not want) to receive foreign funding — which means they can only gain funding indirectly through NGOs or by making the Vía Campesina responsible for activities in that country. The situation in the East and Southeast Asia region improved since the election of FSPI as regional co-ordinator. Unlike its predecessor, Thailand's Assembly of the Rural Poor, which functioned with limited resources, FSPI assigned one staff person who was responsible specifically for work with the Vía Campesina.

The uneven development among regions contributed in some ways to the greater prominence of Latin American regions within the Vía Campesina. CLOC, for instance, has contributed immensely to strengthening ties among organizations of peasants, farm workers, and indigenous peoples throughout Latin America. Given that most Vía Campesina organizations are also members of CLOC, strong relations of co-operation and collaboration were established throughout Latin America through CLOC conferences and congresses, and exchanges and mobilization on common issues. Then too, unlike the Asian regions, work within Latin America was greatly facilitated by cultural and language similarities. Indeed, in an increasing number of cases the Spanish-speaking organizations from the South American, Central American, and Caribbean Vía Campesina regions began to work as one consolidated block rather than as three separate regions.

As a result, some of the Vía Campesina's positions and actions reflect Latin American experiences and perspectives to the exclusion of the interests and concerns of other regions. Perhaps the most obvious case is the joint Vía Campesina–FIAN Global Campaign for Agrarian Reform, which has yet to secure the participation of many Asian Vía Campesina organizations. For example, only two Asian women participated in the International Workshop on Agrarian Reform and Gender held in June 2003 in Bolivia, compared with forty-nine Latin American representatives. This highly skewed participation dynamic influenced the outcomes of the workshop: far less space was allocated to the various cultural and gender dimensions of land tenure, land use, and land rights as experienced in Asia. Henry Saragih, FSPI leader and Operational Secretariat of the Vía Campesina, points out that the Vía Campesina "Position on Agrarian Reform," initially discussed at the Third International Conference, reflected primarily the Latin American experience and has yet to include a human rights perspective as stressed by the East and Southeast Asian delegation. That Latin American organizations dominate discussions of agrarian reform is certainly understandable given the region's long and intense history of struggle for land. But if the Global Campaign for Agrarian Reform or Vía Campesina's "Position on Agrarian Reform" are to be effective tools for mobilization at a global level, they must better reflect the complex and diverse histories, experiences, and perspectives of all of its regions.

Even the prevailing image of the Vía Campesina reflects various aspects of Latin American culture: the green farm caps, *pañuelos*, slogans, and MST-inspired *mistica* have become the Vía Campesina's trademark. On numerous occasions Spanish has been the dominant language of delegation meetings. Consequently, the North American, European, and Asian delegations have often joined their Latin American counterparts in raising their fists and loudly shouting Spanish slogans like *"la lucha continúa"* and *"Viva la Vía Campesina!"* This solidarity had, until recently, rarely been reciprocated with Vía Campesina slogans chanted in Thai, Indonesian, or Kannada.

No doubt the location of the Operational Secretariat — which has been in Honduras since 1996 — has also helped strengthen the movement's presence in Latin America, and the office has played an important role in supporting CLOC. According to Vía Campesina statutes, the Operational Secretariat should rotate among the various regions. In the period leading up to the Third International Conference, ICC members expressed a general hope that the next Operational Secretariat would be placed in one of the Asian regions and thereby significantly improve on the movement's presence in Asia. For various reasons — most of them related to the KRRS — these hopes were crushed at the conference. Many Vía Campesina delegates arrived in India having heard rumours of tensions within the KRRS. The key voice, KRRS president Nanjundaswamy, proved to be noticeably unwilling to discuss the issue or explain the situation, thus leaving delegates to contemplate different scenarios, which led in turn to a lack of clarity, suspicions, and mistrust. As well, prior to the International Conference, Nanjundaswamy had assured the ICC that KRRS would organize a one-million-strong demonstration to be held on October 2 in Bangalore. Yet the KRRS did not get anywhere near that number to participate. Granted, heavy rains probably kept some KRRS members away, but some Vía Campesina delegates suspected that the low attendance was due to the internal divisions within the KRRS.

Many people believed that the divisions were much deeper and stronger than portrayed by Nanjundaswamy. The KRRS president also alienated a number of the women delegates by taking the responsibility of participating in the inaugural ceremony of the Women's Assembly but then delaying the ceremony for hours by his absence and ultimately sending another male official as a replacement. Many women interpreted these actions as dismissive and disrespectful.

The newly elected regional co-ordinator for the East and Southeast Asian region, the FSPI, believed that it lacked the international experience and capacity to take on the role of Operational Secretariat. In the end the final decision was to keep the Operational Secretariat in Tegucigalpa until sufficient capacity was established elsewhere. "In the end this was not a decision about the physical place of the Operational Secretariat — whether it would be located in Bangalore or Tegucigalpa" Nicholson says. "By the time we arrived in Bangalore we knew there were a series of significant problems. In the end, this was a decision about a 'way of working' that entails transparency, democratic decision-making, consensus building, and building relations of trust and respect."

The vitality, exuberance and critical contributions of Latin American regions to the Vía Campesina are not at question here. The Vía Campesina would not be what it is today if there had not been such meaningful participation from Latin America. As more Asian and African organizations join, the Vía Campesina will undoubtedly go through significant shifts. A small sign of times to come occurred at the World Food Summit: Five Years Later, when some delegation members donned Vía Campesina hats of an Asian design — that is, a wide V-shaped hat made of reeds. One of the Vía Campesina meetings at the Summit was opened by a peasant representative from Thailand. Seated in lotus position, with graceful hand movements, he demonstrated a consciousness-raising exercise.

Ultimately the Vía Campesina's capacity to engage in democratic processes that ensure an equal distribution of presence, influence, power, and participation among all regions depends largely on whether or not it acknowledges existing inequalities and actively seeks ways of rectifying these problems. Furthermore, the extent to which the movement succeeds in embracing new organizations as members depends on the mechanisms it puts in place to restrict the power of its current members to act as "gatekeepers" in areas in which national and regional tensions and conflicts exist.

"Let's Organize the Struggle — Land, Food, Dignity, and Life"

As the Vía Campesina continued to grow and worked at consolidating alliances, internal criticisms and conflict became more pronounced. These all came to a head at the Third International Conference, thus shedding light onto important internal struggles within the movement. Quite rapidly, La Vía Campesina turned its gaze inward.

In June 2003, just over ten years after its formal constitutive conference, five representatives from each of the seven regions met in Natoye, Belgium, for a Vía Campesina strategy meeting. Here the Vía Campesina took stock of the global context for dissent following the terrorist attacks of September 11, assessed various aspects of internal functioning, established priorities, and developed strategies for internal cohesion and organizational strengthening (Vía Campesina 2003a, 2003b). Participants identified a whole range of weaknesses: a lack of consistent information-sharing combined with weak communication and co-ordination contradicted the movement's claim to transparent decision-making; a concentration of expertise and responsibility among too few leaders centralized visibility and power; too few (human and financial) resources for regional and thematic work weakened Vía Campesina's presence and effectiveness at all levels; and, the lack of gender equality and youth within the movement clearly narrowed the movement's vision and analysis. The results of this encounter were compiled in "Fourth International Vía Campesina Conference: Themes and Issues for Discussion," a document circulated for further debate during eight regional conferences organized in preparation for the Fourth International Conference of the Vía Campesina scheduled for Brazil in 2004 (Vía Campesina 2004a).

The extensive and consultative preparatory process leading up to the Fourth International Conference was significant. For one thing it effectively decentralized the debate concerning the Vía Campesina's positions, strategies, and internal dynamics beyond the international and national leadership. More locally based leaders and groups in each of the regions wrestled with a number of questions:

- What are our common values?
- How can we make action agendas from the international level more compatible with struggles at the local level?
- How can we ensure that information and national-level proposals are distributed to the regional and international levels?
- How can we strengthen the incorporation of women [and youth] into Vía Campesina and better integrate their interests in Vía Campesina's activities and positions?
- What is the best way of carrying out co-ordinated mobilization at the international level? Organizational styles differ in Bolivia, Mexico, India, and Brazil. Should we find a common form or style of mobilization, or should each organization make its own decisions? (Vía Campesina 2004a: 47–49)

The regions were strengthened by the process as each developed an action plan for future Vía Campesina work within the region and brought new organizations into the fold, thus expanding the movement's perspectives and analysis. Ultimately, the preparatory process empowered the Vía

Campesina as a whole. Having already had full-fledged discussions at the regional level, participants arrived at the Fourth International Conference equipped to move ahead in important areas, both external and internal.

Under the banner "Organizing the Struggle: Land, Food, Dignity and Life," the Vía Campesina's Fourth International Conference took strong stances against international institutions and policies deemed to be detrimental to the survival of family farms (Vía Campesina 2004c, 2004d). The Vía Campesina vowed to take to the streets to continue to radically oppose neo-liberalism by demanding that the "WTO get out of Agriculture" and that national governments promote the viable alternative of people's food sovereignty.

Having analyzed the FAO's recent report on agri-biotechnology, the Vía Campesina declared the FAO's stance to be a pernicious attack on peasant agriculture and demanded that the institution publicly retract its position of promoting GMOs as a solution to world hunger. While rejecting GMOs, the Vía Campesina renewed support for its global seeds campaign.

Through a commitment to reactivate and strengthen its international thematic commissions the Vía Campesina conference consolidated positions and future action plans on seven key issues: food sovereignty and trade liberalization, biodiversity and genetic resources, agrarian reform, gender, sustainable peasant agriculture, human rights, and migration and farm workers. With the integration of the U.S.-based Border Farmer Workers Project, which is working closely with organizations from other continents, the Vía Campesina would now be paying more attention to migration and the rights of migrant farm workers.

One of the most critical issues for the Vía Campesina remains access to land. After all, a landless peasant cannot grow food to bring to market or worry about seeds, and a small farmer needs secure land tenure. Based on the negative experiences of some countries with the World Bank's market-assisted agrarian reform process and ongoing human rights abuses related to land struggles, the Vía Campesina voiced the urgent need for alternatives. It vowed to strengthen and expand the Global Campaign for Agrarian Reform, first launched in 1999. Thanks to the significant contributions from the East and Southeast Asian region, agrarian reform is now increasingly conceptualized from a human rights perspective. Peasant rights to agrarian resources are at the heart of the Vía Campesina's petition to the United Nations Commission on Human Rights for a charter or declaration on peasant rights.

Putting into practice its commitment to gender equality, the Vía Campesina's Fourth International Conference was preceded by the Second International Women's Assembly. This Women's Assembly was remarkable in a number of ways: women from all of the regions actively participated in all discussions; panels had representation from all regions; and the Assembly encouraged numerous cultural exchanges — particularly dances, music, and song. Since the 2000 conference the Vía Campesina had guaranteed gender parity in its leadership by expanding the ICC to include one man and one woman from each of its regions. But as the delegates to the Second Women's Assembly emphasized, formal gender parity is not enough in itself. Given that around the world agricultural politics remains a male-dominated field, the Vía Campesina must continue to work at the local, national, regional, and international levels to ensure women's equality.

The Vía Campesina is also acutely aware of the importance of youth to maintaining vibrant peasant and rural cultures and agricultural practices. In efforts to increase the participation and representation of youth, at its Fourth International Conference the Vía Campesina held its First International Youth Assembly, which brought together ninety-two representatives from thirty-five countries. The youth filled the conference with imagination, creativity, energy, song, and dance, effectively breaking through language barriers. The political message of youth was also clearly heard: they want to stay on the land, they want to produce food, they are convinced that "another agriculture is possible," and through the Vía Campesina they will organize internationally to make this happen.

Interest in belonging to the Vía Campesina continues to grow. The Fourth International Conference formally integrated Africa as the eighth region of the Vía Campesina, which now includes organizations from Mali, Mozambique, Senegal, Madagascar, and South Africa. The Fourth Conference integrated another forty-two organizations into the movement — over half of them Asian — and moved the Operational Secretariat from Tegucigalpa to Jakarta. No doubt, the Vía Campesina's presence is Asia will be strengthened considerably as a result.

Each day of the Fourth Conference began with one of the regions communicating their history, peasants roots, and/or current struggles through theatre, dance, or song. These *místicas* helped break through language barriers and established common ground, accentuating the cultural significance of seed and planting ceremonies, a history of oppression and repression, and a determination to survive against enormous odds. Conference proceedings were often interrupted by various delegations rising up and voicing slogans in different languages. Panel discussions were complemented with songs from various parts of the world. Sessions ended with everyone dancing to Brazilian or East Timor music. In commemoration of Lee Kyung Hae, the Korean farm leader who died in the midst of the WTO's Fifth Ministerial conference, the Vía Campesina vowed to mark September 10 — the "international day of protest against the WTO" — with massive mobilizations for food sovereignty in Seoul, Korea. Many participants who attended the Fourth International Conference said they never before experienced such a powerful sense of community at the international level. The movement was clearly more ready to embrace diversity, learn from each others' experiences, be open to different leadership styles, and prepared to broaden its geographical, cultural, and political presence.

On the road to building an international peasant movement, La Vía Campesina has faced important challenges. Although the movement dreams of autonomy, it is greatly affected by external factors because it moves in the very real world of social movements where political and economic constraints help shape collective identities, strategies, and actions. Dynamics within the peasant movement itself also influenced the path it followed. Internal struggles were part of its journey as differences, debates, and conflicts flared up now and then. At the same time, the Vía Campesina took concrete steps to reach gender equality and to deal with regional and national differences and conflicts. The process leading up to and including the Fourth International Conference enabled local and national organizations to reflect carefully on how best to organize to build food sovereignty. In this work as a whole the Vía Campesina reiterated a firm commitment to building unity within diversity — and thus fostering community.

7. Reflections on the Meanings of La Vía Campesina

> A campesino comes from the countryside. There have always been campesinos. What did not exist before were investors, industrialists, political parties, etc. Campesinos have always existed and they will always exist. They will never be abolished. —Marcelo Carreon Mundo, former member of the National Board of UNORCA, and leader of Ejidos Productores Forestales de la Zona Maya, Quintana Roo, Mexico

Farming families in the North and South responded to the spread of a corporate and neo-liberal model of agriculture by establishing common ground and developing a collective peasant identity — all of which enabled La Vía Campesina to build alternatives to the powerful forces of globalization. The Vía Campesina's experience has a good deal to say about the role and responses of peasants and farmers to globalization in the past decade or so; it has much to say about the relationship between agriculture and development, and transnational social movements.

Walden Bello (2003) argues that the ability of a transnational movement to act effectively depends largely on its capacity to collectively analyze the current global context, define strategic goals and objectives, and elaborate appropriate strategies and tactics. It also depends crucially on the movement's ability to develop structures, processes, and mechanisms to ensure inclusive democratic decision-making and participation (Eschle 2001a). Only then can it continue to accurately represent the interests and concerns of its constituencies.

An examination of the politics of food, then, forces us not only to look at the power dynamics among farmers' organizations, the state, multilateral institutions, transnational agribusiness corporations, and other social actors. It also demands an examination of power relations within the movement itself. Most important in this process are the ways in which peasant organizations around the world are working together to ensure the well-being of rural communities and negotiate an alternative model of development.

The cultural politics of social movements are complex. Building an understanding of them begins with paying close attention to the everyday. It means understanding the impact of external forces on people's daily lives and how movements reshape the world in which they function every day. Thus, resistance is broadened beyond visible confrontations to include partially hidden forms, sites, and strategies based on tradition, cultures, and alternative visions of how the world should be. In this light, resistance encompasses a wide range of practices: constructing collective identities, defining a collective will, developing a collective voice, and carving out social and political spaces. How movements organize themselves can also be a deep exercise in cultural politics because effective change requires "doing politics" differently, through inclusion and participation. This approach represents a direct challenge to the exclusionary politics of dominant structures and processes. To put it another way: if a social movement, confronting a world order that is becoming increasingly exclusionary and in which homogeneity is enforced, defines its opposition by advocating effective participation and embracing diversity, it must build internal processes that reflect these values. It must champion inclusion and diversity in its own internal decision-making processes. The transformatory potential of movements is greatly influenced both by power relations within movements themselves and by the power dynamics in the social and political context in which the movements function.

A Special Political Moment

Since the Vía Campesina emerged in 1993 resistance to neo-liberal globalization has strengthened, and resistance movements are now more organized, co-ordinated, and visible. These movements have now established their own independent international spaces — the World Social Forum and its regional offshoots, for example — to debate alternatives. In 2001 the World Social Forum in Porto Alegre drew over 10,000 participants; in 2002 the number climbed to 50,000 participants. The event has attracted record numbers: in 2003 over 100,000, and in 2005 some 150,000 people. Regional offshoots of the World Social Forum are now being organized around the world. Resistance movements are active at the local, national, and international levels, and there is better and stronger co-ordination between different sectors of civil society (Vía Campesina 2003a). Participation among different sectors of civil society is stronger, and protest actions are decentralized and co-ordinated to occur in many parts of the world on the same day.

In response to the U.S.-driven war on Iraq, global justice movements and peace movements have converged and clearly demonstrated strength in numbers as millions of people from all walks of life marched in the streets of cities and small towns around the world. Despite increased security measures and the (in some cases, brutal) clamping down of dissent in numerous regions of the world following the terrorists attacks of September 11, 2001, resistance remains strong and is growing — again despite *The Economist*'s (perhaps wishful) prediction in 2004 that global justice movements had all but died.

Peasant protest, certainly, continues unabated. For example, in late October 2002 Latin American peasant and indigenous organizations joined others marching in the streets of Quito to protest the Free Trade Agreement of the Americas and demand a meeting with the negotiators. On January 13, 2003, Bolivian peasant and labour organizations closed major roads in rejection of the FTAA and the sale of Bolivian gas to U.S. and Chilean interests. The government responded by deploying over 10,000 military and police personnel. Nonetheless, the protests eventually forced the resignation of President Sánchez de Lozada. In Mexico peasant organizations brought in 2003 with hunger strikes and major mobilizations (the likes of which had not been seen since the 1950s) in desperate attempts to get their government to renegotiate the agriculture chapters of NAFTA. In India, on February 1, 2003, school children joined by farmers, workers, and other social activists formed a 300-kilometre human chain to join the cities of Allahabad, Varanasi, and Jaunpur in the state of Uttar Pradesh to demand that transnational corporations "quit India."

During the WTO's fifth Ministerial conference held in Cancún the Vía Campesina worked hard to ensure that there would be no violence by negotiating well into dawn with the anarchist Black Bloc and other urban youth groups. Following the death of Lee Kyung Hae — an event that so vividly reflects the violence inflicted by the WTO on the world's farmers — the demonstrations led by the Vía Campesina gained more power and helped lead to the WTO's "collapse in Cancún." A Vía Campesina (2003c) press release stated:

> The Fifth Ministerial Conference of the WTO ended... in complete failure.... From September 8–14th we engaged in significant days of struggle, first, within the framework of the International Peasant and Indigenous Forum, and later, in diverse street demonstrations both inside and outside the convention center where the negotiators were concentrated. The peasant and indigenous march... set the tone for the resistance and struggle of the following days.
>
> On September 13 [2003], with patience and great courage, one hundred women from all over the world dismantled piece by piece the barricade that impeded entry to the convention center. The Korean peasants together with a large part of the crowd joined in this action and using thick ropes we tore down the walls. This was a symbol of the WTO that would soon collapse in Cancún. The thousands of police and military stood there ready to quell the protesters but no one was intent on confronting them. Our non-violent confrontation was with the WTO, not with the police and the military....
>
> The collapse of the WTO is a result of a profound crisis within the neo-liberal model. It is urgent that we continue to strengthen our movements, our alternative proposals. Creating an open, transparent and constructive dialogue among ourselves is all the more necessary to advance in our strategies of struggle.

In mid-September 2004 a Vía Campesina delegation arrived in Seoul to join the Korean Farmers' League and the Korean Women Farmers' Association in a memorial service for Lee Kyung Hae, followed by mass demonstrations to protest rice imports into South Korea. These actions were met with violence and repression (Vía Campesina 2004e). Later that month members of the FSPI celebrated National Peasant Day by organizing mass rallies in various provinces of Indonesia to demand respect for peasant rights and genuine agrarian reform (FSPI 2004).

The Vía Campesina also had a strong presence at the WTO Ministerial conference held in Hong Kong in December 2005 — a presence met with swift police action when over 1,300 protesters were arrested and accused of unlawful assembly. Some of the local people did join the Vía Campesina's non-violent actions. As one women said, "I walk with the march because I share your ideas and support your struggle. Farmers in China face the same problems as you since China entered the WTO some years ago" (Vía Campesina 2005).

On the International Day of Peasant Struggle, April 17, 2006, Vía Campesina organizations and allies took to the streets in Palestine, the United States, and Mozambique to demand that peasants' and farmers' rights be respected. In Bangladesh and Brazil peasants engaged in a number of land occupations. In Honduras they demanded genuine agrarian reform, and in India and Ecuador they organized traditional seed fairs. In Indonesia the FSPI celebrated cultural events involving a national rice-harvest ceremony to emphasize the country's self-sufficiency in rice while strongly rejecting the importation of rice. To commemorate those killed in the massacre of MST members a decade earlier, many citizens of Italy, Spain, and France demonstrated in front of the Brazilian embassies and in the streets to demand an end to "Eldorado: 10 years of impunity." The list of peaceful actions of peasant resistance is endless — and with the formation of La Vía Campesina, when peasants and farmers engage in these local efforts, they do so with the knowledge that they are connected with their counterparts around the world.

Amory Starr concludes her study of anti-corporate movements by reminding us of Peter Kropotkin's prescient words, written at the turn of the twentieth century, that after all is said and done, "'The question of bread' is the preeminent social question." She suggests that in today's context, "Centring food in economic and community analysis is an important way to get people to deal with environmental and economic issues" (Starr 2000: 224). Because of humanity's daily connections and interactions with food, this necessity can also highlight the very real threats to, and the roots of, culture and community. Whether resistance movements are fighting privatization of the commons, the imposition of GMOs in food crops, industry's forays into nanotechnology and attempts to expand the use of food irradiation, negotiation of bilateral, regional, and global trade agreements — all of these struggles are deeply connected to agriculture and those who produce food. Every single one of us on this earth is connected to that process, because we must eat that food. We are all dependent on farmers; their struggles for "healthy" farms have an impact on all of us.

Citizens everywhere are expressing a growing distrust of the food system. The outbreak of mad cow disease in Europe and Canada, foot-and-mouth disease in Britain, GMO contamination of corn stocks in Mexico, e-coli food poisoning in the United States, the Asian flu in poultry, and the dioxin episodes in Belgium have fuelled increasing concerns over issues of food safety and food quality. These concerns have in turn spurred a rising interest in alternative food systems. Demands for locally grown, safe, good-quality food are increasing as evidenced by the exponential growth of organic markets.

All of these conditions represent an important political moment for progressive farm organizations. The Vía Campesina in particular is strategically well positioned to assist farm and peasant organizations to challenge different aspects of this global agricultural change and to spearhead peasant activism at the international level. For years we have heard bureaucrats, government representatives, and world leaders repeat the mantra — *there is no alternative to globalization,* the TINA syndrome — that is, the globalization of an exclusionary development model that goes by the name of "economic liberalization." How refreshing to see that peasants and farmers around the world have more imagination, and that they are actively participating in the globalization of another vision of how the world should and could be. In assessing the Vía Campesina's work, Servando Olivarria Saavedra says that members of his organization have come to a new understanding of globalization and its impact.

> We learned that we were not the only ones struggling. Globalization has meant the impoverishment of the majority of communities. All the communities of the world that have been deeply affected, overwhelmed and crushed by this economic globalization — we are organizing ourselves. In other words, we need to globalize this struggle for justice, for the survival of community, for the development of communities. We need to globalize this struggle in the poorest of communities everywhere just as the large capitalists have globalized the economy.

Perhaps farmers' imaginations are more often driven by immediate and practical concerns. After all, it is farmers and peasants who know, feel, and live the daily consequences of this corporate model of agriculture. No farmer, anywhere, actually wants to work every day in a toxic, industrialized farm site. While governments continue to ply the media with the good news that economic globalization is leading to increased exports, rarely, if ever, do they bother to explore what is actually happening down on the farms. The ways of life and the survival of peasants and family farms everywhere are at stake, and so too is the well-being of the environment. Indeed, the very existence of farming families depends on alternative farmer-led development.

The Significance of Being a Peasant

Many years ago Karl Marx predicted that with agrarian capitalism peasants would simply disappear. Today the masters of globalization expect them to succumb to commercialized large farms. Yet peasants are stubbornly refusing to go away. Indeed, in the face of a development model geared to ensure the extinction of peasants and small farmers, the Vía Campesina is redefining what it means to be a peasant or a small farmer. A process of "re-peasantization" is occurring as national and regional organizations proudly embrace the term "peasant" to describe themselves. This is certainly the case for many Latin American organizations formed in the late 1980s and as recently as the early 1990s. Asian organizations too, like the Federation of Indonesian Peasant Unions or the Peasant Movement of the Philippines, are clearly affirming their "peasant" identity. Peasants and farmers belonging to the Vía Campesina are proudly declaring an alternative identity: they declare themselves to be "peasants."

In the English-language literature of Europe the term "peasant" has a restricted meaning tied up in feudalism. In the colonial context, and especially in other languages, its meaning expanded. Thus, *paysan* and *campesino* were always to some extent broader categories. But, even in its broadest usage — *campesino* in Latin America — peasants were viewed as remnants of the past. Their demise was welcomed by capitalists, by national and development planners, indeed, by virtually everyone but the peasants themselves. Resurrecting "peasants" represents an act of resistance. As Nettie Wiebe says:

> If you actually look at what "peasant" means, it means "people of the land." Are we Canadian farmers "people of the land"? Well, yes, of course. And it's important to take that language back.... We too are peasants and it's the land and our relationship to the land and food production that distinguishes us.... We're not part of the industrial machine. We're much more closely linked to the places where we grow food and how we grow food, and what the weather is there.... The language around this matters. It begins to make us understand that "people of the land" — peasantry everywhere, the millions of small subsistence peasants with whom we think we have so little in common — identifies them and it identifies us. (quoted in Edelman 2003: 187)

It is this vision that the Vía Campesina name itself suggests. At the 1993 constitutive conference, delegates from Great Britain declared that the literal translation — "Peasant Road" or "Peasant Way" — would be inappropriate not only because of the derogatory connotation attached to the term "peasant" but also because peasants did not actually exist in the English countryside. Jun Borras recalls that many other delegates argued in favour of using the term "peasant" because a term like "farmer" had connotations "that did not capture the nature and character of the farm sector we do represent." In the end, a compromise was reached; delegates opted not to translate "Vía Campesina" into English.

Reclaiming the meaning of peasant is perhaps one of the Vía Campesina's most important accomplishments. Whether you are a peasant, *paysan, paysanne, campesino, campesina*, small farmer, *agricultor, productor*, rural worker, or indigenous peasant — all have embraced and have been embraced by the Vía Campesina. Those involved in the Vía Campesina do not necessarily distinguish among these terms. As Karen Pedersen, women's president of the NFU (2002–05), proudly declared at a public gathering:

> The language around us is changing all the time. Historically, we were peasants. Then when that term came to mean "backward" we became "farmers." In these days "farmer" has the connotation of inefficiency and we are strongly encouraged to be more modern, to see ourselves instead as managers, business people or entrepreneurs capable of handling increasingly larger pieces of territory. Well, I am a farmer and I am a peasant. Through my participation in the Vía Campesina I learned that I had much more in common with peasants then I did with some of my agribusiness neighbours. I am reclaiming the term peasant because I actually believe that small is more efficient, it is socially intelligent, it is community oriented. Being a peasant stands for the kind of agriculture and rural communities we are striving to build.

If some people in the National Farmers Union are rediscovering their peasant roots, others in Mexico had never doubted them. For instance, Emiliano Cerros Nava, an executive commission member of UNORCA in Mexico, patiently explains, "This debate in the literature... is a fabrication at a higher level, by those who know more. In the countryside, out there, there is no such debate. We continue being peasants. That's the way it is."

This is a politicized identity. It reflects people who share a deep commitment to place, who are deeply attached to a particular piece of land, who are all part of a particular rural community, whose mode of existence is under threat. This place-bound identity, that of "people of the land," reflects the belief that they have the right to be on the land. They have the right and obligation to produce food. They have the right to be seen as fulfilling an important function in society at large. They have the right to live in viable communities and the obligation to build community. All of these factors form essential parts of their distinct identity as peasants; in today's politicized globalization, articulating identity across borders and based on locality and tradition is a deeply political act.

The Vía Campesina has jealously guarded its peasant and farmer-led status. All Vía Campesina representatives are either farming themselves or they have been selected, appointed, or elected by farm organizations. The movement has successfully resisted the persistent intrusions of non-governmental organizations (some well-intentioned and some not so well-intentioned), reformist farm organizations, and international institutions. Often these bodies have either tempted the Vía Campesina with the promise of much-needed funds or tried to redirect its agenda. The Vía Campesina restricts its membership to authentic organizations of peasants, farmers, rural women, farm workers, and indigenous communities who must formally demonstrate agreement with the positions and principles of the movement. In the case of rural organizations that also have urban bases, the Vía Campesina strongly encourages these groups to send their rural representatives to participate in Vía Campesina delegations, meetings, and conferences. Non-governmental organizations cannot be members.

In this way the Vía Campesina has succeeded in clearly articulating and firmly placing in the international arena the needs, interests, demands, and visions of those who actually produce food. In doing so, it has helped focus international agriculture and food deliberations on issues such as agrarian reform, GMOs and the control and ownership of seeds, sustainable agricultural practices, human rights and gender equality in the countryside, and the role of international trade in ensuring food sovereignty.

The Vía Campesina's peasant identity reflects a deep attachment to a shared culture. The production, distribution, preparation, consumption, and celebration of food are all fundamental aspects of rural cultures. Seeds are perhaps peasants' most precious resource — and in many cases a deeply cultural and sacred resource. The Vía Campesina regularly engages in the cultural ritual of exchanging seeds. At numerous international gatherings the Vía Campesina representatives bring seeds from their homelands to exchange with their counterparts from different parts of the world. At the first World Food Summit in Rome the Vía Campesina distributed its declaration "The Right to Produce and Access to Land," with the subtitle "Food Sovereignty: A Future Without Hunger," accompanied with a small package of seeds to all delegates in attendance. Vía Campesina members also brought truckloads of earth into the city to form a small plot of land, where peasants, rural women, indigenous peoples, and farmers from different parts of the world all engaged in a symbolic act of planting seeds. The Vía Campesina closed the NGO Forum on Food Sovereignty by distributing seeds collected from around the world while delegates listened to music and a poem expounding the sacredness of seeds.

In carrying out these kinds of actions the Vía Campesina helps to ground the debates. In gifting, exchanging, or symbolically planting seeds — the essence of life — the Vía Campesina takes the familiar and fundamental elements in peasants' daily reality to impress on others the profound impor-tance of farmers' relationship to seeds and to the land. These actions leave a visual imprint of an important yet very simple message: we, the peasants of the world, take seeds, we plant them and we turn them into food. This is our role in society and it is a vital contribution. We are talking about real people, real issues, real lives.

Globalizing Hope

Farm leaders say that the Vía Campesina makes them feel as though they are part of a much wider community of people who share a similar situation and common values. Fred Tait, a member of the NFU, says, "When I look across my fields at the end of the day I now know that I am not alone." Rogelio Alquisiras Borgos of UNORCA expresses much the same sentiment:

> I think that the Vía Campesina is contributing like a small grain of sand because we are no longer alone in the world. It is contributing... in changing existing relations of domination in the world. Now there are voices that are opposing the interests of the transnationals. For example, as a result of what happened in Seattle, we, who are in the most isolated place in the planet, we saw with open eyes that organizations like the Vía Campesina... shared a vision. The WTO is serving the interests of transnationals and this is something we must confront. In the streets we denounced this injustice to the whole world. Although I was not in Seattle, my organization, which is part of the Vía Campesina, was there and I know we are contributing through our local and national experience.

The goal of La Vía Campesina is to bring about change in the countryside — change that improves livelihoods, enhances local food production for local consumption, and opens up democratic spaces; change that empowers the people of the land with a great role, position, and stake in decision-making on issues that have an impact on their lives. The movement believes that this kind of change can occur only when local communities gain greater access to and control over local productive resources, and gain social and political power.

In recognition of how its member communities are deeply influenced by outside forces, the Vía Campesina's strategy is to help strengthen local and national organizations by building solidarity and unity among a great diversity of organizations, and creating spaces for these organizations to participate in international deliberations on agriculture and food.

Thus the Vía Campesina works in an environment of constant tension and reaffirmation. It is a transnational movement of people defined by place. It is a movement in which participants from around the world seek not only to provide an alternative voice in international forums, but also to use the connections among themselves to build a solid foundation for their lives. They are thus forced to reinforce their identities through the use of a constant referent: the routine of their everyday lives grounded in planting and harvesting. This rootedness — in all its various connotations – is being used both to imagine and to present an alternative present and future, an alternative modernity that embraces innovation and global interaction while not obliterating tradition and the importance of locality.

The Vía Campesina insists that peasants and small farmers have a unique place and critical role in redefining agricultural policies. For far too long rural and food policies have been developed in the absence of those most affected. Since policies and actions of outside forces have an immediate and direct impact on the daily lives of "people of the land," this exclusion can no longer be tolerated. Although the Vía Campesina emerged out of exclusion, this does not mean that it is struggling simply to be included in the existing structures – structures that sought to exclude peasants and small farmers in the first place. Instead, the Vía Campesina insists on defining the spaces, the terms and processes of participation, and in so doing fundamentally change the structures that affect agriculture, both locally and globally.

One of those structures is the prevailing model of "development," and the Vía Campesina has countered the failure of development to solve the persistence of poverty and hunger by putting forth its new conceptual framework of food sovereignty. But to help prevent the usurpation of food sovereignty by outside forces, the Vía Campesina will have to work further on its definitions of the theoretical underpinnings and practical policy applications of the approach. For example, how do peasants envision food sovereignty addressing the links between the right to food and livelihood, ownership and control over productive resources (land, seeds, water), development, culture, gender, ethnicity, and knowledge? How are international institutions responding to the goal of food sovereignty? And how does food sovereignty contribute to the struggles of peasant and small-scale farmers?

Furthermore, the failure of development to significantly address issues of poverty and hunger raises fundamental questions about the conceptualization of development itself. Some 75 percent of the world's poor live in the countryside and depend on the agriculture for survival. For the first time, with the formation of the Vía Campesina, peasants and farmers have a collective voice. Their ability to articulate visions of their world should prompt a wealth of new research to help explain the failures of development and to suggest viable alternatives.

In the meantime Vía Campesina organizations around the world are engaging in a variety of non-violent collective actions ranging from participation and collaboration to non-participation. They engage in negotiations accompanied by mobilization and direct action (Vía Campesina 2000b). In the process the organization redefines what is political. Just like the food justice movements' statement that "eating has become a political act," the Vía Campesina (1999b: 1) asserts that "producing quality products for our own people has also become a political act…. This touches our very identities as citizens of the world." The Vía Campesina's cultural politics redefines what it means to be a peasant or a farmer, redefines what constitutes knowledge and who gets to define and control knowledge, introduces new concepts, and hence helps shape the international agenda.

The formation and consolidation of the Vía Campesina provide living proof, then, that peasant and farm families have not been compliant accomplices during this process of economic restructuring, nor have they been passive victims in the face of increasing poverty and marginalization. Instead, they are actively resisting the globalization of a corporate model of agriculture. Indeed, peasants and farmers are using three traditional weapons of the weak — organization, co-operation, and community — to redefine "development" and build an alternative model of agriculture based on the principles of social justice, ecological sustainability, and respect for peasant cultures and peasant economies. This involves building viable alternatives ranging from small agricultural co-operatives, local seed banks, and fair-trade ventures to reclaiming traditional farming practices. It also means linking these efforts beyond the local by working at the national, regional, and international levels.

In forming the Vía Campesina, peasants and farm organizations effectively transnationalized and succeeded in carving out a space in the international arena. The Vía Campesina is filling that space with peasant voices, articulating peasant demands and peasant alternatives in efforts to resist the imposition of a corporate model of agriculture. The solidarity and unity experienced with the Vía Campesina yield perhaps the most precious gift of all, hope. Hope that "another" agriculture is possible. Indeed, the Vía Campesina enables us to imagine that change is possible and that an alternative project is being created. This is clearly captured in the Vía Campesina's slogan "Globalize the Struggle — Globalize Hope."

Appendix A:
Similarities and Differences among Nicaraguan and Canadian Farm Women

Economic similarities
- Negative effect of general economic instability and economic crisis in the farm community.
- Cheap food policy, high input costs, low prices for produce.
- Pride in being good efficient producers.
- Lack of recognition of the full value of women's work.
- Demand for equal pay for work of equal value.
- Women's jobs tend to be in the lower-paying sector.
- Lack of access to credit for women.
- There are class differences among farmers based on ownership and control of productive property.

Economic differences
- Canadian economic need for survival is not as great as for Nicaragua.
- Economic standard of living is higher in Canada.
- Canada has more mechanized production; Nicaraguan production is more manual.
- In Canada, women own and control more land than do Nicaragua women.
- The banks in Nicaragua do not foreclose on farmers in debt. In Canada farm foreclosure is an everyday occurrence.
- There is no agrarian reform in Canada.
- There are more co-operative enterprises and state enterprises in Nicaragua; in Canada individual farming is most common while a few (5%) enterprises are corporate.

Social similarities
- Lack of adequate rural child care and other support programs for women in production.
- Limiting social structures and values which hinder women's full community involvement.
- Lack of participation of men in child care and domestic work.
- Limited participation of women in policy-making level of the media.
- Right to participate in all aspects of health care as it affects women, e.g. abortion.
- The problem of migration to the cities, deruralization.
- The sustaining of family, life,

Social differences
- Nicaraguan women have a greater capacity and self-assurance in expressing their concerns.
- Level of organization of women is higher in Nicaragua, with greater unity, while Canadian women's organizations are fragmented.
- Greater level of trust among sectors of Nicaraguan women and among the women of each sector.
- Nicaraguan women are alive, active, determined, and committed to changes for their own good, for their family and country; Canadian women tend to be apathetic and disempowered.

children are high priorities for women.
- Both societies are male-dominated in practice.

- Canadian women are more individualistic; Nicaraguan women have collective sense.
- The problem of male domination is more open in Nicaragua. It has more subtle and hidden expressions in Canada.

Source: Reformatted from Women in Agriculture Study Tour (1989: 5–8)

Appendix B:
Common Issues and Struggles of Women Organized in the UNAG and the NFU

Understanding the differences	*Recognizing the common ground*	*Sharing the gender struggle*
• Canada is one of the wealthiest nations in the world, while Nicaragua is one of the poorest nations in Latin America.	• Globalization of an industrialized, neo-liberal, export-oriented model of agriculture is affecting farming families everywhere in similar ways.	• Unequal gender relations.
• Canadian agriculture is highly mechanized and demands huge capital investments. Farm size is increasing while rural depopulation is in the rise. Nicaraguan agriculture is more labour-intensive and is less dependent on capital investment.	• Farmers do not get cost of production.	• Gender division of labour that does not recognize women's reproductive work, does not place equal value on women's productive work and allocates women the more invisible roles in community work.
	• Farmers everywhere are caught in a price-cost squeeze which pushes them to intensify production by increasing their use of farm chemicals.	• Unequal access to and control over productive resources.
• In Canada, farmers represent only 4% of the population, while 44% of the Nicaragua labour force is involved in agriculture.	• Land is being increasingly concentrated in the hands of fewer people.	

Source: Adapted from NFU-UNAG Women's Linkage Committee, n.d.

Appendix C:
The Vía Campesina Gender Position Paper

Background and Analysis

The radical changes that are occurring in the countryside are undermining the economies, cultures and the very lives of rural women all over the world. We, in the Vía Campesina, understand that these threats to women, mothers and the Mother Earth must be analyzed and conscientiously, collectively confronted in order to shape a future that is filled with regenerative energy, justice and hope.

The global neo-liberal economic agenda is designed to enhance corporate profit and concentrate power without regard for the destruction of nature, culture, community or the well-being of people. The impact of these changes are most acute in rural areas where the brutal exploitation of the environment and the people of the land is an immediate, daily experience for millions. Women experience the impact of these changes in different ways than their male counterparts because of their history, roles and relationships. Hence it is fitting and necessary to articulate a gender analysis in order to shape inclusive, just and viable long-term solutions.

The predominant current economic goal of increasing the production of saleable items assigns more value to industrial production than reproduction, manufacturing than nurturing, profits than people. This devalues the reproductive, regenerative forces both of the natural world and in human society. As the bearers of children all women are suffering from this fundamental shift in values. As those who grow food and take care of the land, peasant and rural women are doubly discounted and disadvantaged by the policies and social changes based on these neo-liberal values. These negative changes, coupled with a history of subjugation and voicelessness, often undermine the self-esteem and leadership confidence of rural and peasant women.

However, women of the land are key to the building of healthy, sustainable rural communities, caring for the land and achieving genuine, long-term food security. Rural women produce much of the food that feeds families and local communities. They are historically and currently responsible for protecting and enhancing the bio-diversity which is vital to human survival. They are the beating heart of rural cultures. Genuine rural development, which includes cultural, social, economic and environmental rejuvenation, depends on rural women consciously and courageously taking a leading role.

Principles and Commitments

1. Equality and Human Rights
1.1 Women are entitled to full and equal social and political decision-making.

The barriers to the full democratic participation and leadership of women in these arenas must be systematically erased. Women's perspectives, leadership and energy are essential for the building of just societies.

1.2 Peasant and rural organizations must reflect the key role of women in their organizational structures and policies. Equality and full democratic participation of women within our own organizations must model the social and political equality we are struggling for in all other domains.

1.3 We demand an end to human rights violations in the countryside. The intimidation and brutalization of peasants, which often includes the sexual as well as physical abuse of women and girls, must stop. We denounce the violent displacement of peasants and the militarization of the countryside. Military conflict should be resolved by negotiated processes and include the participation of women.

1.4 The confidence, self-esteem and human potential of women is cruelly undermined by the subjugation and abuse many experience within their own homes. We commit ourselves to respecting women and upholding their right to be free from domestic violence and repression.

2. Economic Justice

2.1 The neo-liberal economic model, which forces everyone into a global competition, is most disadvantageous and unjust to peasant women. It strips them of resources to grow food and forces them into an uncertain struggle for their own and their children's survival. It leaves rural displacement, family and community break down, joblessness, low wages, and economic slavery in its path. Women suffer the most acute and widespread impoverishment under these conditions. Because women bear the biggest cost of these changes, justice demands that they have a larger role in reshaping the economy. The Vía Campesina will lead the way in demanding and demonstrating alternative economic arrangements which give the needs of women and children first priority, rather than relegating them to last place as is currently being done.

2.2 Women have always had, and continue to have, primary responsibility for the food provisions of their families and communities. In order to be able to fulfill that role, women must have access to land in their own right. We are committed to ensuring that women gain security of tenure on land, and have equal access to such credit and training as may be required to enhance their food production.

2.3 Women have a long tradition of gathering, selecting and propagating seed varieties for food and medicinal uses. They are primary protectors of the world's genetic resources and bio-diversity. We oppose the corporate theft and patenting of these genetic resources. Women's traditional knowledge must be honoured and respected and their ability to continue the vital role of protecting and enhancing bio-diversity must never be undermined. The future of humankind depends on this.

2.4 Women who work in the agriculture or rural service sectors for wages must be given wages equal to those of their male counterparts. Wage discrimination on the basis of gender is a fundamental injustice against women. Along with being paid lower wages, women are sometimes made to suffer the psychological and physical damage of sexual harassment in workplaces, and are forced by economic circumstances to endure unhealthy and even dangerous working conditions. This is unacceptable.

3. Social Development

3.1 Our goal of rural development includes the genuine improvement and development of human society, rather than merely the increased production of industrial goods. We are working to achieve a model of rural development which improves education for all rural people, ensuring especially that all children, girls as well as boys, have the opportunity to get schooling.

3.2 We recognize that in the current global context we must build links of solidarity and egalitarian interdependence in order to stave off an enslaving dependence on transnational corporations. In order to resist the corporate onslaught and build cohesive, regenerative communities, the Vía Campesina commits itself to respect the autonomy and human value of all persons and the many unique cultures of peasant communities.

3.3 Rural women must have access to adequate and appropriate health care services. A great deal of unnecessary suffering is caused by the lack of basic health facilities, medicines and trained professionals in the countryside. Health services must never be tied to forced sterilization or acceptance of corporate products such as baby formula.

3.4 Our health, and that of our families, is increasingly endangered by the chemical and biological pollution and lack of good water and soil as a result of modern production methods. The global experimentation with genetically modified seeds and plants is a Russian roulette. These agricultural production practices also reduce our quality of life. Economic globalization undermines any possibility of building a sustainable future. The Vía Campesina will continue to struggle against the environmental destruction which is destroying the health of families along with the health of the eco-system.

Action Plans

* Work to achieve gender parity at all policy-making events within our organizations at the local, national, regional and international levels.
* Achieve the goal of having 50 percent women delegates in all committees and conferences of the Vía Campesina.
* Build leadership among women through concrete training and participation in programs.
* Support the organization of gender workshops for both women and men.
* Ensure that women take positions of decision-making within local, regional, national and international peasant and farm organizations.
* Continue to actively build links of solidarity between peasant and farm women within the Vía Campesina movement through better communication, meetings, exchanges and collective analysis.
* Gender issues should be integrated into all of the following themes of the Vía Campesina: agrarian reform, biodiversity and genetic resources, human rights, food sovereignty and trade and farmer based sustainable agriculture. Develop a strategy of publicity and mass media campaigns on these issues.
* All Vía Campesina initiatives should be implemented and assessed to ensure that they respect equal rights of women.
* All members in all participating Vía Campesina organizations must accept the importance of developing a gender, class and ethnicity perspective and integrate this into their frameworks. The burning problem of inequality between the genders can be solved in the countryside.
* Vía Campesina organizations must build and support literacy training programs, consciousness raising and political training in rural areas. The Vía Campesina demands free education for all women and men.
* The Women's Assembly pointed out that women want equality; they do not want to overcome men. Equality means that women need social, psychological, physical and economical support.
* For this reason Vía Campesina needs better coordination so that there is greater interaction with organizations around the world. To ensure better coordination, coordinators from each country should work together to find solutions to the issues they face at the national level; they should also work closely together to strengthen the work at the international level.

Notes

1. "Where Have All the Peasants Gone? Long Time Passing"

1. There is an extensive literature on the role of the peasantry. Key historical references include Lenin (1954), Chayanov (1966), Moore (1966), Wolf (1966, 1969), Paige (1975), and Scott (1976, 1985). For more recent debates see, among others, Bryceson, Kay, and Mooij (2000), Otero (1998), Bernstein and Byers (2001), and Brass (2000a, 2000b, 2005).

2. Here, Edelman is referring to studies like Michael Kearney's (1996) *Reconceptualizing the Peasantry: Anthropology in Global Perspective.*

3. See, for example, Moyo and Yeros (2005), Wright and Wolford (2003), Branford and Rocha (2002), Edelman (1999), Petras and Veltmeyer (2001), Sinha et al. (1997), Brass (1995), Veltmeyer (1997 and 2000), and Starn (1999).

2. Modernization and Globalization

1. The major regional trade agreements are the Andean Community (formerly known as the Andean Pact), Asia-Pacific Economic Co-operation Forum (APEC), European Union (EU), Mercado Común del Sur (MERCOSUR), North American Free Trade Agreement (NAFTA), South African Development Community (SADC), and the South Asian Association for Regional Cooperation (SAARC). The Free Trade Area of the Americas (FTAA) is still being negotiated.

2. The Cairns Group, named after the town where its first meeting took place, includes Australia, New Zealand, Canada, Argentina, Brazil, Paraguay, Uruguay, Chile, Colombia, Costa Rica, the Philippines, Fiji, Guatemala, Indonesia, Malaysia, South Africa, and Thailand.

3. From an interview with Dr. Fred Perlak in *Food? Health? Hope?* a documentary produced and directed by Deepti Seshadri and Rajani Mani (Bangalore Talkies, India, 2000).

4. Significantly, Hardin (1991, 1998) eventually altered his original notion of the "tragedy of the commons" to that of the "tragedy of the unmanaged commons."

5. See NFU 2000a for an excellent visual description and analysis of the highly concentrated group of corporate players that dominate each link of the Canadian food chain.

6. A number of reports highlight the increase in farmers' suicides in various states. See Dandekar et al. (2005), Government of Andhra Pradesh (2004), Mohanty (2005), and Mohan Rao (2004).

7. Thanks to Nico Verhagen, technical assistant to the International Operational Secretariat of the Vía Campesina, for pointing this out to me.

3. Peasants and Farmers Going Global

1. I was unable to find out when the American Farm Bureau Federation ceased being an IFAP member.

2. Blokland's (1993) notions of *concertación* and "concerted peasant alliances" were included in the package of preparatory documents for the Mons Vía Campesina conference. *Concertación* emerged in Nicaragua and other Central American countries as part of the reconstruction efforts following the civil wars in the region. *Concertación* operates at three levels: 1) within a sector it involves different classes coming together once common interests are identified; 2) working out differences and arriving at commonalities with other sectors; and 3) reaching *concertación* with the state. See Blokland (1995) for an expanded version of the 1993 article.

3. Edelman analyzes the strained relations between NGOs and peasant organizations in Central America (1998a, 1998b) and Costa Rica (1999). Bebbington (1998) discusses the changing roles and subsequent crises of identity and legitimacy of NGOs working in the rural sector in the Andes and Chile. Tadem (1996) traces the history of relations between NGOs and people's organizations in the Philippines.

4. In an interview in 2000 Blokland said that he was now director of Agriterra, an NGO that he said was working with the same vision that had initially been offered to the Vía Campesina. He explained that Agriterra seeks to: "build a strong farmers' movement through north/south and south/south cooperation. This involves exchanges, sharing of experiences among organizations and strengthening organizations' capacity to do advocacy to better represent the interests of farmers in government policies." According to Agriterra's Annual Report (1999: 6) it: "mobilises technical assistance (pool of experts); promotes supplementary financing (including loans, guarantees or risk-bearing investments); facilitates apprenticeships on Dutch farms and in co-operatives; promotes joint ventures (international agricultural brokerage); and pools its own resources as well as public funds together with direct investment capital of Dutch co-operatives)." Agriterra works closely with IFAP: the current chair of the board of Agriterra (Gerard Doornbos) was the president of IFAP, 2000–02, and Blokland (director of Agriterra) was vice-chair of the Development Cooperation Committee of IFAP.

5. These observations were communicated to me in personal conversations with an NGO representative who, for obvious reasons, will remain unnamed.

6. Although no such Code of Principles was ever established, during its Third International Conference the Vía Campesina established the basics of an internal position on international relations and strategic alliances, outlining its strategies, principles, and terms of engagement.

4. "The WTO... Will Meet Somewhere, Sometime. And We Will Be There"

1. Of the forty-four farmer representatives listed in the IFAP delegation to Doha, only eight were from developing countries. See IFAP (2001) for the complete list.

2. The killing of a young protester at the G8 demonstration in Genoa no doubt also contributed to the decision of the FAO and Italian government to postpone the World Food Summit.

3. *Satyagraha* means "truth force," but generally refers to non-violent resistance.

4. Sutherland appears to have misrepresented IFAP's position. Wiebe (2001), who was then president of the NFU, told me in an interview that while IFAP agreed with the general thrust of liberalized trade it also raised a number of clear reservations and caveats to the draft agreement.

5. Some of the main organizations responsible for spearheading the Our World Is Not for Sale strategies and actions leading up to Doha were: the Arab NGO Network for Development, Friends of the Earth International, International Forum on Globalization, Public Citizen's Global Trade Watch, Council of Canadians, Focus on the Global South, Vía Campesina, and World Forum of Fisher Peoples.

6. In spring 2001 the Vía Campesina and Friends of the Earth called a meeting with farmers' organizations and NGOs to discuss joint strategies on trade, agriculture, and food sovereignty. Following this meeting a subgroup was formed to draft the Peoples' Food Sovereignty document (Verhagen 2001). Organizations participating in the Our World Is Not for Sale coalition then formed the Peoples' Food Sovereignty Network to focus more specifically on issues of food, agriculture, and globalization. This network is now called the Agri-Trade Group. The "Priority to Peoples' Food Sovereignty — WTO Out of Food and Agriculture Campaign" was developed by the Agri-Trade Group and launched by the Vía Campesina, COASAD, Collectif Statrégies Alimentaires, ETC Group (formerly RAFI), Focus on the Global South, Foodfirst/Institute for Food and Development Policy, Friends of the Earth Latin America and Caribbean, Friends of the Earth England, Wales and Northern Ireland, GRAIN, Institute for Agriculture and Trade Policy, IBON Foundation, and Public Citizen's Energy and Environment Program.

7. Kwa (2002) provides an in-depth analysis of the WTO's practices by closely examining numerous personal accounts of WTO negotiators from developing countries. For other accounts see *Focus on Trade* (2002), reports from the Coalition of Civil Society groups in Doha (2001a, 2001b), *Agence France Presse* (2001a), and the Joint Statement of NGOs and Social Movements (2002).

8. The petition was signed by Oxfam International, Institute for Agriculture and Trade Policy (USA), Australia Council for Overseas Aid, German Forum for Environment and Development, Research and Information Systems (New Delhi), Canadian Council for International Co-operation, RODI (Kenya), Canadian Foodgrains Bank, GermanWatch, International Gender and Trade Network-Europe, and the International Coalition for Development Action (Brussels).

5. *A Fine Balance: Local Realities and Global Actions*

1. The United States, for example, has attacked (unsuccessfully) the Canadian Wheat Board eleven times. These international trade challenges, which the

CWB considers a form of harassment, can cost the Board anywhere from $2 to $5 million (White 2002: 5). Farm newspapers recently reported on a leaked government document in which bureaucrats were recommending that Canada be willing to give up supply management in the current round of WTO negotiations (Wilson 2002d: 3).

2. The following description and analysis of the IPC was facilitated by access to all pertinent NFU files and documents, such as minutes of the IPC and NFU national board meetings. I also reviewed the Oxfam Global Agriculture Project files, which provided detailed information about various IPC activities.

3. See David Myhre (1994) for a discussion of UNORCA's efforts to restructure the agricultural credit system. Neil Harvey (1990) provides a good analysis of agrarian movements in Mexico during the period 1979–90 and see Barry (1995), de Ita Rubio (1994), Randall (1999), Comisión de Agricultura (2000), and Public Citizen's Global Trade Watch (2001) for in-depth discussions of changes in agricultural policies and the impact of liberalization on peasant agriculture.

4. The divisions among the peasant movements in the Philippines occurred in the framework of major splits in the Philippine left, including the Communist Party of the Philippines, the National Democratic Front, and the National People's Army. See Rocamora (1993, 1994) for an analysis of these struggles, and dKMP (1993) for a brief overview of the KMP–dKMP split.

5. The five Mexican organizations are UNORCA, Asociación Nacional de Empresas Comercializadoras de Productores del Campo (ANEC), Asociación Mexicana de Uniones de Crédito del Sector Social (AMUCSS), Central Independiente de Obreros Agícolas y Campesinos (CIOAC), and the Coordinadora Nacional Plan de Ayala (CNPA).

6. As part of a restructuring of U.N. agencies, the U.N. Commission on Human Rights no longer exists and has been replaced by the U.N. Human Rights Council. The Council met for the first time in June 2006.

7. An international controversy erupted in early 2002 when the results of a scientific study revealed that in some remote areas of two Mexican states (Puebla and Oaxaca) corn varieties had been found to have genetically modified contamination rates of up to 60 percent. This occurred in a country where it is illegal to grow GM corn. See 2002 FoodFirst Backgrounder (8, 2) and Joint Statement on the Mexican GM Maize Scandal (2002) for full discussion.

8. Doris Gutierrez de Hernandez was first elected to the Nacional Congress in Honduras as the alternate deputy from the Department of Francisco Morazan. Subsequently, for the period 2002–06 she was elected as deputy of the National Congress in the same department.

6. *Co-operation, Collaboration, and Community*

1. The NFU was the co-ordinator of this project. The following observations were made from information provided in the final report submitted

to funders by the Vía Campesina Women's Working Group (1999). The project also produced proceedings of each of the three workshops. In my capacity as Technical Support I also participated in the first meeting of this working group followed by the meeting of the ICC. The account of the meetings reflects my observations and the information compiled in the Vía Campesina's Women's Working Group (1996) report of the meeting held in San Salvador.

2. There is some discrepancy in the numbers reported. The internal documentation that immediately followed these events stated that 150 women participated in the Assembly and Congress which meant that women represented 44 percent of all delegates. However, in the absence of having the complete list of delegates the numbers used here are based on information provided in the official proceedings. See CLOC (1997) and CLOC–Vía Campesina (1997) for the full proceedings of the First Latin American Rural Women's Assembly and the II Congress of the CLOC.

3. According to the final declarations of CLOC events in Mexico, the Second Latin American Assembly of Rural Women brought together 180 women. A total of 320 delegates participated in the third congress of CLOC.

4. The following observations are based on an analysis of the proceedings of the Asian Peasant Women's Workshop (1999).

5. The Third International Conference also agreed to amalgamate Eastern Europe with Western Europe, thus reducing the number of regions from eight to seven.

6. The Third International Conference discussed and further elaborated position papers on all of the Vía Campesina key themes, and gender is one of those themes. The NFU, as co-ordinator of the Women's Commission, circulated a first-draft position (in Spanish, English, and French) to members of the ICC and the Women's Commission in late spring 1999 for discussion at the local, national, and regional levels.

7. UPANACIONAL sent two letters to Vía Campesina: the first had no date but made reference to Hurricane Mitch, which suggested that it was probably written in early 1999; the second letter was dated Sept. 14, 2000.

References

Primary sources

Individual interviews conducted by author
Alegría, Rafael, Vía Campesina Operational Secretariat. 10 September 2000, Tegucigalpa, Honduras.

Alfonso Herrera, Ramos, co-ordinator, arts section, Sanzekan Tinemi. 23 March 2000, Chilapa, Guerrero.

Alquisiras Borgos, Rogelio, co-ordinator, arts and crafts section, Sanzekan Timeni. 24 March 2000, Chilapa, Guerrero.

Andrade Reyes, Jésus, staff-person responsible for commercialization, UNORCA. 24 February 2000, Mexico City.

Armenta Bojorquez, Héctor, president, Marcelo Loya Ornelas, Sociedad de Producción Rural. 26 April 2000, Guasave, Sinaloa.

Assadi, Mustafa, professor, Department of Political Science, University of Mysore. 20 November 2000, Mysore, Karnataka.

Basavaraj, G.V., working president, KRRS in Sagar Taluk. 13 November 2000, Goolihalli Village, Avinahalli.

Basavaraj, K.B., member of KRRS. 13 November 2000, Kerematha Village, Avinahalli.

Boisgontier, Christian, leader, Confédération Paysanne. 5 December 2000, Paris, France.

Blokland, Kees, director, Agriterra. 8 December 2000, Arnhem, The Netherlands.

Boehm, Terry, member, national board, National Farmers Union. 21 October 2000, telephone interview.

Borras, (Jun) Saturnino, former representative, KMP, and founding member, Vía Campesina. 19 March 2001, interview by e-mail.

Cabrera López, Teresa, technical support to ARIC Independiente. 10 February 2000, Ocozocoautla, Chiapas.

Cabrera Rosales, Consuelo, former ASOCODE representative, Vía Campesina Women's Commission. 27 April 2001, Guatemala City.

Carreon Mundo, Marcelo, leader, Organización de Ejidos de Productores Forestales de la Zona Maya. 29 February 2000, Felipe Carrillo Puerto, Quintana Roo.

Carrillo, Olegario, former national board member, UNORCA, and elected representative, state legislature of Sonora. 6 May 2000, Chilapa, Guerrero.

Cerros Nava, Emiliano, member, executive commission, UNORCA, Mexico. 23 February 2000, Mexico City.

Chautla Ramos, Brígida, co-ordinator, UNORCA's indigenous and human rights network. 17 February 2000, Mexico City.

Chemerika, Lisa, former participant and co-ordinator, CCAEP. 25 August 2002, telephone interview.

Choplin, Gerard, co-ordinatorm CPE. 12 December 2001, Brussels, Belgium; 11 October 2002, telephone interview.

Easter, Wayne, former president, NFU. 31 January 2002, telephone interview.

Encino Hernández, Porfirio, member, executive commission, and national board member, UNORCA. 21 March 2000, Mexico City.

Flores Castro, Alvaro, president of executive committee, Sanzekan Tinemi. 24 March 2000, Chilapa, Guerrero.

Ganapathiyappa, H., president, Freedom Fighters' Association. 14 November 2000, Sagar, Shimoga.

Gangadhara, K.C., KRRS secretary, Shimoga District. 16 November 2000, Kachinakatte Village, Shimoga.

Gangadhara, K.T., state general secretary, KRRS. 13 November 2000, Shimoga.

Gómez Flores, Alberto, executive co-ordinator, UNORCA. 6 April 2000, Mexico City.

Gutiérrez de Hernández, Doris, technical assistant, Operational Secretariat of the Vía Campesina. 18 September 2000, Tegucigalpa, Honduras.

Hernández Cascante, Jorge Luis, program co-ordinator, UPANACIONAL. 3 March 2001, San Jose, Costa Rica.

Hernández Jiménez, Raquel, secretary, executive committee, Sanzekan Tinemi. 23 March 2000, Chilapa, Guerrero.

Hernández Libreros, José Francisco, responsible for communications, Organizacíon de Ejidos Productores Forestales de la Zona Maya. 28 February 2000, Felipe Carillo Puerto, Quintana Roo.

Hernández Salazar, Edith, responsible for managing supplies, Sanzekan Timemi. 25 March 2000, Chilapa, Guerrero.

Hilario Francisco, Diego, regional co-ordinator, UNORCA, Vera Cruz. 18 February 2000, Mexico City.

Hoff, Dena, national board member, National Family Farm Coalition. 22 October 2002, telephone interview.

Jaimes Chávez, Zohelio, leader, Coalición de Ejidos de la Costa Grande de Guerrero. 25 March 2000, Atoyac de Alvarez, Guerrero.

Kesteloot, Thierry, program co-ordinator, Oxfam Solidarité. 26 November 2000, Brussels, Belgium.

Ladrón de Guevarra, Ernesto, former staff-person, UNORCA. 25 February 2000, Mexico City.

LaPlante, Maxime, leader, Union Paysanne. 15 October 2002, telephone interview.

Ledesma Santos, Rosa, responsible for forestry improvement, Organización de Ejidos Productores Forestales de la Zona Maya. 28 February 2000, Felipe Carrillo Puerto, Quintana Roo.

Magaña, Guerrero, Pedro, former regional co-ordinator, UNORCA, Guanajuato. 13 March 2000, Mexico City.

Meenakshi, G.B., KRRS president, women's wing of Sagar Taluk. 13 November,

Goolihalli Village.

Meneses, Luis, former executive co-ordinator, UNORCA. 7 March 2000, 5 April 2000, Mexico City.

Mungarro Garibay, Lina, co-ordinator, Asociación Mexicana de Mujeres Organizadas en Red (AMMOR). 13 March 2000, Mexico City.

Murrel, Roxanne, program co-ordinator, Oxfam-Canada. 5 February 2002, e-mail interview by author.

Nanjundaswamy, M.D., president, KRRS, and regional co-ordinator, Vía Campesina. 8 November 2000, 9 November 2000, Bangalore, Karnataka.

Nicholson, Paul, leader, CPE, and regional co-ordinator, Campesina. 4 December 2000, Lekeitio, Spain; 22 February 2002, telephone interview.

Olivarria Saavedra, Servando, regional co-ordinator, UNORCA. 29 April 2000, Culiacán, Sinaloa.

Parameshwarappa, M., member, KRRS. 18 November 2000, Chinnikatte, Honnali Taluk, Davangere.

Pedersen, Karen, women's president, NFU. 21 June 2002, Cutknife, Saskatchewan.

Pilar López Sierra, Maria, researcher, CECCAM. 7 April 2000, Mexico City.

Prakash, T.N., associate professor, Department of Agricultural Economics, University of Agricultural Sciences, Bangalore, Karnataka, India. 3 November 2000, Bangalore, India.

Puttanaiah, K.S., president, KRRS. 2 November 2000, District of Mysore.

Qualman, Darrin, executive secretary, NFU. 5 October 2001, Saskatoon, Saskatchewan.

Quevedo Castro, José Luis, secretary general, Comité Regional Campesino Autónomo de Guasave y Sinaloa de Leyva. 26 April 2000, Guasave, Sinaloa.

Rajashekara, T.K., general secretary, KRRS, Sagar Taluk. 14 November 2000, Thavarehalli Villa, Anadaspuram.

Rebollar Domínguez, Laura, technical team member, Asociación Mexicana de Mujeres Organizadas en Red. 8 February 2000, Mexico City.

Riqueño Sánchez, Filipa, secretary, executive committee, Titakititoke Tajame Sihauame. 24 March 2000, Chilapa Guerrero.

Rutherford, Sally, former executive director, Canadian Federation of Agriculture. 8 February 2002, telephone interview.

Santos Jiménez, Victoria Juana, co-ordinator, sustainable agriculture and women's programs, Organización de Ejidos Productores Forestales de la Zona Maya. 2 March 2000, Felipe Carrillo Puerto, Quintana Roo.

Senapathi, K.B., KRRS president, Sagar Taluk. 15 November 2000, Karemtha Village, Avinahalli.

Serrano Castro, Rosa Isela, former president, Asociación Mexicana de Mujeres Organizadas en Red (AMMOR), and national board member, UNORCA. 2 May 2000, on the road from Sinaloa to Guerrero.

Shanmukhappa, Angadi, member, KRRS. 17 November 2000, Shikaripura, Shimoga.

Shivappa, G., member, KRRS. 18 November 2000, Shikaripura Taluk, Shimoga.

Soto Ramírez, Marina, staffperson, Asociación Mexicana de Mujeres Organizadas en Red (AMMOR). 8 February 2000, Mexico City.

Storey, Shannon, former NFU women's president. 6 October 2001, Saskatoon, Saskatchewan.

Suárez, Víctor, co-ordinator, ANEC. 6 April 2000, Mexico City.

Subbanna, K.V., member, KRRS. 18 November, Heggodu, Shimoga.

Thiesson, Stuart, former executive secretary, NFU. 4 October 2001, Saskatoon, Saskatchewan.

Tlacotempa Zapoteco, Albino, general co-ordinator, reforestation and natural resources, Sanzekan Timemi. 24 March 2000, Chilapa Guerrero.

Toner, Conrad, former NFU national board member. 6 May 2002, telephone interview.

Umapathiyappa, G., KRRS president, Shimoga District. 18 November, Sugoor Village, Simoga.

Valenzuela, Alfonso, former national board member, UNORCA, and representative elected to the state legislature, Sonora. 6 May 2000, Chilapa, Guerrero.

Valenzuela Segura, Benjamín, director, SEPRODAC, and national board member, UNORCA. 1 May 2000, Culiacán, Sinaloa.

Venegas, Holanda, secretary, Asociación Mexicana de Mujeres Organizadas en Red. 13 March 2000, Mexico City.

Verhagen, Nico, technical assistant, Vía Campesina Operational Secretariat. 11 December 2001, Brussels, Netherlands; 27 February 2003, telephone interview.

Vidals, Velaria, treasurer, Asociación Mexicana de Mujeres Organizadas en Red. 13 March 2000, Mexico City.

Vuarin, Pierre, program co-ordinator, Fondation pour le Progrès de l'Homme. 5 December 2000, Paris, France.

Vuffray, Gérard, farm leader, Uni-Terre. 24 January 2002, telephone interview.

Wells, Stewart, president, NFU. 22 September 2001, Saskatoon, Saskatchewan.

Wiebe, Nettie, former president, NFU, and regional co-ordinator, Vía Campesina. 16 November 1998, Calgary, Alberta; 28 September 2001, Laura, Saskatchewan; 17 June 2002, Saskatoon, Saskatchewan.

Yam Moo, Dionicio, peasant. 1 March 2000, Felipe Carrillo Puerto, Quintana Roo.

Group interviews conducted by author

Coalición de Ejidos of the Costa Grande de Guerrero. 25 March, 2000, Atoyac de Alvarez, Guerrero.
  Jardiel Jaimes Chávez, member, technical team
  Zohélio Jaimes Chávez, responsible for relations and management
  Leonides Donjuan Cuarca, president, co-operative el Sasanil
  Carmelo Martínez de Jesus, state co-ordinator, UNORCA
  Ignacio Serrano Radilla, responsible for communications
  Irinea Ocampo Bella, president, regional co-operative of loans and savings
  Ramón Millan Flores, responsible for information dissemination

Ejido Chichuahuita. 25 April 2000, Los Mochis, Sinaloa.
   Marco Antonio Quintero Félix, regional co-ordinator, UNORCA
   Elizardo Leyva Angelo, member and president, Comité 30 de Marzo
Organización de Ejidos Productores Forestales de la Zona Maya. 1 March 2000,
   Felipe Carrillo Puerto, Quintana Roo.
   Olga Alguilar Che, responsible for the *traspatio* program
   Diana Marcela Arceo Manrique, responsible for women's groups
   María Yolanda Caamal Pachero, promoter
Union de Ejidos Emiliano Zapata. 27 April, 2000, Los Chinitos, Sinaloa.
   Alejandro Sánchez Dominguez, ejido adminstrator
   Isidro Morales Ramirez, former ejido president (1990–93)
   Félix Luna González, current president
   Octavio Sánchez Belerra, ejido member
   Moisés Barajas Pérez, former ejido president (1989–92)
   Juan Carlos Moreno Martínez, ejido member

Primary documents
Vía Campesina policy position papers, 1993–2003.
Vía Campesina press releases, 1993–2003.
Minutes of meetings and reports, Operational Secretariat for the International
   Co-ordinating Committee of the Vía Campesina, held on:
   21–25 February1994, Lima, Peru
   1–3 April 1994, Krakow, Poland
   1–2 October 1994, Segovia, Spain
   3–4 March 1995, Brussels, Belgium
   8–11 October, 1995, Quebec City, Quebec
   10–11 November, 1996, Rome, Italy
   22 April 1996, Mexico City, Mexico
   9–11 August 1996, San Salvador, El Salvador
   8–9 November 1997, Brasilia, Brazil
   16–20 May 1998, Geneva, Switzerland
   1–2 November 1998, Dakar, Senegal
   10–11 March 1999, Isarn, Thailand
   27 November–3 December 1999, Seattle, United States
   24–25 May 2000, Dresden, Germany
   7 October 2000, Bangalore, India
   31 January–1 February, 2001, Porto Alegre, Brazil
   1–2 September 2001, La Habana, Cuba
   10–12 January 2002 Paris, France.
Minutes of meetings and workshops, Women's Commission of the CLOC/Vía
   Campesina, held on:
   2–3 November 1997, Brasilia, Brazil
   16–17 March 1998, Santo Domingo, Dominican Republic
   13–17 April 1998, Tegucigalpa, Honduras
   7–12 September 1998, San Salvador, El Salvador
   10–11 June 1999, Kingstown, St. Vincent and the Grenadines

8–12 September 2000, Managua, Nicaragua.

Minutes of meetings, Women's Commission of the Vía Campesina, held on:
6–7 August 1996, San Salvador, El Salvador
29 November and 3 December 1999, Seattle, United States
31 August 2001, La Habana, Cuba.

Primary sources: Unpublished documents

Alegría, Rafael. 2001. Letter from Rafael Alegría, Operational Secretariat of the Vía Campesina to Silvio Mazarioli, member of Organizing Committee of the Global Peasant's Encounter, 15 May.

Asian Peasant Women's Workshop. 1999. "Proceedings of the Asian Peasant Women's Workshop." Held on 11–13 August in Bangkok, Thailand.

ASOCODE. 1994. "Informe ASOCODE, Reunión de Seguimiento de la Vía Campesina, Región Norte, Caribe y Centro América." 25 January, Tegucigalpa, Honduras.

Blokland, Kees. 1994. Letter from Kees Blokland to the NFU (Canada), June 3.

CLOC. 1997. "II Congreso Latinoamericano de Organizaciones del Campo." Memoria del Congreso, 3–7 November, Brasília. Sao Paulo: Secretaría Operativa de la CLOC.

CLOC—Vía Campesina. 1997. "I Asamblea Latinoamericana de Mujeres del Campo: Mujeres del Campo Cultivando un Milenio de Justicia e Igualdad." Memoria de la Asamblea, 2–3 November, Brasília. Sao Paulo: Secretaría Operativa de la CLOC.

Coalition of Civil Society Groups in Doha. 2001a. "Civil Society Groups Call on Countries to Reject Power Politics at Doha and an Expanded Agenda." Press Release, 9 November. Received on-line via electronic list serve Qatar_coalition@yahoo.groups.

_____. 2001b. "WTO fails again: The first time was farce, the second time is tragedy." Report from the Coalition of Civil Society Groups in Doha, 15 November. Received on-line via electronic list serve Qatar_coalition@yahoo.groups.

CPE. 1995. "Agriculture Européenne: pour un métier attractif, des campagnes vivantes, des aliments de qualité... changeons la politique agricole!" Communiqué de presse, Mai, Bruselles.

_____. 1997. "Report of the meeting CPE-NGOs." 4 June, Brussels.

Desmarais, Annette. 1994. "Organizing for Change: Peasant Women in Bolivia and Honduras." Unpublished research report. Ottawa, ON: Canadian Bureau for International Education.

Desmarais, Annette, and Nettie Wiebe. 1998. "Peasant Women on the Frontiers of Food Sovereignty." First Quarterly Technical Report submitted to PROWID, 23 January, Saskatoon, Saskatchewan: NFU.

dKMP. 1993. "Five-Year Rural Development Program, 1995–2000." Quezon City, Philippines.

EHNE. 1992. "Informe Estancia de la C.P.E. en Managua del 23-24-92 al 30-04-92." 30 April, Bilbao.

FAO Director-General. 2003. Letter from Jaques Diouf (FAO Director-General) to Antonio Onorati (International Focal Point of the NGO/CSO International Planning Committee), TCD-DG/03/55, 16 January, Rome.

Food Sovereignty Platform. 1999. "Placing Food Sovereignty before Commercial Interests." Position paper. Brussels: Food Sovereignty Platform.

GFAR. 2001. "Un Marco de Cooperación entre Vía Campesina y el Foro Global de Investigación Agropecuaria (FGIA/GFAR)." Propuesta de cooperación mandada a la Secretaría de la Vía Campesina, April, Rome.

IFAP. n.d. "International Federation of Agricultural Producers." IFAP promotional brochure, Paris: IFAP.

_____. 1998a. "Agricultural Trade: Concerns and Consensus among Farmers' Organizations." June, Paris: IFAP.

_____. 1998b. "Rural Poverty and Sustainable Development: A policy Statement by World Farmers." Available at <www.ifap.org/about/wfcpoverty.html> (accessed January 7, 2003).

_____. 2000a. "Some Key Issues for Farmers Concerning a New Round of Multilateral Trade Negotiations. A Policy Statement by Farmers' Worldwide." Results of the 34th World Farmers Congress, Hannover, Germany, May 31.

_____. 2000b. "World Farmers' Congress Report of the Constitution and Membership Committee." Results of the 34th World Farmers Congress, 28–31 May, Hannover, Germany. Available at <http://www.ifap.org/about/wfcreport2000.html> (accessed July 12, 2006).

_____. 2000c. Report of the Standing Committee on Agriculture in Developing Countries, Hannover, Germany, May 24. Available at <http://www.ifap.org/about/wfcagdevelop2000.html> (accessed July 12, 2006).

_____. 2001. "The Doha Agenda for a New round of Multilateral Trade Negotiations." Press Release, November 15. Available at <www.ifap.org/news/nr151101.html> (accessed January 12, 2003).

Joint Statement of NGOs and Social Movements. 2002. "International Civil Society rejects WTO Doha Outcome and the WTO's Manipulative Process." Statement released in January. Received on-line via electronic list serve agri-trade@yahoogroups.

Joint Statement on the Mexican GM Maize Scandal. 2002. Statement prepared for the FAO and the CGIAR. 5 February. Received on-line via electronic list serve agri-trade@yahoogroups.

KMP. 1988. "Position of the Philippines Peasant Movement (KMP) on the GATT Agricultural Negotiations." Presented by Jaime Tadeo to the International Trade and GATT Conference, December, Montréal, Québec.

_____. 1994. Letter from Nati Bernardino, Deputy Secretary General of the KMP to the Vía Campesina. 19 July.

KRRS. 2002. "Bt cotton seeds set afire in Davangere." Available at <http://www.krrsbucottonsetafire.8m.com/> (accessed February 2, 2003).

Managua Declaration. 1992. "The Managua Declaration." Farmers' declaration issued in the framework of the II Congress of the UNAG, 26 April, Managua, Nicaragua.

Marzaroli, Silvio. n.d. Letter and invitational package sent on behalf of the

Co-ordinating Committee to the Operational Secretariat of the Vía Campesina.

NFFC and NFU. 2002. "Farm Groups from U.S. and Canada Unite on GM Wheat Ban." Joint NFFC and NFU Press release, 17 April, Washington, D.C., and Saskatoon, Saskatchewan.

NFU. 2000a. "The Farm Crisis, E.U. Subsidies, and Agribusiness Market Power." Brief presented by the NFU to the Senate Standing Committee on Agriculture and Forestry, 17 February, Ottawa.

_____. 2000b. "National Farmers Union Policy on Genetically Modified (GM) Foods." Passed at the 31st Annual National Convention of the National Farmers Union, 19 November–2 December, Saskatoon, Saskatchewan.

_____. 2002b. "'Free Trade': Is it working for farmers?" Saskatoon, Saskatchewan.

_____. 2003. "Ten Reasons Why We Don't Want GM Wheat." Promotional pamphlet. Saskatoon, Saskatchewan.

NFU International Program Committee. 1996. "Minutes of the meeting of the NFU International Program Committee." 5–7 December, Saskatoon, Saskatchewan.

_____. 1997. "NFU International Program Committee Report on Activities (1996–1997)." 8 July, Saskatoon, Saskatchewan.

NFU-UNAG Women's Linkage Committee. 1990. "NFU-UNAG Women's Linkage Project. Project Proposal to Oxgam-Canada." Saskatoon, Saskatchewan.

_____. n.d. "Common Issues and Struggles." NFU Informational Publication, Saskatoon, Saskatchewan.

NFU-USA. 2002. "Farmers Anticipate Record Lows While Cargill Expects Record Gains." Press Release, January 17, Aurora: Colorado.

Nicholson, Paul. 1992. "Presentación de la CPE al Congreso de la UNAG." 25–26 April, Managua, Nicaragua

_____. 2000. Address to the Third International Conference of the Vía Campesina, 3–6 October, Bangalore, Karnataka.

Peoples' Food Sovereignty. 2001a. "WTO out of Food and Agriculture." Press release, November 6. Available at <www.peoplesfoodsovereignty.org/new/statements.container.htm> (accessed November 13, 2001).

_____. 2001b. "Priority to Peoples' Food Sovereignty — WTO out of Food and Agriculture." Statement released on November 6. Received on-line via electronic list serve agri-trade@yahoogroups.

Paulo Freire Stichting (PFS). 1992a. "Follow-up to the Managua Declaration: Towards an Alternative Development Model. Proposal for a Methology." Document 1, June, Doetinchem, The Netherlands.

_____. 1992b. "Follow-up to the Managua Declaration: Towards an Alternative Development Model. Preparation for discussion: Employment as a starting point." Document 2, June, Doetinchem, The Netherlands.

_____. 1993a. "Follow-up to the Managua Declaration — The Peasant Road towards development alternatives." Documents for the discussions in the Constitutive Meeting of the Preparatory Research Programme of Farmers' Organizations. Doetinchem, The Netherlands.

_____. 1993b. Letter of invitation from the PFS to peasant and farm organizations to attend the gathering in Mons. April 4.

_____. 1993c. "Memoir: Constitutive Meeting of the Peasant Road. Mons (Belgium) 15–16 May 1993." Doetinchem, The Netherlands.

Roppel, Carla. 1996. "Made to Order: Lifeforms and the New Science." A discussion paper for the NFU, Saskatoon, Saskatchewan.

Tadem, Eduardo. 1996. "Reflections on NGO-PO Relations." Paper presented at the NGO Parallel Forum to the II International Conference of the Vía Campesina, 18–21 April, Tlaxcala, Mexico.

Union Paysanne. N.d. "Union Paysanne: pour une agriculture a dimension humaine et des campagnes vivantes." Organizational informational pamphlet, Montréal, Québec.

UNORCA. 2000a. "Agricultura Sustentable en la Zona Maya (Programa Piloto)." Proposal to the Governor of the state of Quintana Roo, February, Mexico D.F.

Vía Campesina. n.d. Pamphlet on the Vía Campesina. Office of the Operational Secretariat, Tegucigalpa.

_____. 1993a. "Mons Declaration: The Vía Campesina Follow-up to the Managua Declaration." Reprinted in Proceedings of the II International Conference of the Vía Campesina (1996). Brussels: NCOS.

_____. 1993b. "Rural Organisations of Vía Campesina Demand Democratisation of World Trade Talks." Press Release, 4 December, Brussels: CPE

_____. 1993c. "The Framework for Action to be developed as a follow-up to the Mons Meeting, May 1993." Brussels: CPE.

_____. 1994a. "Report of the co-ordinating commission from the meeting in Lima, Peru." Held during the First CLOC Congress, 21–25 February (Report dated April 11), Brussels: CPE.

_____. 1994b. "Vía Campesina strongly opposed to GATT Agreement to be signed in Marrakesh and proposes concrete alternatives." Press release, 13 April, Brussels: CPE.

_____. 1994c. "Report of the Co-ordinator of the Activities Commission and 1994 Prosposals." Report prepared by Paul Nicholson, Brussels: CPE.

_____. 1994d. Letter from Paul Nicholson, General Co-ordinator of the Vía Campesina, to the President of the PFS, 5 July, Brussels: CPE.

_____. 1994e. "Summary and Conclusions of the meeting of the Co-ordination Committee Meeting of Vía Campesina." 1–2 October, Segovia, Spain. Brussels: CPE.

_____. 1995. "Minutes of the meeting of the Co-ordinating Commission of the Vía Campesina held in Quebec City." 18–19 October, Saskatoon, Saskatchewan: NFU.

_____. 1996a. "Tlaxcala Declaration of the Vía Campesina." Reprinted in Proceedings of the II International Conference of the Vía Campesina, Brussels: NCOS Publications.

_____. 1996b. "Proceedings of the II International Conference of the Vía Campesina." Brussels: NCOS Publications.

_____. 1996c. "The Right to Produce and Access to Land." Position of the Vía

Campesina on Food Sovereignty presented at the World Food Summit, 13–17 November, Rome, Italy.

_____. 1996d. "Comments on the Final Declaration of the NGO Forum." Statement delivered on November 16 at the NGO Forum.

_____. 1998a. "Stop Agricultural Negotiations in the WTO: We Demand Food Sovereignty for all Peoples, Access to Land and the Right to Produce." Position of the Vía Campesina on the WTO Ministerial Meeting, 17 May, Geneva, Switzerland.

_____. 1998b. "Vía Campesina: A Three Year Plan: Strengthening the Vía Campesina 1999–2001." Tegucigalpa, Honduras: Operational Secretariat of Vía Campesina.

_____. 1999a. "Hoy 12 de octubre lanzamos una campaña global de reforma agraria." Press release, 12 October, Tegucigalpa, Honduras: Operational Secretariat of Vía Campesina.

_____. 1999b. "Vía Campesina Seattle Declaration." Position of the Vía Campesina on the WTO Ministerial Meeting, 3 December, Seattle, United States.

_____. 2000a. Vía Campesina press release at the GFAR, 23 May, Dresden, Germany.

_____. 2000b. "Draft Vía Campesina Position Paper: International Relations and Strategic Alliances." Position discussed at the Third International Conference of the Vía Campesina, 3–6 October, Bangalore, India.

_____. 2000c. "Vía Campesina Gender Position Paper." Position paper approved at the Third International Conference of the Vía Campesina, 3–6 October, Bangalore, India.

_____. 2000d. "The Struggle for Agrarian Reform and Social Change in the Rural Areas." Position paper approved at the Third International Conference of the Vía Campesina, 3–6 October, Bangalore, India.

_____. 2000e. "Food Sovereignty and International Trade." Position paper approved at the Third International Conference of the Vía Campesina, 3–6 October, Bangalore, India.

_____. 2000f. "Bangalore Declaration of the Vía Campesina." Declaration at the Third International Conference of the Vía Campesina, 3–6 October, Bangalore, India.

_____. 2000g. "Biodiversity, Biosafety and Genetic Resources." Position paper approved at the Third International Conference of the Vía Campesina 3–6 October, Bangalore, India.

_____. 2000h. "Proceedings of the Continental Women's Meeting." 3–12 September, Managua, Nicaragua.

_____. 2000i. "Draft proceedings of the First Women's Assembly of the Vía Campesina." 30 September–1 October, Bangalore, India.

_____. 2001a. "Important mobilisations worldwide show strengthening movements against WTO." Press release, 12 November, Tegucigalpa, Honduras.

_____. 2001b. "Vía Campesina Three Year Plan 2001–2003." Tegucigalpa, Honduras.

_____. 2002a. "Vía Campesina will represent farmers and indigenous people's in the mobilization against the FTAA in Porto Alegre." Press release, 2 February, Tegucigalpa, Honduras.

_____. 2002b. "Civil delegation and Vía Campesina meet Arafat in his besieged Head Quarters." Press release, 30 March, Tegucigalpa, Honduras.

_____. 2002c. "Palestine: The international pacifist civil company imposes its presence on Ramallah." Press release, 31 March, Tegucigalpa, Honduras.

_____. 2002d. "Vía Campesina calls for mobilization in front of the Israeli Embassies and offices of the UN." Press release, 1 April, Tegucigalpa, Honduras.

_____. 2002e. "Vía Campesina demands respect for the principle of food sovereignty and [the] right of Palestinian farmers to produce and to remain on their land." Press release, 4 April, Tegucigalpa, Honduras.

_____. 2002f. "The 40 of Moquata strengthen their presence and have sent out today, 11h00 a delegation to give testimonies and relaunch their demands." Press release, 22 April, Tegucigalpa, Honduras.

_____. 2002g. "Report on the participation in the 'Week of the landless' in South Africa." 24 August–1 September, Tegucigalpa, Honduras.

_____. 2002h. Letter from Rafael Alegría to Bruce Moore, co-ordinator of the Popular Coalition to Eradicate Hunger and Poverty. 30 June, Tegucigalpa, Honduras.

_____. 2003a. "Draft Discussion Paper on Vía Campesina Strategies and Action Plan." 7 February, Tegucigalpa, Honduras.

_____. 2003b. "Draft Discussion Paper on Vía Campesina Issues." 26 March, Tegucigalpa, Honduras.

_____. 2003c. "We won in Cancún! The WTO was derailed!" Press release, 23September, Tegucigalpa, Honduras.

_____. 2004a. "Fourth International Vía Campesina Conference: Themes and Issues for Discussion." Vía Campesina Operational Secretariat, Tegucigalpa, Honduras.

_____. 2004b. "Vía Campesina in Geneva at Session of the Human Rights Commission of the U.N." Press release, 4 April, Geneva.

_____. 2004c. Declaration of the Vía Campesina's Fourth International Conference, 14–19 June, Itaici, Brazil.

_____. 2004d. "Borrador de la Memoria de la IV Internacional de la Vía Campesina." 14–19 June, Itaici, Brazil, Operational Secretariat of Vía Campesina, Jakarta.

_____. 2004e. Letter to the President of South Korea and the Chairman of the National Assembly of South Korea, 17 September, Jakarta.

_____. 2005. "Hong Kong Citizens Show Support for WTO Protesters," Press release, 17 December.

_____. 2006a. "La Vía Campesina women occupy a farm in South Brazil." Press release, 8 March.

_____. 2006b. "Statement from La Vía Campesina in support to the women from Rio Grande do Sul (Brazil)." Press release, 24 March.

_____. 2006c. "37 people charged for the action against Aracruz." Press release, 26 April.

_____. 2006d. "Violations of Peasants' Human Rights: A Report on Cases and Patterns of Violence 2006," La Vía Campesina: Jakarta. Annual report prepared by the Vía Campesina. Available at <www.viacampesina.org/main_en/images/stories/annual-report-HR-2006.pdf> (accessed June 5, 2006).

Vía Campesina Women's Working Group. 1996. "Report of the Vía Campesina Women's Working Group Meeting." Held 6–8 August, San Salvador, El Salvador.

_____. 1997. "Peasant Women on the Frontiers of Food Sovereignty." Project proposal presented to PROWID/CEDPA, 29 August, Saskatoon, Saskatchewan: NFU.

_____. 1999. "Peasant Women on the Frontiers of Food Sovereignty: The Vía Campesina Women's Working Group." Final report submitted to PROWID, June, Saskatoon, Saskatchewan: NFU.

Wiebe, Nettie. 2000. Letter from Nettie Wiebe to M.D. Nanjundaswamy, 16 August.

Women in Agriculture Study Tour. 1989. "Working Paper." Study Tour working paper, Saskatoon, Saskatchewan, NFU.

Secondary Sources

Agence France Press. 2001a. "Unfair Trade Creates Breeding Ground for Terrorism: NGOs." 10 November. Received on-line via electronic list serve Qatar_coalition@yahoogroups.com

_____. 2001b. "South Korean Farmers Stage Violent Anti-Import, Anti-WTO Protest." 13 November. Received on-line via electronic list serve Qatar_coalition@yahoogroups.com.

Agriculture and Agri-Food Canada. n.d. "Canada's Agriculture, Food and Beverage Industry: Canada's Organic Industry." Suppliers and Products Fact Sheets. Available at <http://ats.agri.ca/supply/3313_3.htm> (accessed on July 15, 2006).

Agriterra. 1999. "International Co-operation Between Rural People's Organisation." *Agriterra Annual Report.* Arnhem, The Netherlands: Agriterra.

Ahearn, Mary Clare, Penni Korb, and David Banker. 2005. "Industrialization and Contracting in U.S. Agriculture." *Journal of Agriculture and Applied Economics* 37 (2): 347–64.

ALAI-Amlatina. 2000. "Congreso MST: Por un Brasil sin Latifundio." 10 August, Quito, Ecuador. Agencia Latinoamericana de Información — America Latina en Movimiento listserve (received August 10, 2000.)

Allen Douglas, and Dean Lueck. 1998. "The Nature of the Farm." *Journal of Law and Economics* XLI (October): 343–86.

Alvarez, Sonia E., Evelina Dagnino, and Arturo Escobar (eds.). 1998. *Culture of Politics: Politics of Culture: Re-visioning Latin American Social Movements.* Boulder, CO: Westview Press.

Amoore, Louise, Richard Dodgson, Barry Gills, Paul Langley, Don Marshall, and Iain Watson. 2002. "Overturning 'Globalization': Resisting Teleology, Reclaiming Politics." In B. Gills (ed.), *Globalization and the Politics of Resistance.*

London and New York: Macmillan and St. Martin's Press.

Apffel-Marglin, Frédérique, and Stephen A. Marglin (eds.). 1990. *Dominating Knowledge: Development, Culture and Resistance*. Oxford: Clarendon Press.

_____. 1996. *Decolonizing Knowledge: From Development to Dialogue*. Oxford: Clarendon Press.

Araghi, Farshad. 1995. "Global Depeasantization 1945–1990." *Sociological Quarterly* 36 (2): 337–68.

Arcellana, Nancy Pearson. 1996. "Rural Women's Workshop Highlights: From the Fields of Home to the City of Rome." Proceedings of the Rural Women's Workshop, the NGO Forum, and World Food Summit Activities held in Rome, Italy, November 6–16. Manila: ISIS International.

Assadi, Muzaffar H. 1995. "Dunkelism and Peasant Protest in Karnataka: A View from Within." *Social Action* 45 (2) (April/June): 191–204.

Aston, T., and C. Philpin (eds.). 1985. *The Brenner Debate: Agrarian Class Structure and Economic Development in Pre-Industrial Europe*. Cambridge: Cambridge University Press.

Baden, John A., and Douglas S. Noonan. 1998. *Managing the Commons*. Second edition. Bloomington and Indianapolis: Indiana University Press.

Barraclough, Solon, Krishna Ghimire, and Hans Meliczek. 1997. *Rural Development and the Environment: Towards Ecologically and Socially Sustainable Development in Rural Areas*. Geneva: United Nations Research Institute for Social Development and United Nations Development Programme.

Barry, Tom. 1995. *Zapata's Revenge: Free Trade and the Farm Crisis in Mexico*. Boston, MA: South End Press.

Bartra, Roger. 1992. *The Cage of Melancholy*. Translated by Christopher J. Hall. New Brunswick, NJ: Rutgers University Press.

BBC News. 2004. "India PM pledge over suicide farmers." Available at <http://new.bbc.co.uk/bo/pr/fr/-/2/hi/south-asia/3855517.stm> (accessed June 19, 2006).

Bebbington, Anthony. 1998. "NGOs: Mediators of Sustainability/Intermediaries in Transition?" In J. Blauert and S. Zadek (ed.), *Mediating Sustainability: Growing Policy from the Grassroots*. West Hartford, CT: Kumarian Press.

Beckie, Mary Anne. 2000. "Zero Tillage and Organic Farming in Saskatchewan: An Interdisciplinary Study of the Development of Sustainable Agriculture." Unpublished Ph.D. dissertation, Division of Extension, University of Saskatchewan.

Bell, Beverly. 2002. "Social Movements and Economic Integration in the Americas." Citizen Action in the Americas Discussion Paper. Centre for Economic Justice. Available at <http://www.americaspolicy.org/reports/2002/0211soc-mov_body.html> (accessed February 2003).

Bello, Walden. 2000. "Reform of the WTO is the Wrong Agenda." *Food First Backgrounder* 6 (3). Oakland: Food First Institute of Food and Development Policy.

_____. 2001a. "Snapshots from Doha." *Focus on Trade* 70 (November). Bangkok: Focus on the Global South. (Also available at <http://www.focusweb.org>.)

_____. 2001b. "Learning from Doha." Compilation of two presentations presented at the Our World Is Not for Sale coalition meeting, December 7-9. Brussels. Available at <http://www.focusweb.org/publications/2001/learning-from-doha.html> (accessed January 15, 2002).

_____. 2003. The Road to Cancun: Towards a Movement Strategy for the WTO Ministerial in Cancun." Available at <http://www.focusweb.org/popups/articleswindow.php?id+308> (accessed January 20, 2005).

Berkes, Fikret, and M. Taghi Farvar. 1989. "Introduction and Overview." In F. Berkes (ed.), *Common Property Resources: Ecology and Community-based Sustainable Development*. Belhaven: London.

Bernstein, Henry, and Terence J. Byres. 2001. "From Peasant Studies to Agrarian Change." *Journal of Agrarian Change* 1(1): 1–56.

Bernstein, William J. 2004. *The Birth of Plenty: How the Prosperity of the Modern World Was Created*. New York: McGraw-Hill.

Berthelot, Jacques. 2002. "Why NGOs/CSOs should reject the development box." Paper for discussion at the NGO/CSO Forum for Food Sovereignty, 10–13 June, Rome.

Berthoud, Gerald. 1992. "Market." In W. Sachs (ed.), *The Development Dictionary: A Guide to Knowledge as Power*. London and New Jersey: Zed Books.

Beus, Curtis E. 1995. "Competing Paradigms: An Overview and Anaolysis of the Alternaive-Conventional Agriculture Debate." *Research in Rural Sociology and Development* 6: 23-50.

Biekart, Kees, and Martin Jelsma. 1994. *Peasants Beyond Protest in Central America: Challenges for ASOCODE Strategies towards Europe*. Amsterdam: Transnational Institute.

Blokland, Kees. 1993. "Concerted peasant alliances and 'concertation' with society." Paper presented at the Conference on Central American Peasant Organisation: Strategies Towards Europe, 22–23 April, Wageningen, the Netherlands.

_____. 1995. "Peasant Alliances and 'Concertation' with Society." *Bulletin of Latin American Research* 14(2): 159–70.

Blustein, Paul. 2001a. "Protest Group Softens Tone at WTO Talks." *Washington Post Foreign Service,* November 12.

_____. 2001b. "WTO Leader Cautions Against 'Protectionism." *Washington Post*, November 9.

Bonanno, Alessandro, Lawrence Busch, William Friedland, Lourdes Gouveia, and Enzo Mingione. 1994. "Introduction." In A. Bonanno et al. (eds.), *From Columbus to ConAgra: The Globalization of Agriculture and Food*. Lawrence, KA: University Press of Kansas.

Bové, José. 1998. "Report from French Farmers." *Synthesis/Regeneration* 16 (Summer) Available at <http://www.wtowatch.org/library/admin/uploaded-files/Report_from_French-Farmers_2.htm> (accessed January 24, 2003).

Bové, José, and Francois Dufour. 2001. *The World Is Not for Sale*. Interviews by Gilles Luneau and translation by Anna de Casparis. London and New York: Verso.

Boyd, William, and Michael Watts. 1997. "The Chicken Industry and U.S. Capitalism." In D. Goodman and M. Watts (eds.), *Globalising Food: Agrarian*

Questions and Global Restructuring. London and New York: Routledge.

Brass, Tom. 1995. *New Farmers' Movements in India*. London and Portland, OR: Frank Cass Publishers.

_____. 2000a. "Moral Economists, Subalterns, New Social Movements, and the (Re-) Emergence of a (Post-) Modernized (Middle) Peasant." In V. Chaturvedi (ed.), *Mapping Subaltern Studies and the Postcolonial*. London: Verso.

_____. 2000b. *Peasants, Populism and Postmodernism: The Return of the Agrarian Myth*. The Library of Peasant Studies. London and Portland: Frank Cass Publishers.

_____. 2005. "The Journal of Peasant Studies: The Third Decade." *The Journal of Peasant Studies* 32 (1).

Brush, S.B. 1996a. "Whose Knowledge, Whose Genes, Whose Rights?" In S.B. Brush and D. Stabinsky (eds.), *Valuing Knowledge: Indigenous People and Intellectual Property Rights*. Washington, DC: Island Press.

_____. 1996b. "Is Common Heritage Outmoded?" In S.B. Brush and D. Stabinsky (eds.), *Valuing Knowledge: Indigenous People and Intellectual Property Rights*. Washington, DC: Island Press.

Bryceson, Deborah, Cristóbal Kay, and Jos Mooij (eds.). 2000. *Disappearing Peasantries? Rural Labour in Africa, Asia and Latin America*. London: Intermediate Technology Publications.

Burdick, John. 1998. "Transnational Peasant Politics in Central America." *Latin American Research Review* 33 (3): 49–86.

Comisión de Agricultura. 2000. "Cuánta Liberalización Aguanta la Agricultura? Impacto del TLCAN en el Sector Agroalimentario." Camara de Diputados LVII Legislatura. México D.F.: Universidad Autónoma de Chapingo, CIESTAAM y Centro de Estudios para el Cambio en el Campo Mexcano (CECCAM).

Campos, Wilson. 1994. "'We Don't Need All Those NGOs': Interview with Wilson Campos." In K. Biekart and M. Jelsma (eds.), *Peasant Beyond Protest in Central America: Challenges for ASOCODE Strategies Towards Europe*. Amsterdam: Transnational Institute.

Capdevila, Gustavo. 2002. "NGOs Speak Out on Behalf of Poor Farmers at WTO." *Inter Press Service* June 25.

Chayanov Alexander. 1966. *The Theory of Peasant Economy*. Edited by Daniel Thorner, Basile Kerblay and R.E.F. Smith. Homewood, IL: Richard D. Irwin.

Christian Aid. 2001. "Master or Servant? How global trade can work to the benefit of poor people." Media report, November, London: Christian Aid.

Dandekar, A., Shahaji Narawade, Ram Rathod, Rajesh Ingle, Vijay Kulkarni, and Y.D. Sateppa. 2005. "Causes of Farmer Suicides in Maharashtra: An Enquiry." Final Report Submitted to the Mumbai High Court, Tuljapur: Tata Institute of Social Sciences, Rural Campus.

De Ita Rubio, Ana. 1994. *El Futuro del Campo: Hacia una Vía de Desarrollo Campesino. UNORCA,* México D.F.: Centro de Estudios para el Cambio en el Campo Mexicana and Fundación Friedrich Ebert Stiftung.

Desmarais, Annette Aurélie. 1991. "Mexican conference marks start of ongoing alliance of farmers." *Union Farmer* December.

_____. 2002. "The Vía Campesina: Consolidating an International Peasant and Farm Movement." *Journal of Peasant Studies* 29 (2) (January): 91–124.

_____. 2003. "'The WTO... will meet somewhere, sometime. And we will be there'." Part of a series of papers prepared for the project "Voices: The Rise of Nongovernmental Voices in Multilateral Organizations." Ottawa, ON: The North-South Institute. Also available at <http://www.nsi-ins.ca/english/pdf/Voices_WTO_Desmarais.pdf> (accessed July 20, 2006).

_____. 2004. "The Vía Campesina: Women on the Frontiers of Food Sovereignty." *Canadian Woman Studies/les cahiers de la femme* 23 (1).

Dove, Michael. 1996. "Center, Periphery and Biodiversity: A Paradox of Governance and a Developmental Challenge." In S.B. Brush and D. Stabinsky (eds.), *Valuing Knowledge: Indigenous People and Intellectual Property Rights*. Washington DC: Island Press.

Duckworth, Barbara. 2001. "Alberta's ILO policy gets mixed reviews." *Western Producer*, July 12.

Ecologist. 1992. "Whose Common Future? A Special Issue." *The Ecologist* 22(4) (July/August).

Economic Times. 2000. "Anything which is protected gets stifled." July 11.

Economist, The. 1999a. "After Seattle: A global disaster." December 11: 17–18.

_____. 1999b. "The non-governmental order." December 11: 18–19.

_____. 2000a. "Sins of the secular missionaries." January 29: 25–27.

_____. 2000b. "Survey: Agriculture and Technology." March 25: 1–16.

_____. 2001. "Seeds sown for future growth." November 17: 65–66.

Economist, The (US). 2004. "From anarchy to apathy: Anti-globalisation." 371: 14.

Edelman, Marc. 1998a. "Transnational Peasant Politics in Central America." *Latin American Research Review* 33(3): 49–86.

_____. 1998b. "Organizing Across Borders: The Rise of a Transnational Peasant Movement in Central America." In J. Blauert and S. Zadek (eds.), *Mediating Sustainability: Growing Policy from the Grassroots*. West Hartford, CT: Kumarian Press.

_____. 1999. *Peasants Against Globalization: Rural Social Movements in Costa Rica*. Stanford: Stanford University Press.

_____. 2001a. "Toward an Anthropology of some New Internationalisms: Small Farmers in Global Resistance Movements." Paper presented at the American Ethnological Society and the Canadian Anthropology Society, 2–6 May, Montréal, Québec.

_____. 2001b. "Social Movements: Changing Paradigms and Forums of Politics." *Annual Review of Anthropology* 30: 285–317.

_____. 2003. "Transnational Peasant and Farmer Movements and Networks." In H.M. Glasius and M. Kaldor (ed.), *Global Civil Society Yearbook 2003*. London: Oxford University Press.

El Financiero. 2000. "México Globalizado." 7(5443) April 2.

Ervin, Alexander, Cathy Hotslander, Darrin Qualman, and Rick Sawa. 2003. *Beyond Factory Farming: Corporate Hog Barns and the Threat to Public Health, the Environment, and Rural Communities*. Ottawa: Canadian Centre for Policy Alternatives.

Eschle, Catherine. 2001a. *Global Democracy, Social Movements, and Feminism*. Boulder, CO: Westview Press.

_____. 2001b. "Globalizing Civil Society? Social Movements and the Challenge of Global Politics from Below." In P. Hamel, H. Lustiger-Thaler, J.N. Pieterse and S. Roseneil (eds.), *Globalization and Social Movements*. Houndmills, Basingstoke and New York: Palgrave.

ETC Group. 2001. "Globalization, Inc: Concentration in Corporate Power: The Unmentioned Agenda." *ETC Group Communiqué* 71.

_____. 2005. "Oligopoly, Inc. 2005: Concentration in Corporate Power." *ETC Group Communiqué* 91.

European Union. 2001. "New WTO Round slap in the face for Isolationism." E.U. press release, November 14, Brussels.

Ewins, Adrian. 2002. "Special Report on the Saskatchewan Wheat Pool." *Western Producer* May 9.

FAO. 1974. "United Nations: Program of Action of the World Food Conference." Reproduced from United Nations Document E/5587. November 22.

_____. 1996. "Rome Declaration on World Food Security and World Food Summit Plan of Action." World Food Conference, November 13–17, Rome: FAO.

_____. 1998. "Universal Declaration of Human Rights: 50th Anniversary." Informational Pamphlet on the Right to Food, Rome: FAO.

_____. 1999. "Synopsis: The Multiple Roles of Agriculture and Land." Report of the Cultivating our Futures: FAO/Netherlands Conference on the Multifunctional Character of Agriculture and Land. Scoping phase, Rome: Sustainable Development Division of the FAO.

_____. 2000. "Agriculture, Trade and Food Security: Issues and Options in the WTO Negotiations from the Perspective of Developing Countries." Volume II, Country Case Studies, Commodities and Trade Division of the FAO: Rome. Available at <http://www.fao.org/DOCREP/033/x8731e/x8931e01a.htm> (accessed January 14, 2003).

_____. 2001a. "States have an obligation to ensure that nobody dies of hunger — FAO Director-General Jacques Diouf." Press release, September 17, Rome: FAO.

_____. 2001b. "UN Food and Agriculture Organization (FAO) warns: Further slowdown in hunger reduction — In most developing countries the number of hunger even increased." Press release, October 15, Stockholm.

_____. 2002. "Declaration of the World Food Summit: Five years later." Conference held 10–13 June in Rome. Available at <http://www.fao.org/DOCREP/MEETING/004/Y6948E.HTM> (accessed January 15, 2003).

_____. 2004. *State of Food Insecurity in the World 2004*. Rome, FAO.

Feder, Ernest. 1978. "The peasant." *Latin American Research Review* 13(3): 193–204.

Flitner, Michael. 1998. "Biodiversity: Of Local Commons and Global Commodities." In M. Goldman (ed.), *Privatizing Nature: Political Struggles for the Global Commons*. London: Pluto Press and TNI.

Florini, Ann M. 2000. *The Third Force: The Rise of Transnational Civil Society*. Tokyo and Washington DC: Japan Center for International Exchange and Carnegie Endowment for International Peace.

Focus on Trade. 2002. "Doha Special #2." No. 70. November, Bangkok: Focus on the Global South. Available at <http://focusweb.org> (accessed December 11, 2002).

Food First. 2002. "Genetic Pollution in Mexico's Center of Maize Diversity." *Food First Backgrounder* 8(2) (Spring). Oakland: Food First Institute for Food and Development Policy.

Friedmann, John. 1992. *Empowerment: The Politics of Alternative Development*. Cambridge, MA. and Oxford: Blackwell.

Frontline. 2001. "Trade rounds and bounced cheques." Interview with V.P. Singh, *Frontline — India's National Magazine* 18(24) November 24–December 7.

Frontline/World. 2005. "Rough Cut: Seeds of Suicide: India's Desperate Farmers." Aired on PBS . Available at <http://www.pbs.org/frontlineworld/rough/2005/07/seeds_of_suicidlink> (accessed June 19, 2006).

FSPI. 2004. "Report on National Peasant Day in Indonesia." September 24. FSPI: Jakarta.

Gibbs, Christopher, and Daniel Bromley. 1989. "Institutional Arrangements for Management of Rural Resrouces: Common-Property Regimes." In F. Berkes (ed.), *Common Property Resources: Ecology and Community-based Sustainable Development*. London: Belhaven.

Gills, Barry K. 2000. *Globalization and the Politics of Resistance.* Houndmills and New York: MacMillan Press and St. Martin's Press:

Goldman, Michael. 1998. "Introduction: The Political Resurgence of the Commons." In M. Goldman (ed.), *Privatizing Nature: Political Struggles for the Global Commons*. London: Pluto Press and TNI.

González, Gustavo. 2000. "Globalization's Impact: Rural Poverty on the Rise." *Inter- Press Service* November 29.

Goodman, David. 1991. "Some Recent Tendencies in the Industrial Reorganization of the Agri-food System." In W. Friedland et al. (eds.), *Towards a new Political Economy of Agriculture*. Boulder, CO: Westview Press.

Goodman, David, and Michael Redclift. 1991. *Refashioning Nature: Food, Ecology and Culture*. London and New York: Routledge.

Goodman, David, and Michael J. Watts (eds.). 1997. *Globalising Food: Agrarian Questions and Global Restructuring*. London and New York: Routledge.

Government of Andhra Pradesh. 2004. "Report of the Commission on Farmers' Welfare." Report released by the Government of Andhra Pradesh, Hyderabad. Available at <www.macroscan.com/pol/apr05/pol070405Andhra_Pradesh.htm> (accessed July 2, 2006).

Green, Duncan. 2001. "The Rough Guide to the WTO." London: Catholic Agency for Overseas Development (CAFOD). Available at <http://www.cafod.org.uk/policy/wto-roughguide.html> (accessed January 14, 2003).

Handy, Jim. 1994. *Revolution in the Countryside: Rural Conflict and Agrarian Reform 1944-54*. Chapel Hill: University of North Carolina Press.

Hardin, Garrett. 1968. "The Tragedy of the Commons." *Science* 162: 1243–48.

_____. 1991. "The Tragedy of the Unmanaged Commons: Population and the Disguises of Providence." In R.V. Andelson (ed.), *Commons without Tragedy: Protecting the Environment from Overpopulation — A New Approach*. Lanham, MD: Rowman and Littlefield.

_____. 1998. "Extensions of 'The Tragedy of the Commons.'" *Science* 280: 682.

Harvey, Neil. 1990. "The New Agrarian Movement in Mexico 1979–1990." Research paper, Institute of Latin American Studies, University of London.

Heffernan, William. 1998. "Agriculture and Monopoly Capital." *Monthly Review* 50 (3) (July/August).

Heffernan William, and Douglas H. Constance 1994. "Transnational Corporations and the Globalization of the Food System." In A. Bonanno et al. (eds.), *From Columbus to ConAgra: The Globalization of Agriculture and Food*. Lawrence, KA: University Press of Kansas.

Heffernan, William, Mary Hendrickson, and R. Gronski. 1999. "Consolidation in the Food and Agriculture System." Report prepared for the National Farmers Union in the United States. Department of Rural Sociology, University of Missouri, Columbia, Missouri. Available at <www.foodcircles.missouri.edu/whstudy.pdf> (accessed January 5, 2003).

Hendrickson, Mary, and William D. Heffernan. 2005. "Concentration of Agricultural Markets." Available at <http://www.foodcircles.missouri.edu/CRJanuary05.pdf> (accessed June 21, 2006).

Hindu. 2001. "KRRS activists destroy Bt cotton crop." (Shimoga Edition). January 3. Received on-line via electronic list serve viacam17april@yahoogroups.com.

Holt-Giménez, Eric. 2006. *Campesino a Campesino: Voices from Latin America's Farmer to Farmer Movement for Sustainable Agriculture*. Oakland: Food First Institute for Food and Development Policy.

ICRW (International Center for Research on Women) and CEDPA. 1999. "Food Sovereignty in Latin America and the Caribbean: Strengthening the Role of Peasant Women." Report-in-Brief. Washington, DC: ICRW and CEDPA.

IFAD. 2001. *Rural Poverty Report 2001: The Challenge of Ending Rural Poverty*. Oxford: Oxford University Press.

Intercambio. 1993a. "Conferencia de la FIPA en Guadalajara." Publication of the Paulo Freire Stichting (PFS) 1: 19–20.

_____. 1993b. "Peasant Road Block?" Publication of the Paulo Freire Stichting (PFS) 2: 4.

Jazairy, Idriss, Mohiuddin Alamgir, and Theresa Panuccio. 1992. *The State of World Rural Poverty: An Inquiry into Its Causes and Consequences*. New York: New York University Press.

Jelin, Elizabeth. 1998. "Toward a Culture of Participation and Citizenship: Challenges for a More Equitable World." In S.E. Alvarez et al. (eds.), *Cultures of Politics: Politics of Cultures*. Boulder, CO: Westview Press.

Karl, Marilee (ed.). 1996. "Partners for Food Security: The Role of Trade Union, Rural Workers' Organizations, Agricultural Producers' and Farmers' Association, Co-operatives, and Development/Advocacy Organizations in Contributing to the World Food Summit and its Follow-up." Report produced for FAO, Rome: FAO.

Kay, Cristobal. 1995. "Rural Latin America: Exclusionary and Uneven Agricultural Development." In S. Halebsky and R. Harris (eds.), *Capital, Power and Inequality in Latin America*. Boulder, CO: Westview Press.

Kearney, Michael. 1996. *Reconceptualizing the Peasantry: Anthropology in Global Perspective*. Boulder, CO: Westview Press.

Kneen, Brewster. 1995. *Invisible Giant: Cargill and Its Transnational Strategies*. Halifax: Fernwood Publishing.

Korten, David. 1995. *When Corporations Rule the World*. West Hartford and San Francisco: Kumarian Press and Berrett-Koehler Publishers:

Kothari, Rajni. 1995. *Poverty: Human Consciousness and the Amnesia of Development*. London and New Jersey: Zed Books.

Kothari, Smitu, and Pramod Parajuli. 1993. "No Nature without Social Justice: A Plea for Ecological and Cultural Pluralism in India." In Wolfgang Sachs (ed.) *Global Ecology: A New Arena of Political Conflict*. London: Zed Books.

Kwa, Aileen. 2002. *Power Politics in the WTO*. Bangkok: Focus on the Global South.

Lang, Michelle. 2002. "Sask. Loses 26,000 ag workers." *Saskatoon Star Phoenix* February 23: 3.

Lappé, Frances Moore, Joseph Collins, and Peter Rosset, with Luis Esparza. 1998. *World Hunger: Twelve Myths*. Second edition. New York: Grove Press.

Lenin, Vladimir Illyich. 1954. *The Agrarian Question and the "Critics of Marx."* Moscow: Progress Publishers.

Leon, Irene. 1997. "I Asamblea Latinoamericana de Mujeres del Campo: Participación y Igualdad." *Servicio Informativo* November 26, Quito: Agencia Latinoamericana de Información (ALAI).

Lewontin, R.C. 1998. "The Maturing of Capitalist Agriculture: Farmer as Proletarian." *Monthly Review* 50 (3) (July/August).

Lyons, Murray. 2003. "Weed out GM wheat: NFU." *Saskatoon Star Phoenix* February 25: C5, C8.

Madeley, John. 2000. "Trade and Hunger: An overview of case studies on the impact of trade liberalization of food security." October, Stockholm: Forum Syd.

Mander, Jerry. 1996. "Facing the Rising Tide." In J. Mander and E. Goldsmith (eds.), *The Case Against the Global Economy: And For a Turn Toward the Local*. San Francisco: Sierra Club.

Marglin, Stephen. 1996. "Farmers, Seedsmen, and Scientists: Systems of Agriculture and Systems of Knowledge." In F. Apffel-Marglin and S. Marglin (eds.), *Decolonizing Knowledge: From Development to Dialogue*. New York and Oxford: Clarendon Press and Oxford University Press.

McBride, Lynne. 1998. "Farmers Union Active in International Debate." *National Farmers Union News* 45 (1).

McMichael, Philip. 2004. "Global development and the corporate food regime." Paper presented at the Symposium on New Directions in the Sociology of Global Development, XI World Congress of Rural Sociology, July,

Trondheim, Norway.

Mies, Maria, and Veronika Bennholdt-Thomsen. 2000. *The Subsistence Perspective: Beyond the Globalized Economy*. London: Zed Books.

Milner, Helen V. 1988. *Resisting Protectionism: Global Industries and the Politics of International Trade*. Princeton: Princeton University Press.

Mittal, Anuradha, and Mayumi Kawaai. 2001. "Freedom to Trade? Trading Away American Family Farms." *Food First Backgrounder* 7 (4) (October 18).

Mohan, Giles, Ed Brown, Bob Milward, and Alfred B. Zack-Williams. 2000. *Structural Adjustment: Theory, Practice and Impacts*. London and New York: Routledge.

Mohan Rao, R.M. 2004. *Suicides Among Farmers: A Study of Cotton Growers*. New Delhi: Concept Publishing Company.

Mohanty. B.B. 2005. "'We are Like the Living Dead': Farmer Suicide in Maharashtra, Western India." *Journal of Peasant Studies* 32 (2): 243–76.

Molina, Tania. 2000. "De la lucha campesina a la cosecha de votos." *La Jornada* Supplement: 8.

Monks, Vicki, Robert M. Ferris, and Don Campbell. 2000. *Amber Waves of Gain*. Washington, DC: Defenders of Wildlife.

Mooney, Pat Roy. 1999. "The ETC Century: Erosion, Technological Transformation and Corporate Concentration in the 21st Century." *Development Dialogue. A Journal of International Development Co-operation*. Dag Hammarskjold: Uppsala.

Moore, Barrington. 1966. *Social Origins of Dictatorship and Democracy*. Boston: Beacon.

Morton, Peter. 2001. "Trade Talks hold Hope for Poor." *National Post* (with files from *Reuters*), November 15. Received on-line via electronic list serve ag-impact@iatp.org.

Moyo, Sam, and Paris Yeros (eds.). 2006. *Reclaiming the Land: The Resurgence of Rural Movements in Africa, Asia and Latin America*. London: Zed Books.

Murphy, Sophia. 1999. *Trade and Food Security. An Assessment of the Uruguay Round Agreement on Agriculture*. London: Catholic Institute for International Relations.

_____. 2002. *Managing the Invisible Hand: Markets, Farmers and International Trade*. Minneapolis: Institute for Agriculture and Trade Policy.

Myhre, David. 1994. "The Politics of Globalization in Rural Mexico: Campesino Initiatives to restructure the Agricultural Credit System." In P. McMichael (ed.), *The Global Restructuring of Agro-food Systems*. Ithaca and London: Cornell University Press.

Nadal, Alejandro. 2000. *The Environmental and Social Impacts of Economic Liberalisation on Corn Production in Mexico*. Oxford and Gland, Switzerland: Oxfam GB and WWF International.

Netting, Robert. 1993. *Smallholders, Householders: Farm Families and the Ecology of Intensive, Sustainable Agriculture*. Stanford: Stanford University Press.

New Indian Express. 2000. "Quit India, farmers tell MNCs." September 27.

New Left Review. 2002. "Landless Battalions: The Sem Terra Movement of Brazil." Interview with João Pedro Stédile, *New Left Review* 15 (May-June): 77–104.

NFU. 2002a. "NFU supports S.O.D." *NFU Newsletter*, September.

O'Brien, Robert, Anne Marie Goetz, Jan Aart Scholte, and Marc Williams. 2000. *Contesting Global Governance: Multilateral economic Institutions and Global Social Movements*. Cambridge, UK: Cambridge University Press.

O'Neill, Mark. 2002. "Grain farmers already feeling WTO squeeze." *South China Morning Post* January 29.

OECD. 2002. "Organic Agriculture: Sustainability, Markets and Policies." Proceedings from an OECD Workshop, Washington, DC, September. Available at <www.oecd.org> (accessed July 15, 2006).

Office of the Press Secretary. 2001. "President Supportive of New Round of Global Trade Negotiations." Statement by the President of the USA. November 14. Available at <http://www.whitehouse.gov/news/releases/2001/11/20011114-8.html> (accessed January 14, 2003).

Oloka-Onyango, and Deepika Udagama. 2000. "The Realization of Economic, Social and Cultural Rights: Globalization and Its Impact on the Full Enjoyment of Human Rights." Preliminary report submitted in accordance with Sub-Commission resolution 1999/8. Report presented to the United Nations Sub-Commission on the Promotion and Protection of Human Rights, 52nd Session. Document #E/CN.4/Sub.2/2000/13.

Osava, Mario. 2000. "Farmers Protest Transgenic Grain Shipment." *Inter Press Service*, July 25.

Otero, Gerardo. 1998. *Farewell to the Peasantry? Political Class Formation in Rural Mexico*. Boulder, CO: Westview Press.

Oxfam International. 2002. *Rigged Rules and Double Standards: Trade, Globalization and the Fight Against Poverty*. Oxford: Oxfam GB. (Available at <http://www.maketradefair.com/en/index.php?file=03042002121618.htm> (accessed on January 20, 2007).

Page, Brian. 1997. "Restructuring Pork Production, Remaking Rural Iowa." In D. Goodman and M.J. Watts (eds.), *Globalising Food: Agrarian Questions and Global Restructuring*. London and New York: Routledge.

PAHO (Pan American Health Organization). 2002. "The Faces of Poverty: Malnourished, Hungry and... Obese?" Press information, August 1, Washington, DC. Available at <www.paho.org/English/DPI/100/100feature30.htm> (accessed on January 17, 2003).

Paige, Jeffrey. 1975. *Agrarian Revolution: Social Movements and Export Agriculture in the Underdeveloped World*. New York: Free Press.

Parajuli, Pramod. 1996. "Ecological Ethnicity in the Making: Developmentalist Hegemonies and Emergent Identities in India." *Identities* 3 (1–2): 15–59.

Petras, James, and Henry Veltmeyer. 2001. *Globalization Unmasked: Imperialism in the 21st Century*. Halifax and New York: Fernwood Publishing and Zed Books.

Picard, André. 2002. "Growing obesity likely to strain health systems." *Globe and Mail* February 18.

Pollack, Aaron. 2001. "Cross-Border, Cross-Movement Alliances in the Late 1990s." In P. Hamel, H. Lustiger-Thaler, J. Nederveen Pieterse, and S. Roseneil (eds.), *Globalization and Social Movements*. Basingstoke, Hampshire and New York: Palgrave.

Pruzin, Daniel. 2002. "NGOs Welcome, Moore Says." *International Trade Reporter* 19 (1), January 3.

Public Citizen's Global Trade Watch. 2001. *Down on the Farm: NAFTA's Seven-Years War on Farmers and Ranchers in the U.S., Canada and Mexico.* Washington, DC: Public Citizen.

Pugh, Terry. 1990. "Life on Canadian farm a new experience for youth." *Union Farmer* October.

_____. 1994. "Reversing the rural exodus through community development." *Union Farmer* December.

Qualman, Darrin. 2001. "Corporate Hog Farming." In R. Epp and D. Whitson (eds.), *Writing Off the Rural West.* Edmonton, AB: University of Alberta Press and Parkland Institute.

_____. 2002. "Farmers' Opposition to Corporate Globalization and Trade Agreements." Paper presented to the conference From Doha to Kananaskis: The Future of the World Trading System and the Crisis in Governance held in Toronto, March 1–3.

Qualman, Darrin, and Nettie Wiebe. 2000. "The Structural Adjustment of Canadian Agriculture." Paper prepared for the Canadian Centre for Policy Alternatives and the SAPRI/CASA Project, August. Ottawa: Canadian Centre for Policy Alternatives.

Racine, Jean-Luc (ed.). 1997. *Peasant Moorings: Village ties and mobility rationales in South India.* New Delhi: Sage Publications.

Rance, Laura. 2002. "Building farmers' knowledge key to farming's future." *Farmers' Independent Weekly* September 5.

Randall, Laura (ed.). 1999. *Reformando la Reforma Agraria Mexicana.* México D.F.: Universidad Autonoma Metropolitana y El Atajo Ediciones.

Reinhardt, Nola, and Peggy Barlett. 1989. "The Persistence of Family Farms in U.S. Agriculture." *Sociologia Ruralis* 29 (3–4): 204–25.

Reuters. 2002. "ConAgra profit jumps 48 percent." *Western Producer* April 4.

Rist, Gilbert. 1997. *The History of Development: From Western Origins to Global Faith.* London and New York: Zed Books.

Robert, Jean. 1992. "Production." In W. Sachs (ed.), *The Development Dictionary: A Guide to Knowledge as Power.* London and New Jersey: Zed Books.

Rocamora, Joel. 1993. "The Crisis in the National Democratic Movement and the Transformation of the Philippine Left." *Debate: Philippine Left Review* 6 (March): 3–60.

_____. 1994. *Breaking Through: The Struggle within the Communist Party of the Philippines.* Manila: Anvil Publishing.

Roppel, Carla, Annette Aurélie Desmarais and Diane Martz. 2006. *Farm Women and Canadian Agricultural Policy.* Ottawa: Status of Women Canada.

Rosset. Peter. 1999. "The Multiple Functions and Benefits of Small Farm Agriculture." Policy brief 4. Oakland: Food First Institute for Food and Development Policy.

Rucht, Dieter. 1999. "The Transnationalization of Social Movements: Trends, Causes, Problems." In D. della Porta, H. Kriesi and D. Rucht (eds.), *Social*

Movements in a Globalizing World. Basingstoke, Hampshire and New York: Macmillan Press and St. Martin's Press.

Sabean, David Warren. 1984. *Power in the Blood: Popular Culture and Village Discourse in Early Modern Germany*. Cambridge: Cambridge University Press.

Scholte, Jan Aart. 2001. "Civil Society and Democracy in Global Governance." Centre for the Study of Globalisation and Regionalisation (CSGR) Working Paper No. 65/01, University of Warwick.

Scholte, Jan Aart, Robert O'Brien, and Marc Williams. 1998. "The WTO and Civil Society." Centre for the Study of Globalisation and Regionalisation (CSGR) Working Paper No. 14/98, University of Warwick.

Scialabba, Nadia. 2001. "Organic Agriculture Perspectives." Conference on Supporting the Diversification of Exports in Latin America and Caribbean Region through the Development of Organic Agriculture, Port-of-Spain, Trinidad and Tobago, October 8–10.

Scott, James. 1976. *The Moral Economy of the Peasant: Rebellion and Subsistence in Southeast Asia*. New Haven and London: Yale University Press.

_____. 1985. *Weapons of the Weak: Everyday Forms of Peasant Resistance*. New Haven and London: Yale University Press.

_____. 1998. *Seeing like a State*. New Haven and London: Yale University Press.

Shameem, G. Parthasarathy. 1998. "Suicides of Cotton Farmers in Andhra Pradesh: An Exploratory Study." *Economic and Political Weekly* (March 28): 720–26.

Shiva, Vandana. 1993a. "GATT, Agriculture and Third World Women." In M. Mies and V. Shiva, *Ecofeminism*. London, New Jersey and Halifax: Fernwood Publishing and Zed Books.

_____. 1993b. "Homeless in a Global Village. In M. Mies and V. Shiva, *Ecofeminism*. London, New Jersey and Halifax: Fernwood Publishing and Zed Books.

_____. 1993c. "The Impoverishment of the Environment: Women and Children Last." In M. Mies and V. Shiva, *Ecofeminism*. London, New Jersey and Halifax: Fernwood Publishing and Zed Books.

_____. 1997a. "Economic Globalization, Ecological Feminism and Sustainable Development." *Canadian Women Studies/Les Cahiers de la Femme* 17(2) (Spring): 22–27.

_____. 1997b. "The Enclosure of the Commons." *Third World Resurgence* 84 (August): 5–10.

Shukla, S.P. 2001. "The Doha debacle." *Frontline — India's National Magazine* 18 (24) (November 24 – December 7). Available at <http://www.flonnet.com/fl1824/18240170.htm> (accessed January 24, 2003).

Sinha, S., S. Gururani, and B. Greenberg. 1997. "The 'New Traditionalist' Discourse of Indian Environmentalism." *The Journal of Peasant Studies* 24(3).

Smith, Jackie. 1995. "Transnational Political Processes and the Human Rights Movement." *Research in Social Movements, Conflict and Change* 18: 187–221.

Stammers, Neil. 1999. "Social Movements and the Challenge to Power." In M. Shaw (ed.), *Politics and Globalisation: Knowledge, Ethics and Agency*. London and New York: Routledge.

Starn, Orin. 1992. "'I Dreamed of Foxes and Hawks': Reflections on Peasant

Protest, New Social Movements and the Rondas Campesinas of Northern Peru." In A. Escobar and S. Alvarez (eds.), *The Making of Social Movements in Latin America*. Boulder, CO: Westview Press.

_____. 1999. *Nightwatch: The Politics of Protest in the Andes*. Durham: Duke University Press.

Starr, Amory. 2000. *Naming the Enemy: Anti-corporate Movements Confront Globalization*. Annandale, London and New York: Pluto Press and Zed Books.

Statistics Canada. 2001. "Canadian farm operations in the 21st Century: Farm numbers decline in all provinces." Agriculture 2001 Census. Available at <http://www.statcan.ca/english/agcensus2001/first/farmop/01front.htm#top> (accessed June 20, 2006).

Stevens, Christopher, Romilly Greenhill, Jane Kennan, and Steven Devereux. 2000. *The WTO Agreement on Agriculture and Food Security*. Economic Series No. 42. London: Commonwealth Secretariat.

Stirling, Robert. 1999. "Family Farming and the Politics of Sustainability." Presentation to the Annual Convention of the National Farmers Union, November 25, Saskatoon, Saskatchewan.

Storey, Shannon. 1997. "Organizing for Socioeconomic Change: Developing a Handbook for National Farmers Union Women in Saskatchewan." Unpublished MA thesis, Continuing Education, University of Saskatchewan.

Third World Resurgence. 1996a. "Food Security: The New Threats." *Third World Resurgence* 67.

_____. 1996b. "Globalisation of Agriculture and Rising Food Insecurity." *Third World Resurgence* 72/73.

Times of India News Service. 1998. "KRRS destroys Monsanto Cotton Crop in Raichur dist." November 29.

Torres, Filemon, Martin Pineiro, Eduardo Trigo, and Roberto Martinez Nogueira. 2000. "Agriculture in the Early XXI Century: Agrodiversity and Pluralism as a Contribution to Ameliorate Problems of Food Security, Poverty and Natural Resource Conservation: Reflections on Issues and Their Implication for Global Research." Executive summary of issues paper commissioned by the Global Forum on Agricultural Research (GFAR), Rome.

UNCTAD. 2006. "Tracking the Trend Towards Market Concentration: The Case of the Agricultural Input Industry." Report prepared by the United Nations Conference on Trade and Development (UNCTAD) Secretariat UNCTAD/CITC/COM/2005/16. Available at <http://www.unctad.org/en/docs/ditccom200516_en.pdf> (accessed July 3, 2006).

University of Guelph. "Guelph Transgenic Pig Research Program." Available at <http://www.uoguelph.ca/enviropig/> (accessed June 20, 2006).

Urrea, Luis Alberto. 1996. *By the Lake of Sleeping Children: The Secret Life of the Mexican Border*. New York: Anchor Books Doubleday.

USDA (United States Department of Agriculture). 1998. "A Time to Act. A Report of the USDA National Commission on Small Farms." January, Miscellaneous Publications #MP-1545, Washington, DC. Available at <www.csrees.

usda.gov/nea/ag_systems/pdfs/time_to_act_1998.pdf> (accessed February 2003).

Vasavi, A.R. 1999. "Agrarian Distress in Bidar: Market, State and Suicides." *Economic and Political Weekly* 34(32) (August 7): 2263–68.

Veltmeyer, Henry. 1997. "New Social Movements in Latin America: The Dynamics of Class and Identity." *Journal of Peasant Studies* 25(1): 139–69.

_____. 2000. "The Dynamics of Social Change in Mexico and the EZLN." *Latin American Perspectives* 27(5): 88–100.

Vivian, Jessica. 1992. "Foundations for Sustainable Development: Participation, Empowerment and Local Resource Management." In D. Ghai and J. Vivian (eds.), *Grassroots Environmental Action*. London and New York: Routledge.

Welch, Cliff. 2001. "Peasants and Globalization in Latin America: A Survey of Recent Literature." Paper presented at the XXIII International Congress of the Latin American Studies Association. September 6–8, Washington, DC.

Whatmore, Sarah. 1995. "From Farming to Agribusiness: The Global Agro-food System." In R.J. Johnson, P. Taylor, and Michael Watts (eds.), *Geographies of Global Change: Remapping the World in the Late Twentieth Century*. Oxford: Blackwell Publishers.

Whatmore, Sarah, and Lorraine Thorne. 1997. "Nourishing Networks: Alternative Geographies of Food." In D. Goodman and M. Watts (eds.), *Globalising Food: Agrarian Questions and Global Restructuring*. London and New York: Routledge.

White, Ed. 2002. "N.D. farmers renew assault on CWB." *The Western Producer*, September 19.

Wiebe, Nettie. Forthcoming. "Women Reversing Desertification." *Canadian Woman Studies: les cahiers de la femme*.

Wilson, Barry. 2001. "Farmers take loans on their futures." *Western Producer*, July 5.

_____. 2002a. "Is bigger better?" *Western Producer*, May 23.

_____. 2002b. "Farmers borrow to expand, says farm lender." *Western Producer*, June 27.

_____. 2002c. "Wilkinson ready to take world stage." *Western Producer*, August 29.

_____. 2002d. "Gov't advised to compromise on supply management." *Western Producer*, September 26.

Wolf, Eric. 1966. *Peasants*. Englewood Cliffs, NJ: Prentice-Hall.

_____. 1969. *Peasant Wars in the Twentieth Century*. New York: Harper and Row.

Wright, Angus Lindsay, and Wendy Wolford. 2003. *To Inherit the Earth: The Landless Movement and the Struggle for a New Brazil*. Oakland: Food First Institute for Food and Development Policy.

WTO News. 1998. "Asian and US Farmers Oppose WTO Ag Reforms." *WTO News* 1(3) (March 3).

Yakabuski, Konrad. 2002. "High on the Hog." *Report on Business Magazine* September.

Yapa, Lakshman. 1996. "Improved seeds and constructed scarcity." In R. Peet and M. Watts (eds.), *Liberation Ecologies: Environment, Development and Social Movements*. London and New York: Routledge.

Ziegler, Jean. 2003. "Report by the Special Rapporteur on the Right to Food: Mission to Brazil." United Nations Commission on Human Rights, fifty-ninth session, January 3, Document # E/CN.4/2003/54/Add.1.

_____. 2004. "Report submitted by the Special Rapporteur on the right to food, Jean Ziegler, in accordance with Commission on Human Rights resolution 2003/25." United Nations commission on Human Rights, Sixtieth session, February 9, Document # C/CN.4/2004/10.